GW00492783

A New History of Sierra Leone

A New History of
Sierra Leone

JOE A. D. ALIE

MACMILLAN
PUBLISHERS

© Joe A. D. Alie, 1990

All rights reserved. No reproduction, copy or transmission
of this publication may be made without written permission.
No paragraph of this publication may be reproduced, copied
or transmitted save with written permission or in accordance
with the provisions of the Copyright, Designs and Patents
Act 1988, or under the terms of any licence permitting limited
copying issued by the Copyright Licensing Agency, 33–4 Alfred
Place, London WC1E 7DP. Any person who does any unauthorised
act in relation to this publication may be liable to criminal
prosecution and civil claims for damages.

First published 1990

Published by *Macmillan Publishers Ltd*
London and Basingstoke
Associated companies and representatives in Accra,
Auckland, Delhi, Dublin, Gaberone, Hamburg, Harare,
Hong Kong, Kuala Lumpur, Lagos, Manzini, Melbourne,
Mexico City, Nairobi, New York, Singapore, Tokyo

ISBN 0–333–51984–1

Printed in Hong Kong

British Library Cataloguing in Publication Data
Alie, Joe A. D.
A New History of Sierra Leone
I. Sierra Leone, history
966.4
966
ISBN 0–333–51984–1

Cover illustration courtesy of
The Royal Commonwealth Society, London

To the memory of my father
Francis Alie
(who passed away on 17 February 1988)

Contents

List of maps   xii
List of photographs   xiii
Foreword by Akiwande Lasite   xv
Preface   xvi

1 Sierra Leone – the land and the people   1
1.1 Political geography   1
1.2 The people   4
1.3 Political organization   13
     Temne political organization   14
     Mende political organization   16
     Sherbro political organization   17
     Limba political organization   18
1.4 Society and culture   20
1.5 Production systems   25

2 Early external influences   31
2.1 The coming of the Europeans   31
     Bunce Island and the slave trade   35
     Some effects of early European contact   36
2.2 The Mane invasions   37
     Effects of the Mane invasions   38
2.3 Advance of Islam   43
     The Futa Jallon *jihad*   43
     Peaceful conversion   44

**3 The establishment and development of the Sierra Leone
     Colony**   48
3.1 The anti-slavery movement in Britain   48
3.2 Foundation of the Colony   51
     Revival of the Colony settlement   54
3.3 Nova Scotians   55

Governor John Clarkson   57
Zachary Macaulay   59
The Maroons   61
The Nova Scotian rebellion   61
3.4   Crown Colony rule   62
Nova Scotian institutions   63
The Abolition Act   65
Thomas Perronet Thompson   67
3.5   The era of Governor MacCarthy   68
Recaptives manage their own affairs   73
Government and the missions   75
3.6   Krio society   78
Krio achievements   80

4   Commercial exchanges in the hinterland   85
4.1   Indigenous trade   85
4.2   Overseas trade   88
4.3   Sherbro Island   89
4.4   Gallinas country   90
King Siaka   91
The reign of Prince Mana   91
Succession disputes   92
4.5   Trade wars   94
The Masimera-Loko wars   94
The Caulker wars   96
The Yoni wars   97

5   Christian missions in the hinterland (c.1600–1900) 101
5.1   The early missions   101
5.2   Later missions   104
5.3   The Mendi Mission   105
5.4   Further advance inland   108
Conclusion   110

6   The declaration of the Protectorate   112
6.1   Non-annexation policy   112
6.2   The Native Affairs Department   115
The Resolutions of 1865   117
6.3   Pressures for the declaration of a Protectorate   118
6.4   Samori Toure and European imperialism   120
The Frontier Police   124
The Waima incident   125
6.5   The Protectorate is proclaimed   126
6.6   Notes on some Colony personalities   127
Sir Samuel Lewis   127
James C. E. Parkes   129

7   The structure and operation of local government   133
7.1   Early Protectorate administration   134
7.2   Protectorate grievances   135
      The hut (house) tax war   140
7.3   Some Protectorate leaders   143
      Madam Yoko   144
      Bai Bureh   145
      Nyagua   146
      Kai Londo   147
      Almamy Suluku   148
7.4   Consolidation of Protectorate administration   149
      The Native Administration system   152
      Changes in provincial administration   154
      District Councils   156
7.5   Local government in the Colony   157
      Freetown City Council   158
      Rural Area Councils   160
      Tribal Headmen in Freetown   161
      Sherbro Urban District Council   162

8   Constitutional and political developments 1863–1945   165
8.1   The 1863 constitution   165
8.2   The railway workers' strike and anti-Syrian riots   168
8.3   Congress politics   169
      Sierra Leone branch   173
      1924 Constitution   174
8.4   The 1926 strike   175
8.5   The Haidara rebellion   176
8.6   Wallace-Johnson and the Youth League   177
      Aims of the Youth League   178
      Assessment of the Youth League   180
8.7   Decline of the Krio   182

9   Economic and social changes during the colonial era   187
9.1   Transportation   189
9.2   Agriculture   192
      Export crops   192
      The subsistence sector   193
9.3   Mining   195
      The impact of mining   197
9.4   Banking and manufacturing industry   198
9.5   Social developments   200
      Education   200
      Medical establishments   203
      Pipe-borne water and electricity   204

10   Transfer of power   207
10.1   The Protectorate Assembly   207
10.2   The Stevenson Constitution   208
10.3   1955–6 countrywide riots   211
        Freetown general strike   211
        Provincial disturbances   212
        The 1958 Constitution   213
10.4   Political parties   214
        The National Council of Sierra Leone   214
        The Sierra Leone People's Party   214
        The United Progressive Party   215
        The Kono Progressive Movement   215
        The People's National Party   215
        The United National Front   216
        The All-People's Congress   217
10.5   The Independence Constitution   217
10.6   An architect of Sierra Leone's independence   218
10.7   The impact of colonialism   219

11   Politics since independence   224
11.1   The Milton Margai era   224
11.2   Sierra Leone under Sir Albert   227
        The 1967 elections   231
11.3   Military rule   236
11.4   The Siaka Stevens regime   239
        Establishment of the Republic   241
11.5   The New Order   245
        Why Momoh?   245
        An assessment of the Stevens regime   248
        Foreign policy   250
        The Mano River Union   251

**12   Social, cultural and economic developments since
        independence**   258
12.1   Social developments   258
        Education   258
        Health and social facilities   260
        The role of NGOs   261
12.2   Cultural developments   262
        Music   264
        Literature and drama   264
        Art and craft   266
12.3   Economic developments   266
        Minerals   266
        Industry and commerce   266

	Agriculture	268
	Financial institutions	269
12.4	Some factors affecting rapid economic development	271
	The future	273

Appendix 1	Governors of Sierra Leone	276
Appendix 2	Governor Clarkson's Prayer for Sierra Leone	278
Appendix 3	Sir Milton's Independence Message	280
Appendix 4	The National Anthem	282
Appendix 5	The National Flag	283
Appendix 6	Coat of Arms	284
Appendix 7	National Honours and Awards	285
Appendix 8	President Momoh's Inaugural Speech	287

Index 293

List of maps

1 Sierra Leone: relief 2
2 Sierra Leone: main rivers 3
3 Sierra Leone: present-day administrative regions 5
4 Sierra Leone: ethnic groups 8
5 Sierra Leone: Mane sub-kingdoms 39
6 Sierra Leone: Colony settlers 52
7 Governor McCarthy's parish plan 70
8 Trade routes and trade centres in the hinterland, 86
seventeenth to nineteenth centuries
9 Standard treaty-signing missions in the hinterland, 123
showing T.J. Alldridge's route
10 Administrative boundary changes, 1896–1945 136–7
11 Evolution of the transport network, 1918–46 170–71
12 Agricultural production. Two further cash crops, tobacco 191
and sugar cane, were cultivated after independence,
mainly in the Northern Province.
13 Main minerals exploited in Sierra Leone during the 196
colonial period. Bauxite and rutile were mined
subsequently.
14 General election results, 1967, by constituency. The 234–5
following four constituencies are not represented, being
added just before the election:
Kono Central (APC win), Kenema North-East (SLPP
win), Koinadugu South-East (APC win) Port Loko South-
West (APC win).
15 Mano River Union States: Sierra Leone, Liberia and 252
Guinea
16 Integrated Agricultural Development Project Areas 270

List of Photographs

Nomoli figures 7
Figure probably used in fertility rites (Kru and Mende) 7
Weaving country cloth 22
A caravel of the fifteenth century 32
The Dutch admiral, de Ruyter 34
The English abolitionist Granville Sharp 49
The English abolitionist William Wilberforce 50
European and African craft off the coast of Sierra Leone, 52
   early nineteenth century
British anti-slavery squadron in action 66
Regent Village at the time of the Rev. W.A.B. Johnson 71
A view of Regent, where Samuel Crowther was schoolmaster 76
   in 1830
Bishop Crowther 81
The main gate to the Harford School, with the Intermediate 108
   building in the background
Sir Samuel Lewis 128
A carving of Bai Bureh 140
Peace talks between kings, queens, chiefs and Europeans at 166
   Freetown in the 1880s
Mrs Constance Cummings-John, one of the Youth League 179
   candidates in the 1938 Freetown City Council elections; the
   first woman mayor in Freetown, 1965–66
City Hall, Freetown 181
I.T.A Wallace-Johnson (1895–1965) addressing a political 181
   meeting
The Queen Elizabeth II Quay 188
Fourah Bay College in the nineteenth century 201
Bo School 202
Dr Davidson Nichol in 1971 202

Connaught Hospital 203
Dr H.C. Bankole-Bright (1883–1958) 209
The Duke of Kent, representing Queen Elizabeth II, shakes 213
   hands with Sir Milton Margai after handing over the
   independence documents
Houses of Parliament, Freetown 220
Sir Milton Margai 225
Sir Albert Margai 228
Oil refinery, Freetown 231
Lieutenant-Colonel Juxon-Smith 237
Dr Siaka Stevens 240
President Siaka Stevens as President of the OAU in Freetown, 243
   1980
President Momoh at the State Opening of Parliament, 1986 246
The Mano River Union Bridge 251
Fourah Bay College 259
The Siaka Stevens Stadium, Freetown 263
In traditional costume, a dancer celebrates Moslem New Year 263
   in Port Loko
Craft centre, Freetown 265

Acknowledgements

The author and publishers wish to acknowledge, with thanks, the following
photographic sources.
J. Allan Cash p. 240
Associated Press pp. 213, 228, 237, 243
Church Missionary Society pp. 76; 81
Mary Evans Picture Library p. 50
Hulton Picture Company pp. 32; 49; 66; 71; 166
IMPADS pp. 188, 202 top; 220, 251; 259; 263 top and bottom; 265
Royal Commonwealth Society pp. 22; 179; 202 bottom
Topham p. 34
Werner Forman Archive p. 7 top and bottom
Other photographs are courtesy of the author

Cover illustration is courtesy of the Royal Commonwealth Society, London

The publishers have made every effort to trace the copyright holders, but if
they have inadvertently overlooked any, they will be pleased to make the
necessary arrangements at the first opportunity.

Foreword

I agreed to write the foreword to this book because I consider it to be a valuable contribution to the study of our national history.

Some years ago, the School Certificate/General Certificate of Education Ordinary Level syllabus of the West African Examinations Council (WAEC) was changed to give greater emphasis to the study of the national histories of the countries belonging to this international examining body. Whilst pupils in Nigeria and Ghana had access to several books, Sierra Leonean teachers and pupils faced an uphill task with only a handful of books. This situation is being changed by recent publications, and Mr Alie's book is a welcome addition to this growing list. The book also comes at a time when the National Teaching Syllabus is being implemented. It will give students a deeper knowledge of the history of our country.

The book is divided into twelve chapters which follow the general pattern set in the WAEC syllabus. Each chapter is sub-divided into topics, and ends with references which guide students to sources of additional information. The inclusion of questions is to be commended. They serve as useful aids for students preparing for examinations in secondary and post-secondary educational institutions.

The book is well-written in simple language. It fills a major gap and should prove extremely useful to our students.

Akiwande Lasite
Principal
Sierra Leone Grammar School
Freetown

Preface

During the colonial era very little thought was given to the promotion of African history and culture in our educational institutions. Most colonial educationists had stubbornly refused to appreciate that Africa had a history worth talking about.

The regaining of political independence by African countries from the late 1950s and beyond saw the gradual restructuring of many institutions, for example, the educational system. Consequently, national histories began to form an integral part of the curricula. These histories aimed, among other things, at interesting the youth in their heritage.

A significant milestone in the development of African history occurred in the mid-1960s when African and Africanist historians, under the auspices of UNESCO, undertook one of the most ambitious projects of this century, namely, the writing of an eight-volume *General History of Africa* designed to put African history in its proper perspective.

A New History of Sierra Leone is a modest contribution to the corpus of national histories that have been appearing on the African continent. It is written with three kinds of people in mind:

- secondary school pupils and college students studying courses in Sierra Leone history, and teachers for whom it will serve as a source book;
- Sierra Leonean policy-planners in whose hands lies the destiny of most of their countrymen and women. A systematic study of the past will, no doubt, enhance their work, for 'the further back they look into the past, the more into the future they can see';
- the general reader and the visitor to Sierra Leone who want to widen their knowledge of the history of Sierra Leone.

All of these people will certainly find *A New History of Sierra Leone* stimulating and informative.

The book provides an in-depth survey and readable account of Sierra Leone's political, socio-cultural and economic development from early times to the present day. Each of its 12 chapters makes extensive use of the most recent research materials, some of which are not normally easily accessible to many readers. Thus, the reader is presented in this single volume with the most up-to-date and authoritative information on aspects and phases of Sierra Leone's past. Let me here record my sincere thanks and gratitude to all those eminent scholars whose works were consulted. They are too many to name here. I also wish to thank the following people who in various ways contributed to the success of the project:

- Professor A. J. G. Wyse, Head of the Department of History, Fourah Bay College (FBC), University of Sierra Leone (USL), Dr Glennon Graham of the Department of Liberal Education. Columbia College, Chicago, USA, Mr Christopher Fyfe, Reader in African History, Edinburgh University, Scotland, United Kingdom and Mr E. D. A. Turay, Senior Staff Tutor, Institute of Adult Education and Extra-Mural Studies, FBC, all of whom read the manuscript and offered very useful advice;
- Mr Patrick Korneh, Lecturer, Department of Sociology, FBC, for putting a lot of sociological and anthropological materials at my disposal;
- Mr M. E. Ajayi Coomber, Senior Lecturer, Department of English, FBC, who painstakingly proofread the final manuscript;
- Mr S. J. A. Nelson, Cartographer, Department of Geography, FBC, for drawing the maps;
- the academic staff of the Mechanical Engineering Department, FBC, especially the Head, Dr J. G. M. Massaquoi and Mr Ansu M. Koroma, for giving me access to their computer facilities; and
- the staff of FBC Library for their willingness to assist at all times.

Three renowned historians – Professor C. P. Foray, Principal, FBC, Professor C. Magbaily Fyle, Director, Institute of African Studies, FBC, and Dr Arthur Abraham, formerly Senior Lecturer in the History Department, FBC – have contributed greatly to broadening my horizon on Sierra Leone history. I am therefore very grateful to them.

Let me express my deep gratitude to my wife Mary, for her moral support and encouragement during this academic exercise.

Joe A. D. Alie
Department of History
Fourah Bay College

1 Sierra Leone – the land and the people

1.1 Political geography

Sierra Leone is a small country on the west coast of Africa, totalling 27 925 square miles (73 326 sq. km). It is roughly circular in shape, extending from north to south a maximum distance of 210 miles (332 km), and from west to east a distance of about 204 miles (328 km). It is bounded on the west and south-west by the Atlantic Ocean, and on the north-west, north and north-east by the Republic of Guinea and on the east and south-east by the Republic of Liberia.

The country has three main relief regions – the Freetown Peninsula mountains, the lowlands, and the highlands of the east and north-east. There are seven main river systems which are evenly distributed over the country. They flow from the north-east to the south-west into the Atlantic Ocean. Most of these rivers are navigable for some miles upstream from the sea, until progress is blocked by rapids and sandbanks. The nation's first towns grew from trading settlements at their heads of navigation.

Two main seasons are noticeable in the country – the dry season and the wet (rainy) season. The dry season begins about mid-November and lasts until April. During this period temperatures can rise as high as 32 degrees Centigrade (90°F). The dry season is dominated by the cold, dry and dusty Harmattan wind which blows from the Sahara Desert. The wet season begins with sudden squalls of rain and thunder, sweeping westwards across the country from the highlands.

[1]

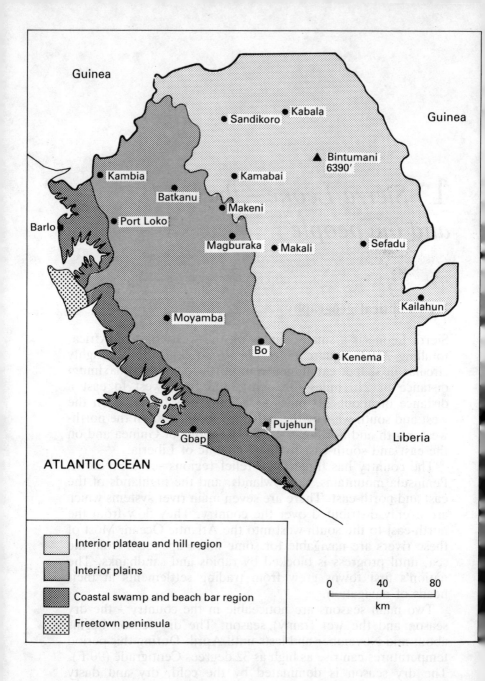

1 Sierra Leone: relief

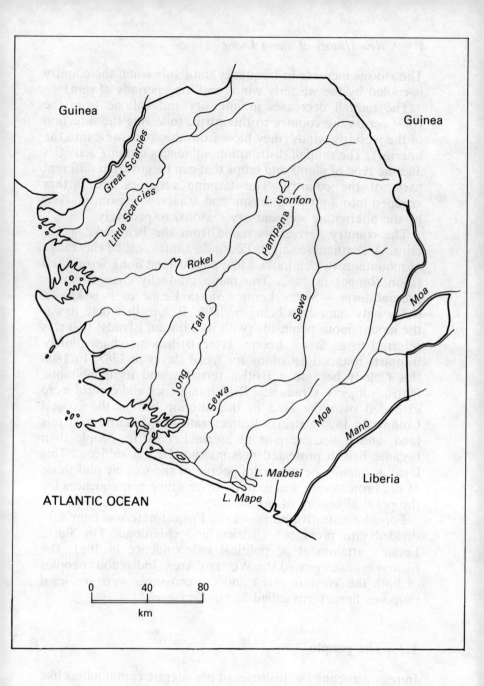

2 Sierra Leone: main rivers

The storms increase in frequency until July when the country is cooled by the westerly winds and long periods of rain.

The rainfall decreases in intensity and volume from the coast across the country to the north, following the direction of the westerly winds (they blow from the south-west into the interior). The rainfall distribution influences farming activities and the type of plants and crops that can be grown in different parts of the country. The farming activities are further grouped into a growing season and a harvest season, marked by the alternating wet and dry seasons, respectively.

The country derives its name from the Peninsula mountains. A Portuguese sailor, Pedro da Cintra, called this range of mountains (which looked like a crouching lion) *Serra Lyoa* (Lion Range) in 1462. The name gradually changed to its present form – Sierra Leone. Sierra Leone as it is known today only came into being in 1896. Before that date it was the mountainous peninsula (with its adjacent islands) that was referred to as Sierra Leone. Here British merchant philanthropists founded a Colony for freed slaves in 1787. In 1808 this Colony became a British territory and its inhabitants, British subjects. Gradually, British influence and control were extended over the land in the interior behind the coastal Colony. In 1896 a British Protectorate was declared over this land, and it became part of Sierra Leone. Its people then became British protected persons, not British subjects. This legal distinction between the people of the Colony and those of the Protectorate was to have far-reaching consequences for the political history of the country.

For administrative purposes the Protectorate was later subdivided into provinces, districts and chiefdoms. On Sierra Leone's attainment of political independence in 1961, the Colony was designated the Western Area. Indigenous peoples of both the Western Area and the provinces were for legal purposes henceforth called Sierra Leoneans.

1.2   The people

In reconstructing the histories of pre-literate communities like the early peoples of Sierra Leone, the historian has to depend on a number of important sources – for example, archaeological research. Unfortunately, however, archaeologists have

Guinea

Guinea

○ Kabala

KAMBIA   BOMBALI   KOINADUGU

○ Kambia

Northern Province

● Makeni

○ Port Loko   ○ Magburaka   KONO

PORT LOKO   ○ Sefadu

■ Freetown   TONKOLILI

WESTERN
AREA   ○ Kailahun

See inset   ○ Moyamba   BO   **Eastern Province**

MOYAMBA   ● Bo   KAILAHUN

Southern Province

ATLANTIC   Kenema ●

OCEAN   KENEMA

Bonthe ○

BONTHE   ○ Pujehun

PUJEHUN   Liberia

Greater Freetown

Mountain

0   8

km

FOREST RESERVE   Waterloo   0   40   80

York   Koya   km

York

Western Area
(Greater Freetown Municipality
and Rural Area Councils)

International boundary ——————
Provincial boundary —·—·—·—
District boundary — — — — —
National Capital ■
Provincial headquarters ●
District headquarters ○

3 Sierra Leone: present-day administrative regions

done very little work in Sierra Leone. But it is clear from
their few findings that people lived in the present area of
Sierra Leone a very long time ago. An examination of tools
discovered in a cave in Yengema, for example, in the Kono
District suggests that people inhabited that area at least 2500
years before Christ. These early inhabitants, like others elsewhere, at first used stone and wooden tools until they learned
how to use and work with iron. They then began to make
better and more durable tools out of iron. Huge smelting sites
have been discovered in Koranko country, but unfortunately
they have not been dated.

The people lived in small communities, but we do not know
for certain who they were. By the time Portuguese traders
began to appear on the West African coast in the mid-
fifteenth century, certain groups had already established
themselves firmly in many areas in what is now Sierra Leone.
On the coast were a host of communities such as the Baga,
Bullom, Krim and Vai. The Portuguese called these coastal
peoples the Sapes. In the north-west were the Temne and
Loko, and further to the north lived the Limba. The Banta
were found in the south-west while the Kissi and Kono lived
in the east.

Each group tended to be isolated from the others and there
was very little internal migration. Fear of war, suspicion of
people from other groups, problems of social cohesion within
the group and possible breakdown of traditions were all factors affecting ethnic diffusion.

The early peoples of Sierra Leone seem to have been
affected by certain invasions, such as those of the Mane (see
2.2). Some groups were absorbed in the process, and others
were displaced, while new groups were formed subsequently.
Over a long period of time, new communities also came in a
rather peaceful manner and settled in various parts of the
country. Like the early inhabitants, these later immigrants
also at first lived separate from others. But the growth of
trade, provision of Western educational and medical facilities,
improvement in transportation systems, mining, agriculture
and migration have tended to draw the groups closer
together.

Today, there are at least 17 ethnic groups in the country.
These groups have been divided into three language categor-
ies – Mande, Mel and others. The Mende, Vai/Gallinas,

Nomoli figures

Figure probably used in fertility rites (Kru and Mende)

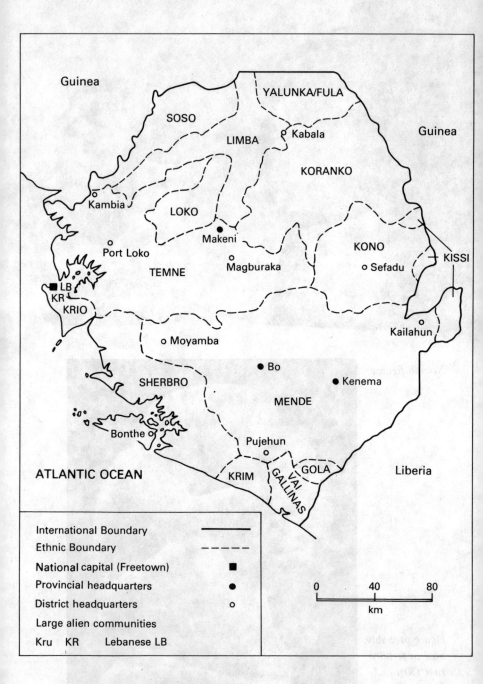

4 Sierra Leone: ethnic groups

Kono, Loko, Koranko, Soso, Yalunka and Mandingo belong to the Mande. The Temne, Bullom/Sherbro, Kissi, Gola, and Krim form part of the Mel group. The others are Limba, Fula, Krio and Kru. The two largest communities are the Mende and Temne, each accounting for about 31 per cent of the population.

The Mende, who are believed to be descendants of the Mane, were originally in the Liberian hinterland. The Mende began moving into Sierra Leone slowly and peacefully in the eighteenth century. They established small groups of settlements based on hunting and subsistence agriculture. A subgroup of the Mende – the Kpaa Mende – made a dynamic move in the early nineteenth century. They had strong military tendencies. The Kpaa Mende dislodged the Banta and pushed them southwards towards the coast. A Kpaa Mende state, with Taiama as its capital, was then created in the former Banta empire. Other Mende leaders were to transform their original farming settlements into fortresses. In many cases these chiefs made agreements with the original inhabitants, offering protection in return for allegiance. Sometimes they killed the leaders and enslaved their followers. By this method, the Mende rulers were able to create large political entities. Other important Mende sub-groups were the Kɔ̀ɔ̀ (upper) Mende and the Sewa or Middle Mende. Today, the Mende occupy roughly one-third of the total surface area of Sierra Leone in the southern and eastern regions.

The Temne claim to have come from Futa Jallon, which is in present-day Guinea. They established a commercial empire on the north-west coast of Sierra Leone before the fifteenth century. A Mane warrior organized them into an important political group in the 1560s. By the late eighteenth century, the Temne had virtually occupied the Sierra Leone peninsula and certain sections of the northern interior. There were two main groups – the Sanda Temne who were found in the north, and the Yoni who lived to the south of the Sanda. It is believed that the Yoni were the older inhabitants. Smaller Temne groupings included the Kholifa and the Konike.

The Temne were divided into about 25 patrilineal clans (ɛ̌ bona) each claiming descent from some heroic ancestor. The social significance of the clan rested on the bond it created between all men possessing it. Originally, marriages were allowed only outside one's ɛ̌ bona, but later marriages within

the ɛ̆ *bona* became frequent. The ɛ̆ *bona* name was transmitted from father to children and a woman belonged to the ɛ̆
bona of her father. With each ɛ̆ *bona* was associated a totem,
usually an animal, fish or bird and sometimes a plant – which
members of the ɛ̆ *bona* may not see, touch, eat, kill or use as
firewood, and so on. Taboo-breakers could be afflicted with
certain bodily diseases.

The Limba are the third largest and one of the oldest
communities in Sierra Leone. They have no tradition of origin
and maintain that they have always lived in Sierra Leone. It is
believed that their first settlement was around the Wara Wara
hills in the northern interior. The Limba later spread southwards and westwards to occupy areas in Temne and Loko
country. By the mid-nineteenth century five sub-groups were
identifiable among the Limba. In the extreme north were the
Wara Wara, and south-west of them lived the Tonko. The
Sela lived to the north-east of the Tonko, while the Biriwa
and the Saffroko were found further south. The dialects of
these groups were different, sometimes partially incomprehensible to each other.

Each Limba belonged to one of the many clans scattered
throughout the country. Clan membership was acquired
through the father. Strictly, no one was allowed to marry
someone of the same clan. Each clan had one or more totems,
usually an animal or bird, which it was forbidden to eat. And
each clan 'owned' a particular country. For example, the
Konteh 'owned' Biriwa; the Mansaray, Wara Wara. This
dominant clan provided the king.

The Vai and the Kono are related people who split up some
time ago. Oral tradition states that there was shortage of salt
in Konosu, the original home of the Vai and the Kono, which
is somewhere in present-day Guinea. The people therefore
decided to set out *en masse* in search of salt water. After
travelling for many months, some of them got tired and decided to settle in approximately the present Kono homeland,
where they later founded three states – Lei, Sando and Soa.
The more adventurous ones continued the journey in search
of salt water and told the others as they departed: '*O maa
kônô, kanii na*' ('You wait for us, we will return'). So the
group that stayed behind and 'waited' became known as
Kono, while those that moved towards the sea never returned
but called their land Kanina ('those that will return').

Table 1.1 The people of Sierra Leone: location and affinities

Group	Location	Remarks
Mande language group		
Mende	Throughout Southern and Eastern Provinces	Assimilated most neighbours
Loko	Mostly Bombali District	Related to Mende linguistically; heavily influenced culturally by Temne
Kono	Kono District	
Vai (Gallinas)	Pujehun coast	Offshoot of Kono; now largely assimilated by Mende
Soso	North-western border of country	Bulk of the group in Guinea
Yalunka	Northern Koinadugu	Related to Soso
Koranko	Koinadugu	
Mandingo	Dispersed over entire country	Spread as religious teachers, traders, warriors
Mel group		
Temne	South-western half of Northern Province, Freetown	Widely dispersed throughout country, especially in diamond areas
Sherbro (Bullom)	Most of coast; especially Bonthe, Moyamba	Northern Bullom absorbed by the Temne
Krim	Coastal Pujehun and Bonthe	Sherbro; being absorbed by the Mende
Kissi	Eastern border, Kailahun, Kono	Bulk of group in Liberia and Guinea
Gola	South-eastern border	Bulk of group in Liberia, largely absorbed by Mende
Others		
Limba	Bombali, Kambia and Koinadugu north of the Temne	One of the oldest groups
Fula	About half in Bombali, Koinadugu, rest scattered throughout country	Part of Fulani, extending from Senegal to Nigeria
Kru	Freetown	Bulk of group in Liberia
Krio	Western Area	

(Adapted from Cartwright, *Politics in Sierra Leone*, p. 14)

[11]

Some writers have suggested that the Portuguese called these people 'Gallinas' because bush fowls abounded in their country (the Portuguese term for hens is *gallinas*). This is plausible, but it is also possible that Gallinas is a corrupt form of Kaninas.

The Loko are akin to the Gbandi of Liberia and the Mende. (The Mende and the Loko call each other *Njagbe* (nephew), a mutually unacceptable term.) It is believed that the Loko were offshoots of a Mane expeditionary force sent against one of the defected Mane viceroys in the 1550s. This force was probably prevented from returning to its base by the Temne, so the Loko stayed around the present Port Loko territory. They were heavily influenced by the Temne.

The Koranko are related to the Mandingo. The Koranko began to arrive in Sierra Leone from Guinea in about 1600. After a few skirmishes with the Kono and the Yalunka, they finally settled to the north and west of Kono country.

The Soso and the Yalunka are a branch of the same people. Soso and Yalunka tradition maintains that they arrived in Futa Jallon some time after the Temne and Baga had created a powerful state to the east of Futa. Because of increase in population, the Soso began to spread out into north-western Sierra Leone in about the seventeenth century. In Futa Jallon there were occasional clashes between the Yalunka and the Fula, culminating in the subjugation of the Yalunka by the Fula until the early decades of the eighteenth century, when they threw off the Fula yoke and moved south. The Yalunka subsequently built a state at the extreme north of Sierra Leone.

The Bullom are among the oldest inhabitants on the Sierra Leone coast. They were invaded by the Mane warriors in the sixteenth century who in the process 'cut the Bullom tribe into two parts'. The northern branch were assimilated by the Temne and the Soso. The southern branch came to be known as Sherbro, a name which was derived from Sherabola, a Mane viceroy who imposed his rule on them towards the end of the sixteenth century. The Sherbro today occupy the south-western coastal region of Sierra Leone from the Ribbi River, south of the peninsula, to the neighbourhood of the lower course of the Bum River, about 90 miles (145 km) to the south-east. Sherbroland extends inland for distances of from 15 to 30 miles (24–48 km). The Sherbro were among the first to make contacts with Europeans, and some of the leading families, the Caulkers, Clevelands, and others have European ancestors.

The Krim are a coastal people akin to the Sherbro and live to the south-east of the Sherbro. They speak a variant of Sherbro and culturally appear to be very close to the Sherbro. The Sherbro call them *Akima*, meaning 'those who ran away'.

The Gola, the majority of whom live in the Liberian hinterland, are also among the earliest inhabitants of Sierra Leone. They occupy some land east of the Gallinas on the present Liberian border with Sierra Leone.

The Kissi say they migrated from the upper Niger before the fifteenth century. They were attacked by the Koranko who pushed them towards the eastern border with present-day Guinea.

The Mandingo and the Fula began arriving in Sierra Leone in the seventeenth century. The first immigrants were mostly traders and Islamic teachers. The Mandingo came mainly from the Sankaran region in Guinea while the Fula came from Futa Jallon and Senegal. They subsequently settled in various parts of the country.

The Krio community, who largely inhabit the Western Area, came into being in the mid-nineteenth century as a result of the integration of such disparate groups as the Original Settlers, Nova Scotians, Maroons, Recaptives and immigrants from the Sierra Leone hinterland (see Chapter 3).

The Kru began arriving in the Sierra Leone Colony from Liberia in the 1790s. They were mostly seamen. As their numbers increased, land was acquired for them near the shore beyond Sanders Brook in the west end of Freetown. The Kru started a settlement on this land which they called Kru Town. Some Kru later ventured into the hinterland to work at the timber factories.

1.3   Political organization

Let us examine the pre-colonial political organizations of some of the ethnic groups, namely, the Temne, Mende, Sherbro and Limba. All these groups had, by the second half of the nineteenth century, created large states with highly-developed political systems. Traditional rulers were, on the whole, not autocratic, for everybody was subject to the same laws. No ruler could exempt himself from the rules of customary law simply because he was a king. Subjects could appeal against their chief. Moreover, kings almost always acted in concert with their principal advisers. If the king wanted to declare war, for instance, he first held a meeting with his advisers. If they felt that the war was unjust, or that the enemy was very strong, they could withhold their support and give orders for peace despite the king.

Temne political organization

There were many Temne kingdoms in the interior, but some were quite small. Many of the kingdoms had been formed in areas originally occupied by other groups. Sometimes, these groups were pushed out of their areas, as was the case with the Loko in Bake Loko (Port Loko). At other times, the Temne took advantage of their numerical strength to impose their will on the earlier groups. Many Koranko kingdoms were lost to the Temne in this way. The most important Temne kingdoms in the nineteenth century were Koya, Yoni, Marampa, Masimera, Kholifa, Konike, Tane and Gbonkolenkeh.

The principal ruler of a Temne kingdom was the *O'bai* (king), who was usually selected from among ruling families. He was generally someone with an outstanding quality. The king was assisted by ministers called *kapr* and some titled women (*bôm kapr*). The king and certain chiefs were required to undergo elaborate installation (*kantha*) ceremonies in the hands of secret-society officials. Once they had gone through *kantha* ceremonies they were regarded as sacred. They could not, customarily, be deposed. The *kantha* ceremonies and training, which sometimes lasted for a year, ensured that the king and his subordinates were made aware of their responsibilities to the populace. When the king left *kantha* he ceremonially bought the country from his subjects.

The king was a *primus inter pares* (first among equals) who enjoyed a great deal of influence among his sub-chiefs. To ensure that he did not abuse his position, he was subjected to various restrictions and taboos, and was expected to conduct himself in conformity with the injunctions and norms of the secret society in charge of his position.

There was, however, no mechanism for deposing a king, and a Temne king was king for life. He was the custodian of the country's land and keeper of the sacred things of rulership. When he passed away (a king never died but returned to Futa, the alleged home of the Temne), certain parts of his body would be preserved and these would be used in the rituals connected with the installation of a successor. If the king died in circumstances which made it impossible to recover these essentials, it would be very difficult to install a successor. This was why the king was never allowed to go to war.

Next to the king was the *Kapr Mesim* (Prime Minister). He was the king's main adviser and intelligence officer and was the custodian of the king's regalia. He pronounced the death of the king and served as the chief mourner and guardian (*obarin*) of the king's widows. He acted as regent (*Pa Rok*) when the king died. Below the *Kapr Mesim* were the *Kapr*. They were given names according to the portfolios they held. The most important ministers were:

Kapr Loya – the Attorney-General. He advised the king on legal matters and deputized for him in court.

Kapr Kuma – the Finance Minister. He was responsible for collecting and keeping tributes and taxes for the king.

Kapr Gbogboro – the Minister of Food and Agriculture. He was responsible for preserving food for the royal family; he also supervised work at the royal estate farms.

Kapr Fenthe – the Minister of Health. He also saw to it that the entire kingdom was kept clean and tidy.

Kapr Soya – the Minister of Defence.

Those chiefs who did not go through *kantha* ceremonies were not regarded as sacred. They owed their position to the king's pleasure. Each Temne country was a political entity which was sub-divided into sections under the control of section chiefs. Each section contained a number of villages ruled by headmen who performed administrative, judicial and ritual duties.

Top-level decisions were taken by a council comprising the king, his ministers and senior secret-society officials. The secret-society bush generally served as the meeting-place, and decisions taken there were final. The Poro or the Ragbenle was predominant in political matters (see pp. 17–18), except in mainly Muslim areas. In such areas the ministers of government were called the *Almami*. However, ceremonies for the installation of the king remained essentially the same in Islamic and non-Islamic areas.

Mende political organization

Dependence and security were important features of Mende society and they seem to have dictated the pattern of Mende settlements. These settlements consisted of 'open' villages/ towns and war-towns. The latter were well-stockaded and were primarily concerned with defence purposes. Dependants lived in the open villages. They were mostly engaged in carrying out economic activities, such as farming for the war-town.

Arthur Abraham has suggested that two types of states were noticeable in Mendeland in the last few decades of the nineteenth century. These were the 'personal amorphous states' and the territorial states. Each state was ruled by a king. The personal amorphous states had a fluid state system. They had no very sharp lines of demarcation and their boundaries depended on the personality of the king. Subjects in these states identified themselves with the king rather than with the state. The state was held intact and stability was maintained only according to the ability of the king. Among such states were those of Makavoray of Tikonko, Nyagua of Panguma, Mendegla of Joru and Kailondo of Luawa.

The territorial states, on the other hand, had fixed boundaries and did not depend for their stability on the character of the king. The state existed and survived in spite of the king who was more or less a *primus inter pares*. A sub-ruler in a territorial state could become as powerful as the king if he had the force of character. Of this type of state there were Lugbu, Bumpe and the Kpaa Mende.

The king in both types of states was generally someone who manifested the greatest skill in leadership and there was no definite rule of succession to the kingship. The king was elected by an electoral college which comprised several leading personalities in the state. He governed with a council of state which included certain sub-chiefs, learned elders and other 'big' men. But this council rarely met as a body because of communications and other difficulties. So the actual administration of the state fell in the hands of the king and a much smaller council.

One of the most important officials in this council was the *Lavai* or Speaker. He was usually a close relative of the king. The Speaker acted as intermediary between the people and the king. He received complaints and disputes and passed on the king's orders to the sub-chiefs. He also ensured that these orders were carried out. The Speaker was the king's principal adviser and deputy. When the king died, the Speaker acted as regent.

The king depended heavily on the Poro in the maintenance of customary law and behaviour. He was rarely deposed and if for any reason he was unable to perform his functions, a regent was appointed. The king was generally referred to as *Maada*, that is, grandfather. His main source of revenue was tribute collection. Subjects also worked his state farm (*manja*).

Each state had a number of countries/chiefdoms. Each consisted of many stockaded towns and open villages. Njama, a country in the Kpaa Mende state in the 1870s, for instance, was made up of nine stockaded towns and two large open villages. Taiama, also in the same state, comprised nine stockaded towns and seven open villages. Wende, in King Makavoray's state, had thirteen towns. A sub-ruler exercised authority over each country. Problems of communication, however, forced these rulers to delegate authority. The ruler's governing council usually consisted of town chiefs and heads of prominent lineages.

Below the country was the war-town (and its satellites) which was the smallest unit of local administration. The war-town was under the control of a chief who had had some military experience. Two or three retired warriors generally assisted him in planning military strategies.

Sherbro political organization

Traditionally, the *Bei Sherbro* was king of all Sherbro country. Under him came various provincial and other sub-chiefs. The position of the *Bei Sherbro* was not hereditary, but strictly elective. The election, which took place in the Poro bush, was conducted by a council of titular chiefs called *feh-feh*. The king-elect was then put into *kungk* by the Poro officials and there instructed in ethnic law and custom. The king was not a semi-divine ruler. He resided at Yoni on Sherbro Island.

The *Bei Sherbro* exercised a measure of control over the other chiefs by hearing appeals against them and always presided at the election of a chief. He and his sub-chiefs became wealthy through trade. When the king died, a regent, called the *Shambo*, carried out the business of government until a successor was elected.

The Poro 'inner circle', which consisted of leading Poro officials and the king, served as executive council and tribunal of the society. It decided policy and was the court of final appeal. It was this body which decided on intervention in wars and on matters of Sherbro relationships with other communities. It also placed a ban on actions which might harm the economy of the whole country; for example, the over-fishing of certain waters, or the gathering of palm nuts at certain times. In addition to its judicial functions, the 'inner circle' was consulted about every important event in the community.

Sherbro country was divided into provinces which were ruled by sub-chiefs. These chiefs usually came from matrilineal ruling families. They all had titles; namely: *Ta Bongay* of Nongoba, *Sei Bureh* of Torma Bum, *So Kong* of Imperi, *Sei Kama* of Jong, *So Fa* of Cha, *Ya Kumba* of Tasso (Kagboro). In order to avoid anarchy, the death of a provincial chief was never announced until a successor was elected. The powers of a provincial chief were never well-defined but varied according to his personality and character. Each province was sub-divided into sections under the control of lesser chiefs.

Thus, politically and judicially, the *Bei Sherbro*, Poro 'inner circle' and senior chiefs occupied the three most important positions among the Sherbro. Among them the policy of the whole country was decided.

Limba political organization

Each Limba country (*kekein*) was governed by a *Gbaku* (king). Each country usually consisted of a major town (where the king lived) and several smaller towns and villages (*mĕti*). The king was selected by the most important men in the country and he was generally someone who had shown some outstanding quality. In some Limba countries, particularly in the north and west, the king and some of his sub-chiefs had to undergo *kantha* ceremonies.

The king's functions were many and various. He was the chief judge, and the source of accumulation and redistribution of wealth in his kingdom. He also had control of the secret societies. He derived a lot of wealth from trade and tributes.

Unlike other communities like the Mende or Temne, the Limba did not have many officials standing between the king and the people. This was mainly because of the close personal relationship between him and his subjects. Many Limba kingdoms did not therefore have a precise system of officials. Exceptions existed in those areas that were influenced by the Temne, where their organizations resembled the Temne type. The Limba political system also recognized the principle of representation, that is, that people had a right to advise their ruler, and that anyone with the ability to speak well and wisely should be given the opportunity to do so either personally to him, through his *sesa* (cousins) or through one of his *bayahain* (big men).

A virgin or legally unmarried girl called the *basaraka* had special ritual duties towards the king. She was always near him when a sacrifice was being offered. She accompanied the king on his tours and fetched him water. The *basaraka* generally lived in comfort and luxury and commanded great respect. In those areas where the king went into *kantha* before installation, she accompanied him. A king's sister or cousin often advised and warned him and also accompanied him on visits. She decided cases between him and his wives. The king's senior wife also had some influence over him and was often consulted on major issues.

There were various checks against abuse of powers by the king. For example, if he became too ruthless, people deserted him and this would belittle him in the eyes of other kings and cause him shame (*kulahu*). The concept of *kulahu* was a central one among the Limba and was closely connected with the king's desire to rule well and get a good reputation for himself and his family. Certain officials like the *sesa* and *basaraka* told him the truth without fear or favour. Also, if a king became too unpopular his son was not likely to succeed him. An incompetent or bad ruler was often persuaded to resign.

Villages were controlled by headmen called *bathagba*.

These paid regular visits to the king and brought him presents. The village was an economic, religious and social unit. Each village formed its own company (*kune*) which went out to work in turn on various household farms. In each village there was a sacred bush for initiation.

1.4   Society and culture

The basic social unit among the hinterland communities was the household. It consisted of a man, his wives and children, and frequently also blood and affinal relatives – for example, junior brothers and their wives, and unmarried sisters – as well as dependants and slaves. The household was usually under the charge of a man. Succession of household headship often passed from father to eldest son, then to brothers.

Descent and inheritance were largely patrilineal, although a man stood in special relationship to his mother's brother, whose blessing was considered more important than that of a father. The Sherbro believed in matrilineal descent. Their kinship system, based on matriclan or ram, traced descent from female members of the family. Thus a man's heirs to his property were his sisters' children, and widows were generally inherited by the brothers of the deceased. Marriage was prohibited within the ram and breaches of these prohibitions were known as *simongama* (incest).

Marriage transactions were usually conducted by parents or other senior relatives. The groom was required to pay dowry to the family of the girl. This might consist of livestock such as cows, goats and sheep. Marriage transactions were celebrated by dancing and feasting. A man could marry as many wives as he could afford. Polygamy was often an economic necessity. With many men being killed in wars, there was a surplus of women; and women and their children were also needed as farm workers. Moreover, society did not encourage spinsterhood or prostitution. Plural marriages conferred prestige on a man and were regarded as a sign of affluence. Additional wives ensured an increased number of children, and a large group of kinsfolk added to security. For the women, marriage increased their status in the community. Through marriage they obtained social and economic opportunities. A married woman could not be easily molested by men and if the woman

was a trader she could be allowed to retain some of the profit.
The husband was obliged to care for his wives for as long as
they stayed together. He could also offer gifts occasionally to
his in-laws and assist them in many ways.

In traditional law women were treated as minors. Consequently, they were never allowed to hold supreme political
positions. Politics and government were the business of men.
Women could, however, become town and village heads,
especially in Mende country.

The man was also dominant in the household and a woman
was regarded legally as a dependant of her husband. A
woman was entitled to only one husband at a time. When the
husband died, his surviving wife could be inherited by one of
his relatives. If the woman refused, then her parents (or her
new husband) were expected to refund her brideprice to her
late husband's relatives. Women worked hard on the farms,
but had little say in the disbursement of the proceeds from the
farm. In certain cases, however, a woman could make her
own little farm. She could obtain a divorce if she had a good
case to advance.

Among certain communities, for example, the Sherbro,
Kono and Kissi, children were named according to the order
in which they were born. There was one series of names for
boys and another for girls. Thus the first male child of Sherbro parents was called Tcho, the next Kòng, then Baki, Sò,
Reke, Kothong. Similarly for girls, Boi, Yema, Kona,
Mahen, Tchoko, Yoki, Nebang. Among the Kono and the
Kissi the children were named in the order of their birth by
the woman, irrespective of who may be their father. In Kono-
land the first male child was Sahr, the next Tamba, then Aiah,
Komba, Kai, Safia and Mani. The girls were named Sia,
Kumba, Yei, Finda, Bondu, Tiwa and Mani. The Kissi used
the following names: Sahr, Tamba, Fayia, Fallah, Nyuma,
Halii, Kundu (male), Sia, Kumba, Finda, Tiwa, Yawa, Ten-
neh and Sona (female).

The ordinary working unit was the domestic family. For the
busier farming season, outside help could be obtained, and
various organizations were formed to provide such assistance.
Some of these were the *kugbe* and *bembe* found among the
Mende. The *kugbe* was a body of young men and women who
assembled during the clearing, hoeing and harvest seasons to
work in farms in their neighbourhood. They were usually

Weaving country cloth

rewarded for their work with food and drink. The *bembe* was a band of a dozen or so young men who offered services to farmers on a wage basis. Also several households, or sometimes a whole village, worked each other's farms in turn.

The activities of the people were sustained by religious beliefs. They believed in the existence of a supreme god who was usually approached through lesser gods. These might be rocks, hills, special trees or some carvings. The Temne called their supreme god *Kru Masaba*, the Kono *Yaata*, the Limba *Kanu Masala*, the Sherbro *Hobatoke*, and the Mende *Mahin Ngewo*. Periodic sacrifices were made to the god. Religious priests performed rituals for success in economic pursuits. They sometimes acted as herbalists, treating both mind and body. The people believed in life after death and some anticipated joining their family and friends in the hereafter. They showed great sorrow at the loss of a relation.

Twins were thought to possess extra-human powers. So when they were born, elaborate ceremonies were performed to welcome them in this world. It was believed that if twins did not like their parents they would bring ill-luck in the family. Consequently, a special altar was always erected in a corner of the parents' room where regular sacrifices of palm oil, kola nuts and cowrie shells were made to placate the twins.

One religious object that played an important role in the lives of many coastal and some interior communities was the *nomoli*. It was usually made of soapstone and was believed to be invested with supernatural powers. *Nomoli* was generally buried in the farm for a successful harvest or kept in the home as a guardian spirit. Sometimes, it was kept in a temporary farm shelter and regularly fed with small portions of the farmer's cooked rice. By its side was a small whip with which it was ceremonially flogged and told to bring plenty of rice.

Among the Kissi a similar figure, called *pomdo*, was also associated with the ancestral cult. The person who discovered it in the ground used it as a medium of contact with one of his immediate ancestors. The Temne and Bullom sometimes used unsculptured stone called *atonga* to contact their ancestors.

Old people were generally accorded a lot of respect, for old age was associated with wisdom. A young person had to speak with deference to an elder. Age was also a very significant factor in determining selection to high political office. Young men were generally barred from holding supreme positions. Apart from the king and a few elders, who sometimes amassed a lot of wealth and lived in comfort, there was hardly any social difference in people's status within any society. Old and invalid people were taken care of through the extended family system.

Kings and other rich people kept slaves, for one way of assessing a man's wealth was by the number of slaves he had. But these slaves, who might be called subjects, serfs or dependants, were not harshly treated. This was why they rarely revolted against their masters. Slaves generally became part of their master's household and it was not always easy to distinguish between a slave and a free man. Slaves provided a large labour force and were used to work farms or as porters. If a slave gave good service, he could be allowed to own property or marry within a master's household. Gradually, he became part of the extended family. A slave who excelled himself could become a big man. Ndawaa, a sub-ruler in one of King Makavoray's countries, was once a slave. In Yalunka country, however, slaves (*konyena*) constituted a special class. They came from the non-Yalunka population, for a Yalunka was never made a slave in his own country. Only prisoners of war were sold. A male *konyena* could marry only within his class, but a free man could marry a female *konyena*. She became free on the night of her wedding. The offspring of this marriage were considered free men.

Education was functional and relevant to the needs of society. The ultimate goal was to produce an individual who was honest, respectful, skilled, cooperative, and who could conform to the social order of the day. Most of the learning was done informally through participation in ceremonies and rituals, imitation and demonstration. For instance, boys and girls were involved in practical agriculture, fishing, weaving, cooking, carving, and so on.

Secret societies served as institutions for higher learning. The main societies were the Poro or Wonde for boys, and the Bondo or Sande for girls. Boys and girls were admitted into these societies when they reached puberty.

In the Poro the boys learned special skills and acquired knowledge of medicine, politics and government. Boys were taught to bear hardship without complaint and grow accustomed to it. The Wonde (which was confined to Kpaa Mende-land) was concerned largely with military training. In the Bondo girls were instructed as to their attitudes towards their husbands, other men, and their fellow wives. In addition, there was some training in homecraft, sex matters and child care. The societies created a sense of comradeship and unity among members irrespective of family, clan or ethnic affiliation. The period of training could last for several months and sometimes for a year, especially for boys. Circumcision was the final stage in some of these institutions, after which the boy or girl graduated with a new status, a young adult.

As previously mentioned, the male societies, especially the

Poro and the Ragbenle, sometimes performed political and economic roles. They were often involved in the crowning and burial of kings and other important local officials. They also acted as checks against the abuse of power. In times of crisis, major decisions were taken in the society bush. The Poro even acted as arbitrator in chiefdom disputes. It could promulgate general laws and regulate trading practices.

There were other cult associations that performed a variety of functions. The Humoi society, for instance, regulated sexual conduct among the Mende. The society was headed by a woman and its rules constituted the rules of marriage and mating. The Humoi forbade incest (*simongama*), which was a heinous offence, and prohibited certain kinds of sexual behaviour for the community as a whole. It was forbidden to have sexual intercourse with a girl under the age of puberty, or with a person in the bush at any time, or with a pregnant woman (other than one's wife) or nursing mother. A brother could not sit on his sister's bed and vice versa, and a man was not allowed to shake hands with the mother of any woman with whom he had had sexual dealings.

Barrenness was usually attributed to the woman concerned having trespassed on a Poro sacred bush. The remedy lay in initiating the woman superficially into the Poro. Illnesses of various kinds in the case of a man could be traced to his having intruded in the Bondo bush during Bondo sessions. He could obtain a cure by paying a fine to the society members and being 'washed' by them.

Some societies, like the Gbangbe among the Koranko, involved training in the detection of witchcraft. The Sherbro had a potent medicine called *Pok*, on which persons suspected of crime and witnesses in court were sworn. If they swore falsely (being guilty of the offence they denied) or if they gave false evidence, they were affected by the *Pok*. It could 'eat' their intestines or sexual organs or force their eyes out of the sockets. Such persons would die unless treated by the *Pok*. This society excluded women from membership.

1.5 Production systems

Until the advent of Europeans in Sierra Leone, the indigenous peoples depended entirely on African products for their socio-economic needs. Most of the products were generally consumed in their areas of production, though a few important ones found external markets. Those peoples who lived inland farmed and raised cattle. They grew rice, cassava, yams, millet and vegetables. Sometimes they hunted and fished to supplement their food. The coastal peoples lived mainly on fishing and salt-manufacturing.

Manufacturing industry   Compared to modern methods, all industry was organized on a very small scale. The unit of production was a single craftsman and his apprentices, usually his children. In certain cases craft guilds were formed to expand production. Goods produced were normally exchanged by barter.

One of the essentials of diet not available in many areas in Sierra Leone was salt. The coastal areas were the main producers of salt and people often travelled long distances towards the coast in search of this precious commodity. Mandingo and Koranko Muslim traders from the northern region visited the coastal countries to procure salt and in the process helped to islamize some of the people they came into contact with.

Salt was produced by three methods: the collection of salt deposited on the leaves of mangrove trees at high tide; the evaporation of sea-water; and the extraction of salt from salt-encrusted mud.

To prevent the salt from dissolving under humid conditions, the salt was carefully rammed into hampers known as *ta sanka* in the Samu area (Kambia region). Salt was a very valuable commodity. Ten *sanka* of salt could buy a slave, and for four to ten *sanka* of salt and a piece of cloth a wife could be obtained.

Oil extraction was an important socio-economic activity. It was mainly done by women. Oil was obtained from nuts (palm-kernel nuts, coconuts and ground nuts) and palm fruits.

Palm-kernel oil   The nuts of palm-oil fruits were dried and cracked open manually. The nuts were grilled over an open fire in pots or pans and the grilled nuts pounded in a mortar and boiled with water. The oil was then scooped off the top of the boiling mixture.

Coconut oil   There were several ways of extracting oil from coconuts but the most common was the cooking method. The dried coconut was grated or pounded, mixed with warm water and squeezed by hand. A milk-like liquid was obtained, which was allowed to settle for some time, to separate the cream from the water. The cream was then scooped off and boiled. The oil was obtained by straining the mixture when cooled.

Groundnut oil The groundnuts were shelled and grilled. The grilled nuts were skinned by placing them on a mat and rolling a wood block over them, or by rolling them under a stick and then winnowing them. The skinned nuts were ground to a paste in a mortar and boiling water added. The mixture was stirred until the oil separated from the paste. The oil was then scooped off the surface and heated in order to boil off any remaining water.

Palm oil The palm fruits were placed in clay-lined pits and covered so that the fruits could ferment. Some fresh fruits were later boiled and added to the fermented fruits and mixed for a long time with the feet. Gradually the oil rose to the surface and was then skimmed off. Boiling water was added to the remaining fruits in the pit to obtain more oil. The oil so obtained contained a large amount of water which was removed by boiling the mixture.

Another method was to boil and pound the fruits until a mass containing oil, fibre and unbroken nuts was obtained. After kneading, the mass was sieved to remove unbroken nuts and fibres. The liquid mixture was boiled to break the oil and water emulsion. The oil then floated to the surface and was skimmed off.

Oil was used for cooking and for preservation of food. For example, fried fish could be kept in oil for a long time without the fish going bad. Oil was also an important ingredient in soapmaking and was used by women as cosmetics. Oil further provided a source of income for both men and women.

Soap-making was another important enterprise of the people. The principal ingredients in the manufacture of soap were ashes and palm oil. The ashes were obtained by burning the peelings of certain crops. The Mende commonly used a soft wood called *kobei*. The ashes were dissolved in water and then filtered. The filtrate was boiled and in the process palm oil was added. The soap thus obtained, commonly called 'country soap' (or black soap), was a valuable aid to hygiene. It was a medicated and medicinal soap, used for general washing and for the cure of such diseases as yellow fever and malaria.

Sierra Leoneans early learned to mine and utilize their supplies of two important metals – gold and iron. Most of the gold was alluvial and was obtained by panning. Some of this gold was used for the manufacture of jewellery and ornaments, and for religious rituals. Iron was found in rocks in the northern interior and was mined by open-cast methods. Iron workers were organized in close communities of blacksmiths who jealously guarded their secrets of smelting, forging and tempering the metal. Their skills were directed mainly to the production of weapons and tools. The Yalunka became famous blacksmiths, and among them blacksmiths' families constituted a privileged class. Skilled Yalunka and Koranko smiths travelled all over the country to barter their wares such as hoes, matchets and knives.

Skilled carvers made sculptures out of ivory, wood or stone, some of which were used in religious ceremonies. Potters made pots out of clay, and in the northern interior leather was made out of hides. Beautiful mats were woven, mainly from vegetable fibres. Cotton was available in many areas and this led to the development of textile industry in Sierra Leone. In some areas like Mende country, cotton seed was mixed with rice and broadcast by hand upon the upland rice-fields. Further to the north-east, cotton was extensively grown in Sankaran, Solima, Kono and upper Koranko countries and was an important trade item of that region. The technical skill involved in cloth manufacture was provided by people who had learned the arts of spinning and weaving, and who knew how to extract dyes from vegetable juice such as camwood and indigo. The cloth produced was popularly called 'country cloth' and was a multi-purpose commodity:

(a) It served as wearing apparel and could be used as bedding, a blanket, for making hammocks or for burial purposes.
(b) It was used as a currency to buy goods, discharge debts, or pay workers. For example, a carpenter in Mende country was often paid four or five country cloths for building a house. A slave was valued at 20 country cloths.
(c) Some wealthy people decorated their parlours or rooms with country cloths. The cloths were also used to decorate chairs used by newly-graduated Bondo girls.
(d) The gift of a white country cloth was a symbol of peace.

Warriors exchanged it if they did not wish to fight against each other.

Thus, although the economic system was rather rudimentary, it nevertheless satisfied the needs of the society.

References

Abraham, Arthur (1978), *Mende Government and Politics Under Colonial Rule* (Sierra Leone and Oxford University Press).

Anya, Oji (1973), 'The Sherbro in the Nineteenth Century – A Coastal People in Transition', MA (USL).

Atherton, J. H. and M. Kalous (1970), 'Nomoli', *Journal of African History* (JAH), Vol. II, no. 3.

Clarke, J. I. (1969), *Sierra Leone in Maps*, 2nd edition (University of London Press).

Dorjahn, V. R. (1966), 'The Changing Political System of the Temne', *Africa*, Vol. 30.

Finnegan, Ruth (1965), *Survey of the Limba People of Northern Sierra Leone* (HMSO, London).

Foray, C. P. (1977), *Historical Dictionary of Sierra Leone* (Metuchen, New Jersey).

Fyle, C. Magbaily (1979), *The Solima Yalunka Kingdom* (Nyakon, Freetown).

Fyle, C. Magbaily and Arthur Abraham (1976), 'The Country Cloth Culture in Sierra Leone', *ODU – Journal of West African Studies*, XXX.

Ijagbemi, E. A. (1977), 'Oral Tradition and Emergence of Temne Chiefdoms', *Africana Research Bulletin* (ARB), Vol. III, no. 2, March.

Ijagbemi, E. A. (1978), 'Rothoron (The North-east) in Temne Tradition and Culture: An Essay in Ethno-history', *Journal of the Historical Society of Sierra Leone* (JHSSL), II, I.

Little, Kenneth (1949), 'The Role of Secret Society in Cultural Specialization', *American Anthropologist*, Vol. 51, no. 2.

Little, Kenneth (1967), *The Mende of Sierra Leone* (London).

McCulloch, M. (1964), *The People of Sierra Leone* (International African Institute, London).

Sawyerr, Harry A. E. (1964), 'Ancestor Worship – The Mechanics', *Sierra Leone Bulletin of Religion* (SLBR), Vol. 6, no. 2, December.

Sawyerr, Harry and W. T. Harris (1968), *The Springs of Mende Belief and Conduct* (Sierra Leone University Press).

Questions PART A (For School Certificate/'O'Level Candidates)

1 Give a brief survey of the indigenous people of Sierra Leone.
2 Describe the pre-colonial political and social organizations of *one* of the following communities:
   (a) the Temne   (b) the Mende   (c) the Sherbro   (d) the Limba.
3 Describe the way of life of the people of Sierra Leone in the pre-colonial period.
4 Of what importance were secret societies (cult associations) to the people of Sierra Leone before the colonial era?

5   How important were *three* of the following in the life of Sierra Leoneans
    in pre-colonial times?
    (a) the salt industry
    (b) oil extraction
    (c) soap-making
    (d) metal industries
    (e) country cloth.
6   Describe some of the cultural features associated with traditional agri-
    culture in pre-colonial Sierra Leone.

Questions PART B (For College/University Students)
Additional reading required.

1   Consider the view that traditional Sierra Leone society was a male-
    dominated society.
2   How democratic were pre-colonial political institutions in Sierra Leone?
3   What secure conclusions can the historian of the pre-colonial Sierra
    Leone hinterland reach about the pattern of royal succession and the
    constitutional powers of rulers?
4   Discuss the nature and relevance of traditional educational systems in
    Sierra Leone.

2 *Early external influences*

For a very long time the indigenous peoples of Sierra Leone, especially the early inhabitants, lived largely in a world of their own. They maintained some trading and other contacts with their immediate African neighbours but the overall effects of these contacts were minimal. From the mid-fifteenth century, however, Sierra Leoneans were to be affected by a series of invasions which were to produce varied and long-lasting effects on their society. The first of these new influences came from European traders anxious to discover new outlets for commerce. The Europeans were soon followed by a group of Mande-speaking peoples called the Mane, whose invasions radically altered Sierra Leone's socio-cultural distribution. Black Muslim elite groups began infiltrating into the country from the north in the seventeenth century and by the close of the nineteenth century, Islam had become the way of life of many Sierra Leoneans.

2.1 The coming of the Europeans

The Portuguese were the first Europeans to visit Sierra Leone and, indeed, the west coast of Africa in the fifteenth century. They were soon followed by the Spanish (who were then called Castilians). But the Castilians gave up their interest in West Africa after the discovery of the Americas in the late fifteenth century. The Portuguese became the pioneers of the trade between Europe and West Africa. There were many reasons for this. They were the first to solve most of the technical problems that had previously made it impossible for Europeans to undertake long voyages of exploration. The

[31]

Portuguese succeeded in building the *caravel*, which was a
sailing ship that used large triangular sails instead of oars.
They also invented certain navigation instruments such as the
compass, which enabled sailors to find their way on the high
seas. Moreover, the Portuguese had ousted the Muslims from
their lands, many of whom had acted as middlemen in the
trade between Europe and Asia. Politically, Portugal was
enjoying peace and stability, whereas the other European
nations were engaged in civil disputes and external wars. The
Portuguese political leadership was also prepared to finance
voyages of exploration.

A caravel of the fifteenth century

A Portuguese sailor, Alvaro Fernandez, anchored in the estuary of the Rokel in 1447. In 1462 Pedro da Cintra called the peninsula Serra Lyoa. The estuary soon became an important source of fresh water and wood for Europeans on their way to and from India. Thus, the name 'watering place' came to be associated with the estuary.

In 1482 Portuguese traders began to build a fort on an island at the end of the bay, but it was later demolished. The traders gradually established themselves all along the coast and its surrounding country. Port Loko became one of their major trading centres. European goods like swords, kitchen and other household utensils and attractively-coloured ready-made clothes were exchanged at first for gold brought from inland and for the fine ivory works of the Sapes. Beeswax was also needed for making candles. The opening of European plantations in the New World (the Americas) in the 1550s and beyond, however, made slaves the major commodity that the Portuguese and, later, other Europeans sought in Sierra Leone. The slaves were needed to work in the plantations.

Some Portuguese married African women and set up families of Afro-Portuguese; others attempted to introduce Christianity among the local peoples.

As Portuguese activity increased in Sierra Leone and elsewhere on the coast, their language came to serve as a trade language between them and their West African contacts as well as between West Africans speaking different languages. It has also been suggested that the technical form of the Bullom boats was derived from a Portuguese model.

By the 1650s, however, Portugal had ceased to count as one of the most influential countries in Europe and its diminished stature adversely affected its ventures, commercial and otherwise.

About the mid-sixteenth century England became interested in the West African coast and English merchant adventurers began trading along the Guinea coast. Together with the French, Dutch and Danish, they proceeded to break the monopoly which the Portuguese had secured in the trade. In 1562 an English slaver, John Hawkins, paid his first visit to Sierra Leone. He captured some 300 slaves from Tagrin on the Sierra Leone River and sailed with them. This encouraged him to make another call shortly afterwards. This time he met a hot reception, for as soon as his men landed at Tagrin to fill

The Dutch admiral, de Ruyter

their water-casks they were set upon. They had to flee for their lives. Another English trader, Francis Drake, came to Sierra Leone in 1579.

The British traders tried to monopolize the trade of certain areas by operating chartered companies – for example, the British Royal African Company (BRAC). They built forts on important islands such as Bance (Bunce) Island, Sherbro Island and Tasso Island. But many of these forts were attacked by other European rivals. For example, the BRAC fort at Tasso Island was sacked in 1664 by a Dutch officer, Admiral de Ruyter, because some Dutch traders had been maltreated. After the attack de Ruyter inscribed his name and those of other Dutch and English sailors on a stone which he buried near the present King Jimmy Wharf. This stone was discovered in April 1923 when engineers were carrying out construction work on the wharf. A model of the 'de Ruyter Stone' is presently kept in the Sierra Leone Museum in Freetown. The BRAC's strongest fort on Bunce Island was captured by an African force led by rival Afro-Portuguese traders in 1728.

After its defeat BRAC withdrew from Sierra Leone, but some of the company's agents remained behind, along with other Englishmen. They married into powerful local chieftaincies along the coast and on the islands south of the Sierra Leone peninsula. At least four of the resulting Afro-British families – Caulkers, Tuckers, Clevelands and Rogers – were to continue to play a significant role in their areas into the twentieth century. These families and others maintained personal ties in England. They, as well as some of the coastal chiefs, sent their children there for Western education, often under the guidance of English firms that were their trading partners.

How trade was conducted   Coastal rulers had welcomed the European traders in the hope that they too would benefit from the trade. So they arranged that all major trade transactions should be carried out only on the coast. The European trader was therefore forbidden to go into the interior to trade and had to pay rents and other tribute to the coastal rulers for permission to trade. The ruler was the trader's landlord and the trader became the ruler's 'stranger'. The landlord was responsible for his stranger's security as well as for his actions.

As trade developed, more European goods were exchanged for ivory, beeswax, cowhides, camwood, some gold and slaves. Some dishonest traders like John Hawkins had tried to kidnap slaves and run away with them. In order to discourage this bad practice, coastal rulers began to demand hostages of a ship's crew as insurance against ungentlemanly conduct by European slave-dealers.

Bunce Island and the slave trade

During the Atlantic slave-trade era certain islands and points on the Sierra Leone coast became important slave centres. One such area was Bunce Island, located in the Sierra Leone

River about 20 miles (32 km) above modern Freetown.

When the BRAC withdrew from Sierra Leone, their fort on Bunce Island was taken over by the London firm of Grant, Sargent and Oswald in 1750. The firm established a shipyard, employed more African workers and assembled a fleet of small vessels to ply the southern coastline in search of slaves. Most of the slaves bought by the company were taken to South Carolina in the North American colonies to be resold to rice planters in Charlestown and other rice-growing centres in South Carolina, for it was soon discovered that slaves from Sierra Leone and its neighbourhood were very good rice-growers.

Danish merchants also became interested in the Bunce Island trade, and by the 1780s these merchants were buying some 2000 slaves a year at Bunce Island. At Bunce Island today one can still find a cannon from a Danish ship dated 1780 and the grave of a Danish ship captain who died in 1783. There was money to be made by anyone who could bring slaves from Sierra Leone to South Carolina. It has been suggested that the descendants of slaves taken from Sierra Leone and its neighbourhood gave birth to a distinctive group of Black Americans in South Carolina and Georgia, who today are called the Gullah. The Gullah language reflects significant influences from Sierra Leone and the surrounding areas. The Gullah speak a variant of Krio (like other descendants of slaves in the Caribbean), but a very large proportion of rural Gullah have preserved traditional songs and fragments of stories in Mende and Vai. They use Sierra Leonean rural names like Vandi, Ndapi, Sanie, Tamba (masculine) and Kadiatu, Fatmata, Hawa and Isata (feminine). They also make baskets and fishing nets which are very similar to those made in the rural areas of Sierra Leone.

Some effects of early European contact

These effects could be summarized under five main headings:

   (i)   introduction of foreign goods;
  (ii)   establishment of European settlements;
 (iii)   encouragement of the trade in slaves;
 (iv)   introduction of Christianity;
  (v)   Afro-European unions.

These have been discussed above, but further comments will be made on some.

The goods brought by Europeans helped to change the life-style of many coastal peoples. For example, they began to dress in European clothes, eat European food and use European utensils. Unfortunately, however, a larger influx of cheap European goods, particularly textiles and metalware, forced many indigenous craftsmen out of business. This in turn led to a decline of local industries. The use of Portuguese as a trade language was to have some effect on the Temne and, later, the Krio languages, for these two languages today contain a certain number of Portuguese words. It is significant that the Temne word for Europeans in general is *Poto*, no doubt a corrupt version of 'Portuguese', since the Portuguese were the first Europeans with whom they came into contact. Demand for slaves to work in the American plantations led to an increase in the incidence of warfare. Some Portuguese even took part in these wars. Accusations of crimes became more rampant and miscarriage of justice became common, for 'guilty' persons were generally sold as slaves.

2.2 The Mane invasions

The Mane hailed from the Mali empire. Their leader, Queen Masarico, had offended the emperor and had to leave the city. She took along large numbers of followers and moved southwards. These followers were later transformed into a conquering army which overran vast territories and many nations. The army's ranks were swelled with recruits to such an extent that for sustenance it became necessary for them to eat some of the defeated peoples.

On reaching the Atlantic coast, Masarico and her troops travelled westwards. The Mane were finally based in the Cape Mount area of Liberia close to the eastern Sierra Leone frontier by the 1540s. At Cape Mount they had a serious battle against the Bullom, in which Masarico's son, running into a Bullom ambush, was killed. Queen Masarico died shortly afterwards from grief and old age. The Mane later conquered the Temne and by 1555 they had succeeded in subduing all the coastal communities.

The success of the Mane could be attributed to certain factors. The Mane were better fighters and they had an efficient military organization. They had stronger weapons and often used poison on these weapons to make them more powerful. They also used larger and faster war canoes and could thus transport many soldiers and military equipment at greater speeds. Some Europeans aided the Mane in their war efforts in the hope that they could obtain war captives as slaves. The coastal peoples lived in isolated communities and made no serious effort to unite and effectively challenge the Mane. They were also probably afraid of the Sumba; these were fierce fighters and cannibals drafted into the Mane army on their way to Sierra Leone. When the Mane forces appeared before a given village, they would send an emissary bearing cloth and arms. To accept was to recognize Mane rule; to reject was not only to risk defeat in battle, but also to be under the further threat of being eaten by the Sumba. As it was, the reputation of the Sumba, enhanced by rumour, was enough to spread terror and a disinclination to resist.

Encouraged by their victories on the coast, the Mane then set about conquering the Sierra Leone interior groups. They incorporated most of their defeated enemies, such as the Bullom and Temne, into their ranks. These soon adopted Mande family names like Kamara, Bangura, Kanu, Kagbo, Konte, Koroma, Silla, Toure.

But the Mane were not always victorious. They had little success against the Limba and Yalunka, who resorted to guerrilla warfare. An attempt to subjugate the Soso also backfired. While the Soso were on the run, they poisoned all the food they left behind. Many Mane soldiers ate this food and died. At this juncture, the Soso decided to go on the offensive and, led by Fula horsemen, they stormed the Mane. The Mane forces fled in disorder, but the Soso were familiar with the land because of their earlier contact with the Sapes; they therefore pursued the fleeing Mane forces and killed large numbers.

Effects of the Mane invasions

The Mane invasions produced wide-ranging effects in Sierra Leone. These include political, military, ethno-linguistic, economic and cultural effects.

Political effects   The Mane warleaders divided the areas they had conquered among themselves, and proclaimed themselves kings. Four Mane sub-kingdoms were thus established. The first was the kingdom of the Bullom, which extended northwards from Tagrin Point and included the Isles de Los (off Conakry in modern Guinea). Mitombo, or Logos, the second kingdom, was centred on Port Loko. The third, the kingdom of Sierra Leone or Boure, ran inland from the Sierra Leone peninsula, which it embraced, to merge with the fourth, the kingdom of Sherbro. The Mane rulers in Sierra Leone owed

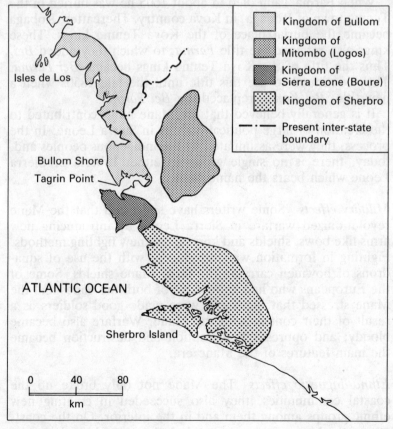

Kingdom of Bullom

Kingdom of Mitombo (Logos)

Kingdom of Sierra Leone (Boure)

Kingdom of Sherbro

Present inter-state boundary

Isles de Los

Bullom Shore

Tagrin Point

ATLANTIC OCEAN

Sherbro Island

0   40   80
km

5   *Sierra Leone: Mane sub-kingdoms*

allegiance to a paramount ruler in Cape Mount and if they failed to honour their obligations to this overlord, a new force would be sent against them.

A Mane general who commanded great respect among the local inhabitants was Farma Tami (*Farma* in Mandingo means 'governor') who came from the east. He set up the kingdom of Mitombo among the Temne, Baga and Loko in the 1560s. He was generally addressed as 'Emperor of the Sapes'. He is said to have brought many areas under his rule. Tami's capital was at Koya. Though he was very powerful, he was not autocratic. He was assisted by certain senior male officials, such as *Naimbana* (who acted as regent when the king died), *Pa Kapr*, *Naimsogo*, and 'Mammy Queens': *Bome Pose*, *Bome Warah* and *Bome Rufah*. Their positions were elective.

When Farma Tami died in about 1605 he was buried in the Temne town of Robaga, in Koya country. Thereafter, Robaga became the burial place of the Koya Temne kings. These kings also retained the title *Farma*, to which they added *Bei*. Thus the title of the Koya Temne kings became *Bei Farma*. They continued to use this title until the late 1850s when a new title, *Bei Kanta*, replaced the *Bei Farma*.

It is generally believed that the Mane kings contributed to the creation of large political entities in Sierra Leone. In the process, they were assimilated by the indigenous peoples and, today, there is no single group in either Liberia or Sierra Leone which bears the name Mane.

Military effects   Some writers have suggested that the Mane revolutionized warfare in Sierra Leone by introducing new arms like bows, shields and knives, and new fighting methods. Fighting in formation was introduced, with the use of squadrons of bowmen carrying the large Mane shields. Some of the Europeans who had knowledge of both the Sapes and the Mane stressed that the Sapes were made good soldiers as a result of their contact with the Mane. Warfare also became bloody; and oppression, disruption and destruction became the main features of the Mane era.

Ethno-linguistic effects   The Mane not only broke up the coastal communities, they also succeeded in creating new ethnic groups among them and in the interior. On the coast, one of the Mane viceroys, Sherabola, imposed his rule on the southern Bullom in the late sixteenth century, resulting in the formation of a new community called Sherbro. (*Sherbro* was probably a corrupt form of Sherabola). A new language also evolved called Sherbro which is slightly different from the Bullom language. The Loko are another product of the Mane. One of the Mane armies (a Toma-Gbande force) invaded Logos (Port Loko) and subsequently established the kingdom of Mitombo there in the mid-sixteenth century. The Mende were, however, the largest group to have emerged from the Mane invasions. The Mane made their greatest impact around the Gallinas and Cape Mount, and it is suggested that the Mende may have emerged from this region. Most writers agree that the Mende represent the Mane fusion with the Gola and Kissi, while the Loko represent the same Mane elements fused with the Temne. The Loko are akin to the Mende and the Gbandi of Liberia. The Limba in fact call the Loko 'Gbande' while the Gbandi themselves say their brothers left them at an early date to fight in a war in the west. The Temne also call the Mende *Ò Měni* (a close reference to the Mane).

Economic effects   These were negative. Many Sapes were forced to work for the Mane rulers and many more were sold to Europeans as slaves. Sape trade with the northern interior was also disrupted. By 1564 Sherbro Island had been transformed into a real granary and Sape labour was used to produce an abundance of millet, root crops and palm wine. The Sapes were harshly used, and in some cases they made desperate efforts to throw off the Mane yoke, if only by flight. Some Bullom revolted against their Mane king, Shere Mambea, in 1572. The king was forced to seek outside help before he could contain the rebellion. Over a thousand of his subjects also withdrew to the bush, leaving behind most of their property. With the help of some Portuguese, many Sapes escaped to such places as the Cape Verde Islands.

Mainly on the basis of their salt manufacture, the Sapes had been able to attract trade from Futa Jallon and elsewhere. The Fula and the Yalunka supplied cloth, cattle and gold, supplemented by iron and dyes from Soso country. The Mane invasions forced this interior trade to find an outlet further north (on the Nunez), and the coastal distribution southwards had to stop. Fortunately, by the end of the sixteenth century conditions had become settled enough to permit a resumption of this trade.

Cultural effects These were mixed. The Mane invasions severely impaired Sape creativity, because most of their skills were destroyed. In the early sixteenth century the Sapes had become famous for their raffia and ivory works, carving to European specifications items like salt-cellars, spoons and dagger hilts. A Portuguese visitor, Valentim Fernandes, wrote that 'the men in this country are the cleverest Negroes where manual art is concerned, they make salt-cellars and spoons of ivory. And also it does not matter what one sketches, they will carve it in ivory.' But these artistic skills did not survive the Mane invasions. It is also clear that a number of stone figures like the *nomoli* and *pomdo* were lost in the wave of successive Mane invasions. For the coastal peoples the encounter with the Mane must indeed have been a traumatic experience.

In at least one respect the Mane made a positive contribution to the domestic skills of the Sapes, and that was in the working of iron. They improved on the iron industry of the local population. It is also possible that the Mane brought techniques of weaving cotton. Formerly, most of the cloth used on the coast came from the distant northern interior. But with the advent and consolidation of Mane power particularly in the south-east, the indigenous peoples began to manufacture their own cloth. The Mende and Kono especially took to this art.

The Mane also brought some war-medicines which were fairly effective. Special priestesses, kept in secluded places, were charged with the responsibility of preparing these medicines. Men could visit them only in special circumstances. The Mane raised the status of women and strengthened existing female secret societies. Women further gained a privileged position in certain politico-cultural organizations. The office of the *Mabole* in the Poro society, for example, is held by a woman. It commands the highest respect and has an integral role in the ceremonial life and purpose of that organization. Male secret societies like the Poro, Ragbenle and Simo were strengthened and given political roles.

The Mane invasions therefore greatly affected Sierra Leone, producing both negative and positive effects.

2.3 Advance of Islam

Some of the early agents of Islam in Sierra Leone sought to promote their religion by force, through the Futa Jallon *jihad*. But force was not the main instrument of Muslim expansion into Sierra Leone. The normal pattern was through peaceful means by long-distance traders, missionaries and teachers.

The Futa Jallon jihad

This *jihad* was waged more for political and economic reasons than for the conversion of non-Muslims to Islam. It was begun in 1727 by Fula Muslim traders in Jallonkadu, the home of the Yalunka. These Fula wanted to take over the government of Jallonkadu and then control the trade of the region, from which they were benefiting greatly. The *jihad* was used to achieve this objective.

The *jihad* was led by a pious scholar, Karamokoh Alfa, and his cousin Ibrahim Suri, a great general. They succeeded in overthrowing the Yalunka. Thereafter, the Fula changed the name of the kingdom to Futa Jallon.

The war dislodged many peoples, who dispersed over a wide area. For example, the Soso, converted or unconverted, were pushed south and west. Some groups settled at first peacefully among the Limba whom they later conquered. Many Limba were forced to move towards the mountains where they built high, inaccessible towns to be safe from invaders. Other groups moved towards the coast and dominated the Baga, Temne or Bullom, north of the Scarcies. Some Soso migrants were given shelter in Port Loko where they were allowed to build their own town, Sendugu. Some Mandingo also settled among the Loko.

The *jihad* contributed partly to the islamization of northern Sierra Leone. The Solima Yalunka, who were living just outside Futa Jallon, came under Fula rule after the Fula had built their strong state. As the Solima Yalunka became Muslims, they sent many of their elders and sons of chiefs to study Islam at Futa. These new converts helped to spread Islam in parts of Koranko and Limba countries. Many conquered peoples also became Muslims, and eventually new Muslim towns appeared in these conquered areas. Some Muslim Yalunka and Koranko moved into Kissi and Mende countries, where they helped to spread the Islamic faith. Many aspects of Islamic influence, like the use of charms and amulets (*sebe*) and the use of the Arabic script, were adopted in many of these areas.

Many of the immigrants became so powerful in their new areas that they gained political power. The Soso that settled in Port Loko increased their strength to such an extent that they were able to take over the government of Port Loko. They were led by the Sankoh family. Some Yalunka became chiefs among the Koranko and Kissi. A Mandingo who had helped the Loko in war was eventually made king and his descendants ruled alternately with a Loko king. A Fula became chief in Yoni country and non-Limba chiefs ruled the Limba. So over a wide area it became usual for peoples to have rulers of alien origin.

Meanwhile, the Fula started making too many demands on their subjects. The Koranko attempted to rebel, but failed. The Solima Yalunka, who were finding Fula domination unbearable, refused to help the Fula in their war against the Sankaran in the 1770s. This greatly annoyed the Fula, who then killed all the Yalunka studying in Futa. The Solima Yalunka retaliated by killing all the Fula in their own country. The Solima Yalunka general, Tokba Asana, then declared war on Futa. He allied with the Sankaran leader Konde Braima. Together they advanced on Futa Jallon. There was a long struggle from which the Fula emerged victorious. The Solima Yalunka were forced to disperse. They built a fortified town in the mountains at Falaba in about 1780.

The Futa–Solima wars continued on and off for many years. The Solima Yalunka continued to remain united in their struggle against the Fula, and even after the wars they remained together and so formed the Solima state around Falaba. Though they accompanied their rebellion with a rejection of Islam, aspects of Islamic influence were retained. The Arabic script was widely used, and so were charms and amulets for protection against sickness and evil spirits. Some Solima leaders also continued to practise Islam.

Peaceful conversion

Long-distance traders, missionaries and teachers from the northern territories were instrumental in the spread of Islam in Sierra Leone. Islam gained influence among Sierra Leoneans because Muslim migrants possessed resources which were highly valued by the local people. Muslims were welcomed because they brought wealth in the form of trade and they provided jobs for the local residents. Their caravans required guards, porters and guides, and local merchants and rulers gained wealth through trade. Muslim scholars were highly literate in Arabic and this earned them a favourable place in the courts of the interior kings where they served as clerks, interpreters and advisers. The use of Arabic was also valued for religious purposes. Religious charms written in Arabic were believed to provide the possessor with protection from injury or disease and assured victory in war and success in economic pursuits. Islamic rituals and the Arabic language were thus perceived by the populace as having spiritual powers which could be transformed into practical advantage. Muslim holy men were thought to have great spiritual powers which allowed them to predict the future. Muslim religious leaders also encouraged traditional practices like sacrifice, polygamy and slavery, which Christianity condemned. These also tended to attract many people to Islam.

Many Muslim traders established themselves along the caravan routes and acted as hosts or landlords to the long-distance traders, providing the services along the trade routes necessary for the exchange of goods. They housed traders and stored their goods; they either bought the goods themselves or contacted potential buyers. They also mediated between sellers and buyers, helped to establish the exchange rate and fulfilled the services of broker and moneylender. Often they provided carriers along trade routes.

As these Muslim trader–landlord families settled in a town, they used their wealth and prestige to obtain land. Sometimes, they maintained private armies to guarantee security of trade. They bought slaves to farm their land and strengthen their armies. They established schools, built mosques and provided Arabic letter-writers for local chiefs. The services they provided for the chiefs – the bringing of wealth through trade, provision of foodstuffs and luxuries, military support in case of attack, education for their children – usually led to intermarriages with chiefly families, increase in landholdings, and the granting of sub-chieftaincies to members of trading families. The settlement of Muslim families at Gbinti and

Foredugu (where the Bunduka family from Senegal obtained chiefdoms), in Yalunka country (where the Mandingo Samura clan established itself), and at Madina and Biriwa (Mandingo Mansaray clan) is a good example of this process. Several families settled in Freetown gained prestige in the same way.

Muslim missionaries and teachers called Karamokoh or Alfa or Foday also built mosques and Koranic schools in many areas in the country. In the mid-nineteenth century, for example, a famous Muslim scholar and teacher, Foday Tarawally, built an Islamic college in Kambia which attracted several young people. These later helped to spread Islam in their home areas.

Koranko Muslims travelling through Mendeland and the coastal countries in search of salt were persuaded to stay and take wives because of their mystical powers associated with Islamic practices. Thus, the Kallon of Kailahun, Kenema and Pujehun districts are descended from a Koranko ancestor named Va Foray Kallon or Foray Sasabla (*sasabla* is the term used by Sierra Leoneans for the Muslim rosary). A colonial officer was to later remark that in Mende country no important event was conducted without first consulting the 'Moriman' who 'looked ground'.

Thus towards the end of the nineteenth century, a sizeable proportion of the Sierra Leone population had become Muslim, even if only nominally.

References

Fyfe, Christopher (1979), *A Short History of Sierra Leone* (Longman).
Fyle, C. Magbaily (1979), *The Solima Yalunka Kingdom* (Nyakon, Freetown).
Kup, A. P. (1970), *Sierra Leone – A Concise History* (David and Charles, Canada).
Opala, Joseph A. (1987), *The Gullah – Rice, Slavery and the Sierra Leone – American Connection* (USIS, Freetown, Sierra Leone).
Rodney, Walter (1970), *History of the Upper Guinea Coast, 1545–1800* (Oxford).
Skinner, David E. (1971), 'Islam in Sierra Leone in the Nineteenth Century', Ph D (University of California).
Skinner, David E. (1977), 'Islam and Education in the Colony and Hinterland of Sierra Leone, 1750–1914', *Canadian Journal of African Studies*, X, 3.
Turay, A. K. (1979), 'The Portuguese in Temneland: An Ethno-Linguistic Perspective', JHSSL: Vol. 3, nos 1 and 2.

Questions PART A

1 How did the arrival of the Portuguese in the mid-fifteenth century affect Sierra Leone?
2 What were the general effects of European contact with Sierra Leone up to the mid-eighteenth century?
3 Who were the Mane? Briefly explain how their invasions affected Sierra Leone.
4 Why were the Mane able to defeat the coastal communities in Sierra Leone?
5 What caused the Futa Jallon *jihad* and how did it affect Sierra Leone?
6 Discuss the political effects of the Futa Jallon *jihad* in Sierra Leone.
7 What factors were responsible for the spread of Islam in Sierra Leone?

Questions PART B

1 What was the nature of European relations with the coast of Sierra Leone during the period 1447–1770?
2 'The Atlantic slave trade altered relations between the rulers and the ruled in Sierra Leone.' Discuss.
3 'The material culture of the Sapes collapsed under Mane pressure.' How accurate is this statement?
4 Discuss the political and ethno-linguistic effects of the Mane invasions in Sierra Leone.
5 What was the nature of the interaction between Mande and non-Mande elements in northern Sierra Leone before the mid-nineteenth century?
6 How successful was Islamic penetration into Sierra Leone before 1850?
7 'The Futa Jallon *jihad* was a political rather than a religious movement.' Discuss.

3 The establishment and development of the Sierra Leone Colony

3.1 The anti-slavery movement in Britain

The background to the founding of the Sierra Leone Colony settlement was the growing opinion that slavery was illegal in Britain. Until the 1780s, however, few Englishmen had given serious thought to the evils of slavery and the slave trade. One such man was Granville Sharp. From the 1760s Sharp became involved in the act of freeing slaves brought to England by their masters from the Americas.

The Sommerset case Sharp sponsored the famous Sommerset case in 1772. A slave, James Sommerset, had brought action against his master Stewart, for his freedom. The Chief Justice, Lord William Murray Mansfield, ruled that under English law it was not possible for a master forcibly to remove his slave from England with the intention of reselling him (as Stewart intended). Sommerset's lawyer also remarked that the air of England was too pure to accommodate slavery. Sommerset was set free. But the Chief Justice did not declare a complete prohibition of slavery, nor did he say that any slave who came to England became a free man.

Thus, the status of the slaves in England was unaffected by this decision. After the American War of Independence many of those black slaves who had fought for the British went to

[48]

Nova Scotia in Canada, but a significant number found their way into England. They led miserable lives in England as most of them were unemployed. Sharp and his friends made tireless efforts, often at great personal inconvenience, to alleviate the sufferings of these blacks, but it soon became clear that private charity could not cope with the growing numbers of poor blacks. The Poor Law officers in London, who normally cared for paupers, bore no responsibility for the blacks because the laws stipulated that paupers were to be supported by their parish of origin. And the place of origin of these blacks was Africa. This was probably why a decision was later taken to resettle the poor blacks in Africa.

The abolitionists, including Sharp, Thomas Clarkson, Henry Thornton and a leading member of the British Parliament, William Wilberforce, founded the Society for Effecting the Abolition of the Slave Trade in 1786. They also formed a Committee for the Relief of the Black Poor to provide food and medicines for London's poor blacks.

The English abolitionist Granville Sharp

The English abolitionist William Wilberforce

The committee members also took up a scheme proposed by Dr Henry Smeathman, a botanist who had visited Sierra Leone earlier and rendered a favourable report on the climatic conditions. He had proposed an agricultural settlement of Africans and whites in Sierra Leone. The plan attracted the attention of London's poor blacks as well as Sharp and his friends. The blacks soon elected headmen who made representations to the abolitionists to assure them of their willingness to come out to Sierra Leone. They even said that one of their number, who was a native of Sierra Leone, had assured them that they would be well received in Sierra Leone.

Sharp promoted Smeathman's idea and envisaged a free and independent community. So he named the proposed settlement 'Province of Freedom'. This province, it was hoped, would serve as a nucleus for the spread of Christianity and European civilization in Africa. Sharp then drew up a constitution for the intended settlement. The prospective settlers would govern themselves by the old English system of frankpledge. The settlers were to be guided by the traditions, customs and laws of England at all times, although they could make laws in their common councils. Provision was also made for the election of a governor by the settlers themselves as well as of a governing council. Capital punishment was prohibited and there was to be a speedy trial of suspects. Moreover, half of the jury in every case were to be of the same ethnic group as the accused. Other matters dealt with in the constitution included police duties, free labour and agrarian reform.

The British Government was requested to provide funds for the intended settlement. The British Government, which was anxious to rid Britain of undesirable jobless blacks as they were potential troublemakers, agreed to provide the money.

Sharp was prepared to take in any industrious Protestant Europeans who could teach craft to the black settlers. Twenty artisans, a town-major to build fortifications, five doctors, a sexton and a chaplain were among the group of settlers that embarked for Sierra Leone. Smeathman, who had been appointed Agent Conductor, died just before the party could set sail. His friend, Joseph Irwin, then took charge of the settlers. He was to accompany them to Sierra Leone and, on arrival, was to have the town laid out in lots and built. The whole expedition was expected to cost about £15 000.

3.2 Foundation of the Colony

On 8 April 1787 a total of 411 immigrants, including some white girls, left for Sierra Leone under the command of Captain T. Bouldon Thompson of the British navy. Thompson was to help the settlers found a colony in Sierra Leone. The settlers arrived on 10 May and the following day Thompson went ashore to negotiate for land with King Tom, a sub-chief of the Sierra Leone peninsula. In return for some £59 worth

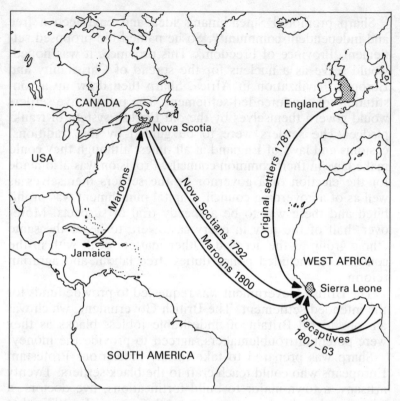

6   *Sierra Leone: Colony settlers*

European and African craft off the coast of Sierra Leone, early nineteenth century

of trade goods – beads, iron bars, tobacco and rum – King Tom and his officials were cajoled into giving up the shore from the watering place to Gambia Island, a stretch of nine or ten miles (16 km), a depth of 20 miles (32 km). On 15 May the settlers disembarked and cut their way through the bush to the top of the hill overlooking the watering place (near where State House is now situated) where they planted the British flag.

The Original Settlers (as they came to be called) then began a new settlement which they called Granville Town in honour of their benefactor Granville Sharp.

Problems of settling down   The settlement suffered severe reverses caused by many factors such as bad weather, illness and disputes over land. The settlers arrived during the rainy season when it was difficult to put up permanent homes. They had spent a long time at sea and were weakened by the voyage. Many began to fall victim to disease and the climate. Four months after their arrival, 86 of the settlers died of malaria and dysentery. About that same number had died on the voyage. The high mortality rate continued throughout the rainy season. In the circumstances it became very difficult to maintain order. However, Thompson did his best. He finally left on 16 September 1787.

When the rains lessened, the settlers began to put up permanent homes. Following Sharp's instructions, they divided their settlement into tithings and hundreds. A tithing consisted of a group of ten families. Each tithing elected on annual basis a leader called a tithingman. Every ten tithingmen in their turn elected a hundredor, also on annual basis. The tithingmen and hundredors formed the governing council. A Governor was also elected. The first Governor was Richard Weaver. Soon the new Colony was plagued with political problems. Personal rivalries made it difficult for the Governor and Council to function efficiently.

Then there were problems connected with agriculture. The settlers knew nothing about tropical agriculture. They brought English seeds which could not thrive in the Colony. As starvation threatened the settlers, many of them began to barter their property with the neighbouring Temne for rice. Some drifted away to work on passing ships or for slave traders. Weaver's successor, James Reid, then wrote to Sharp requesting that he send some business agent to help them until their crops were well-established.

In answer to Reid's request, Sharp sent a ship under the command of Captain John Taylor with fresh supplies plus 39 new immigrants, who were mostly whites, in June 1788. But King Naimbana, who was more powerful and influential than King Tom (and who had been away when the first settlers arrived), refused to allow these new immigrants to disembark until a new treaty was signed. For £85 worth of trade goods, King Naimbana also gave up claims to the shore on 22 August 1788. The new treaty between King Naimbana and Captain John Taylor superseded King Tom's treaty with Thompson in 1787. The new ship's arrival raised the hopes of some of the settlers, and many of those who had run away came back.

Some of the settlers and a few of the whites sent to develop the Colony abandoned the settlement completely and took to trading in slaves. The European ship captains constantly harassed the settlers and were also very unruly. At one point they burnt down one of the native settlements near Granville Town. The new king, Jimmy, reacted by burning down Granville Town in 1790. This attack brought to an end Sharp's dream of establishing a 'province of freedom' in Africa.

Revival of the Colony settlement

The abolitionists were saddened by these unfortunate developments in the Colony. They approached the British Government for financial assistance to revive the Sierra Leone settlement, but this met with failure. Some of the abolitionists then proposed that a company of merchants be formed to take over the administration of the Colony and alleviate its economic distress.

In 1790 the abolitionists formed the St George's Bay Company and the following year it received its charter as the Sierra Leone Company. Henry Thornton, who was banker, was elected Chairman of the company. The company hoped to promote Christianity, commerce and Western civilization in the Colony. It disallowed slave trade in the Colony and promised to open schools for all Colony children.

Under the company's direction, the Colony was to be ruled by a governor and seven councillors, all appointed by the company directors in London and not by the colonists. The new situation was to create disappointment, unrest and revolt in the Colony.

The company sent an agent, Alexander Falconbridge, to Sierra Leone in 1791 to refound the Colony. Falconbridge gathered the former residents of Granville Town (who numbered about 50) to establish a new Granville Town near Fourah Bay. He also helped the settlers to plant a few crops and put up some buildings. He organized a militia and gave the people arms to defend themselves. After staying for six months Falconbridge returned to report to his masters. He took along King Naimbana's eldest son, John Frederick. Sharp took care of the boy and rebaptized him Henry Granville. Falconbridge came out again to Sierra Leone in 1792 where he died.

3.3   Nova Scotians

The Nova Scotians were the next important group of settlers that arrived in the Colony. They were black slaves who had fought for the British in the American War of Independence in exchange for their freedom and some land after the war. The American victory forced these black loyalists and other white loyalists to emigrate to the British settlement of Nova Scotia in Canada. It was from this settlement that they acquired their name.

However, as a result of disappointments and frustrations in Nova Scotia, they sent a protest mission led by Thomas Peters to Britain to seek redress. With the cooperation of the British Government, the Sierra Leone Company was able to make arrangements for the transfer of the Nova Scotians to Sierra Leone. Lieutenant John Clarkson of the British navy accompanied Thomas Peters to Nova Scotia in 1791 to oversee the repatriation arrangements. John Clarkson was the younger brother of Thomas Clarkson, who was one of the most important members of the Abolition of the Slave Trade Committee. He had shown keen interest in his brother's activities for the abolition, and he supported Granville Sharp's plan for the settlement of free Negroes in Sierra Leone.

Many factors compelled the Nova Scotians to emigrate to Sierra Leone. There was first of all the desire for land. After patiently waiting for eight years, many of them began to lose all hope of ever getting the land promised them. Closely connected with the land problem was the desire for independence. Nova Scotians felt that they were still slaves working for white masters. In Africa they would finally break the chains of dependence and bondage, and work on their own land. They also wanted security in their independence. Some loyalists feared that they would be tricked some day and be caught as slaves. Africa was too far away from North America for such a possibility. Besides, slavery was now illegal in the Sierra Leone Colony. Then there was the need for religious freedom. There was much restriction on worship placed on the blacks in Nova Scotia, and John Clarkson's assurance that they would be free to worship in their own manner no doubt encouraged the black pastors to emigrate. Nova Scotian black chapels had helped to create a sense of community life. It was therefore not uncommon to see an entire congregation wanting to emigrate to Sierra Leone.

It is important to note, however, that some blacks had bought land in Nova Scotia and were conveniently settled. For example, of 151 men from Shelburne and Birchtown who were accepted by Clarkson, 105 were owners of some property. And the land promised to the Nova Scotians was still there. The overriding factor of the Nova Scotian exodus was independence. Clarkson not only offered land, but the promised land. A farm in Nova Scotia was no substitute for an entire country in Africa.

John Clarkson believed that he had the full authority of the directors of the Sierra Leone Company to make commitments on their behalf and to interpret the settlement terms to the Nova Scotians (these had not been agreed upon before his departure from England). He felt that the constitution drawn up by Sharp in 1787 was still in operation in the Sierra Leone Colony and everything he said to the Nova Scotians was based on this constitution. He therefore promised the Nova Scotians free land in Sierra Leone. Each family was to be allocated farm lands as follows: twenty acres for a man, ten for his wife and five for each child. Clarkson went on to say that any taxes paid by the Nova Scotians would be 'for charitable purposes, such as the maintenance of their poor, the care of the sick and the education of their children'. He also made it quite clear to the would-be immigrants that they would have full control in the running of their own affairs.

Unknown to Clarkson, however, as he was making these promises to the Nova Scotians, the Sierra Leone Company was drawing up detailed provisions for the administration of the Colony. The Colony would be effectively run by the company and not by the settlers.

Some 1200 black loyalists left Nova Scotia early in 1792 and arrived in Sierra Leone on 28 March. A few of them had died on the way. They founded a new settlement at the old Granville Town which they named Free Town to symbolize that they were a free and independent people. Nova Scotians, too, experienced major problems of survival such as inhospitable climate. The other problems were caused mainly by the company's employees.

Governor John Clarkson

When the Nova Scotians arrived, Clarkson was made Superintendent of the Sierra Leone Colony. The settlement under Clarkson struggled through its first few weeks successfully; by August the remainder of the Original Settlers at Granville Town joined the new community at Free Town. By the end of the rains the new settlement began to show signs of its future development. The first houses were built along regular streets which Clarkson named after the twelve directors of the Sierra Leone Company.

But he encountered some difficulties. Thomas Peters challenged his right to head the Colony and accused the whites of being responsible for their sufferings. Those Nova Scotians who were loyal to Peters planned a rebellion, but the plot backfired. Clarkson then publicly reprimanded Peters, accusing him of ingratitude. The white officials began to fear that Peters and his team aimed at replacing them with a black government.

Peters' ambition was shattered when he was found guilty of theft. Despite this disgraceful end, Thomas Peters must be honoured for injecting new blood into the Colony. If he had not braved the oceans to plead the Nova Scotians' cause in Britain, the Colony settlement would hardly have prospered. For it was the Nova Scotians who gave a new lease of life to the Sierra Leone Colony settlement.

Confusion and mismanagement also besieged the Clarkson

administration. Some settlers seldom reported for work and most of the company's white employees were lazy and irresponsible. They were more interested in moving around in fancy clothes than with superintending the plantations. They quarrelled daily over their respective authority and paid more attention to parading their troops than to preparing a settlement. Their wives remained on board the ships in the harbour, gossiping, quarrelling, and stirring up trouble. The soldiers pilfered the stores they were supposed to guard, got drunk, and abused the black settlers.

The governing body of the Colony proved unworkable. The councillors disagreed on nearly all major issues. Following a protest by Clarkson to the company directors, the Council was dissolved and replaced with a governor and two councillors. Clarkson was then formally appointed Governor of the Colony and was given wide powers.

In spite of his new powers Governor Clarkson continued to rule by persuasion, preaching to the Nova Scotians, pushing them to action, pleading with them to end their hatred for and distrust of the Europeans, thus hoping that their trust in him would be transferred more generally to the company itself. His policy did bear some fruit. By the end of 1792 Clarkson wrote that the Colony gained strength daily. Poverty continued to be a problem, but the Nova Scotians were growing produce in their gardens, and raising hogs; fishing boats went out daily; and enterprising settlers went to Gambia and Bunce Island to trade.

Before Clarkson left he had made some attempt to establish a more effective control of the settlers. He again divided the settlement into tithings and hundreds. This system provided the settlers with a means of organization by which they effectively protested against company government in the following years.

Governor Clarkson left Sierra Leone in December 1792, but not before he had preached an important sermon to the settlers and offered his famous 'Prayer for Sierra Leone'. This prayer has over the years acquired almost divine attributes and it can be seen today displayed in many homes in Sierra Leone. (See Appendix 2.)

Governor Clarkson was coolly received by the company directors in England. Though he had saved the Colony from ruin, the directors were annoyed at the promise of land he had made to the Nova Scotians, which later became an embarrassment to the company and a major source of grievance in the Colony. Clarkson was relieved of his duties in 1793 and thereafter he became a banker.

Zachary Macaulay

Macaulay was Governor of the Colony in the years 1794–95 and 1796–99. He first worked as a book-keeper for a Scottish company on an estate in Jamaica, eventually rising to become manager of the estate. In Jamaica, Macaulay was disgusted at the evils of slavery. Unable to alleviate the hardships of the plantation slaves, he resigned his position in Jamaica and returned to England. He eventually came into contact with the Chairman of the Sierra Leone Company who arranged for his appointment as Governor of Sierra Leone in 1794.

Macaulay's departments were grossly understaffed, which compelled him to do almost all the work. He was a judge, a school-teacher and a preacher. In addition, he was his own secretary, his own postmaster, his own envoy. He posted ledgers and corresponded regularly with the company directors. He made regular friendly calls on neighbouring chiefs. He also tried to establish some order in the Colony.

Meanwhile, the problems of the colonists continued to increase. For example, cargoes sent from England often proved inappropriate or deficient. In place of crucial building supplies, watering cans arrived. Cement and flour were soaked in sea-water. Marking out and allotting land went very slowly. Most of the immigrants were sustained by company rations and allotments, and some found employment putting up buildings and laying out streets.

The Napoleonic wars between France and Britain adversely affected the Colony. A French naval squadron bombarded the Colony for two weeks in September 1794, and by the time they left, the Colony lay in ruins. Eight months after this French attack, Macaulay went to Britain on leave.

By the time he returned in 1796 the Sierra Leone Company was exploring various avenues for raising money to rebuild Free Town. He was then authorized to impose quit-rents. Each settler was charged one shilling for every acre of land used. This met with vehement opposition because the settlers (particularly Nova Scotians) considered it immoral on the part of the company to charge them for land that had been promised to them 'free of all expense'. The settlers also complained about the company's refusal to honour its pledge to them. Before they left Nova Scotia, each settler family had been promised at least twenty acres of land in the Sierra Leone settlement, but on their arrival got only one-fifth of the promised land. Governor Macaulay tried to pacify the settlers by giving them the full allotted land, but the settlers would not accept, because the quit-rent was tied to the new offer.

The Sierra Leone Company then accused the Nova Scotians of ingratitude, pointing out that the latter were enjoying many unpromised services like free schools for their children, free medical care, credit facilities, and so on. The dispute over the tax issue continued for a long time. The Nova Scotians were convinced that payment of quit-rents (which were fifty times higher than those demanded in Australia) amounted to acceptance of company rule and a denial of their own rights of self-government. They also believed that quit-rents were a threat to the value and security of their land. The quit-rent issue was to have profound influence on development in the Colony, particularly on agricultural development. Most Nova Scotians abandoned agriculture and sought solace and sustenance in other pursuits, particularly commerce and building and made tremendous success of them.

Amidst all these problems Macaulay still found time to expand the Colony. He built a Governor's House on Thornton Hill (named after Henry Thornton) and extended Free Town westwards as far as the sea. Free Town then looked more like a European or American commercial town of the nineteenth century. By 1796 the city comprised 300–400 houses. A uniform currency was provided and a people's militia was organized, mainly to foil external aggression. In an attempt to regularize marriages in the Colony, rules were drawn up which recognized as valid and legal only those marriages that were performed by the chaplain. Another rule made it obligatory on fathers to maintain their illegitimate children.

Macaulay finally left for England in April 1799. He took along 25 boys and four girls to be educated in England in the hope that they would eventually return to Sierra Leone to spread Christianity and European civilization.

The Maroons

The Maroons were the third major pioneer group of settlers in the Sierra Leone Colony. They were blacks from Jamaica who had revolted against slavery and maintained their independence in the mountains, until they were conquered in 1796 by the British, who deported a large number to Nova Scotia. They requested transfer to Africa and some 550 of them were sent to Sierra Leone in 1800.

The Nova Scotian rebellion

Nova Scotians were imbued with ideas of freedom and liberty. They had suffered much for the sake of freedom in America and were therefore not prepared to be submissive in Africa. Sensing this, Governor John Clarkson had arranged for tithingmen and hundredors to be elected to serve as a form of local government below the level of the Governor and Council. By 1798 they had formed two chambers that were intended to cooperate with the British Governor in writing the Colony's rules and regulations. In 1799, however, the British Crown granted a new charter to the Sierra Leone Company which had the effect of returning all authority to the company and its Governor, leaving no features of representative government. This move, together with the quit-rent issue, was too much for the Nova Scotians to bear. So in 1800, led by Isaac Anderson, James Robertson, Nathaniel Wansey and Ansel Zizer, the quondam Nova Scotian tithingmen and hundredors gave notice to Governor Ludlam that they were no longer going to submit to the company's authority, but were going to take over the administration of the Colony. The Governor tried to arrest the ringleaders, and an armed rebellion broke out. Reinforced by other dissidents, the Nova Scotians almost overwhelmed the company's forces, but for the timely arrival in Sierra Leone of the Maroons and a detachment of the Royal African Corps. Their arrival turned the scales in favour of the company against the Nova Scotian insurgents. The rebellion was suppressed and the ringleaders punished. The rising had profound effects, especially on the Nova Scotians. Firstly, it made the British lose faith in the Nova Scotians as instruments of modernization. From then onwards all kinds of disparaging remarks were made about them. Secondly, the rebellion discouraged the Sierra Leone Company from bringing more American blacks to Sierra Leone because the company felt that it was these blacks who were creating all the problems in the Colony.

There were constant quarrels between the Koya Temne (whose land had been sold to the settlers) and the Sierra Leone Company over land. By the treaty of 1788 King Naimbana had promised on behalf of himself and his successors to give up any claim to the Colony land forever. But according to Temne law the land had only been leased, not sold, for land was not saleable. When company officials refused to sign a new treaty with Naimbana's successor, Bei Farma, he became angry. He and his sub-chief (also called King Tom), in alliance with Nova Scotian rebel Wansey, then proceeded to attack the company's new fort on Thornton Hill on 18 November 1801. Wansey had warned that the fort was a threat to the Temne.

After a fierce struggle the company's forces gained the upper hand and went on the offensive. Many Temne settlements were destroyed and King Tom fled. He took refuge with Mandingo and Soso chiefs on the Scarcies where he planned another invasion, but was easily defeated. He was then persuaded by Dala Modu (a Soso chief then living just north of the Sierra Leone Colony) to give up fighting. In 1807 the Koya Temne signed a dictated peace treaty with the British, by which they renounced all claims to the Colony land.

3.4   Crown Colony rule

When the Sierra Leone Company revived the Colony in 1791 it invested £235 000 there and established factories for marketing goods and produce at reasonable prices. The company did not intend to make huge profits, but it was hoped that its business would pay and yield the shareholders a reasonable return for their investments.

However, the company began to experience serious problems in 1793. In that year its store ship was destroyed by fire. The following year French warships attacked the Colony and destroyed property worth £55 000. An attempt to meet some of the reconstruction costs through the imposition of quit-rents backfired. Agricultural investments too proved a failure. The company was therefore hard-pressed to generate funds to keep the Colony going.

Company officials eventually approached the British Government for financial assistance. They were able to influence British parliamentarians, and from 1796 the British Government began to make annual grants to the company. Starting with a grant of £4000 in 1796, the amount was raised to £10000 per annum in 1798.

About this same time Britain was looking for a naval base for the protection of her shipping in West Africa, and the Colony's natural harbour was well-placed to fulfil this need. In December 1803 a Special Committee was appointed to look into the condition of the Colony.

Following the committee's report, the annual grant was raised by £4000 for the purposes of defence. Still, financial problems, threats of insurrection from within, and fears of attack from without continued to plague the company and to prevent it from thriving as a commercial venture. Henry Thornton finally requested that the British Government assume full responsibility for governing the Sierra Leone Colony. The British Government accepted the offer and on 1 January 1808, the Colony was transformed into a Crown Colony.

Nova Scotian institutions

Following a series of reverses in the Colony – Temne attacks, French invasion and settler rebellion – the Sierra Leone Company was forced to surrender the Colony to the British Crown in December 1807. The company had failed, but the Colony had not. That the Colony continued to exist in 1807, and even beyond, lay, in the words of John Peterson, in the resilience of its Nova Scotian population in the face of hardship. The major characteristic of the Nova Scotian settlers was their independence. Independence, which at times went so far as open defiance of the company government, provided the settler with the minimal requirements for survival. Nova Scotian independence was manifested in three main areas – in their religious, political and economic organizations.

Nova Scotians depended heavily on their churches and religious leaders to direct their affairs. It was the religious leaders who had organized them to migrate to Sierra Leone. Nova

Scotian chapels became the vital centres of public opinion and communal action, and the preachers to a large extent became the key to government. Three groups of religious bodies were represented in the Nova Scotian population – Baptists, Members of the Countess of Huntingdon Connexion and Methodists. There was, however, no denominational rivalry among the groups. For a people twice uprooted from their homes, and with bitter experiences of treachery and slavery, Christianity was a unifying force which welded the Nova Scotians together.

Though the Province of Freedom had failed, one of its most important manifestations was allowed to continue – the system of tithingmen and hundredors. These elected officials later developed into an effective pressure group against the administration. For example, they protested several times about quit-rent and land allocations. The colonial administration eventually recognized that tithingmen and hundredors were a force to reckon with. In 1796 Governor Macaulay began to consult them on major proposals and obtain their approval of future legislation. They proposed a host of laws which the Governor and Council adopted.

When the governors insisted on implementing the quit-rents, Nova Scotian leaders became more anti-government. In 1799 they declared that only they had the right to legislate since Nova Scotians owned the land in the Colony. Europeans, they demanded, should pay taxes. Events moved with a certainty which led directly to the settlers' rebellion of 1800, directed by the officially-elected Nova Scotians, originally intended by the company to keep order. The timely arrival of the Maroons and the successful suppression of the rebels by the government ended the most dramatic manifestation of independence among the settlers during the period of company rule.

The economic life of the community provided further evidence of Nova Scotian independence, of the existence of their own province of freedom. Many Nova Scotians became wealthy through trade. Nova Scotians were thus able to build for themselves out of trade a firm foundation for their society. A good number of them were also artisans.

Thus, faced with considerable hardship and frustration, the Nova Scotians had proved resilient and adaptable in their new situation. With the spirit of independence shown in their churches, their governmental institutions, and in their economic life, they had, according to Peterson, given a new meaning to Sharp's original dream of a province of freedom. To them went the credit for the fact that as the British Government took over the Colony, and as the Recaptives began to come ashore in 1808, there was a vital community of freed slaves upon which the subsequent history of the settlement was built.

The Abolition Act

The founding of the Colony settlement did not put an end to the struggle for the abolition of the slave trade. Wilberforce and others continued to press on and by the early nineteenth century, they began to see more positive signs of success. Their efforts were aided by certain developments in the West Indies and in Britain itself. Many British plantation-owners in the West Indies were now running their plantations at a loss, for slave labour was no longer profitable. The planters therefore thought that prohibition of the slave trade would be to their advantage, since it would then be easier for them to compete with the French sugar-producers, who relied less on slave labour. Many slaves were also revolting against their masters, so the will to retain many slaves was no longer strong. Some people, including a few Africans living in England, also pointed out that British traders would in the long run make more money, if they treated Africans as customers not merchandise, that is, if instead of selling them, they sold them goods. Lord Granville and Charles Fox, who became Prime Minister and Foreign Minister, respectively, in Britain in 1806, were both in favour of the prohibition of the slave trade. Given this background, it became easier for the British Government to declare the slave trade illegal.

Thus, in 1807 Britain passed the Abolition Act which made slave trading illegal for British subjects. The Act stipulated that any British subject caught trading in slaves would be fined £100 per slave. On the other hand, if anyone liberated slaves, he would receive £40 for a man, £30 for a woman and £10 for every child under the age of fourteen. The Act banning the slave trade was a great triumph for the abolitionists. William Wilberforce received an ovation in Parliament. The USA also forbade the importation of slaves in 1808. Other countries followed suit.

In 1807 also, the directors of the Sierra Leone Company founded the African Institution with the primary objective of finally ending the slave trade through the improvement and 'civilization' of the African peoples. This institution was able to influence the British Government to establish a Vice Admiralty Court in Free Town for the trial of slave captains and the release of slaves. The Abolition Act and the setting-up of the court were to have important consequences for Sierra Leone.

The British navy was charged with the responsibility of capturing slave vessels. Many such vessels were brought to Free Town and their human cargoes released. These became known as Recaptives or Liberated Africans. From about 2000 in 1807, the Colony's population grew rapidly due to the large influx of Recaptives there. In 1825 the population had reached 11 000 and in 1840, 40 000.

British anti-slavery squadron in action

A Liberated African Yard, the Kings' Yard, was established for the reception of the Recaptives, many of whom arrived in a deplorable and emaciated state. On their arrival the Recaptives were registered and named before being sent to found villages near Free Town. Others, especially the children, became servants or apprentices to earlier Colony inhabitants. Some were drafted into the British army.

Thomas Perronet Thompson

T. P. Thompson was the first Crown Colony Governor. Born in 1783 in Hull, England, Thompson graduated with a Bachelor of Arts degree from Queen's College, Cambridge, at the age of nineteen. He then entered the Royal (British) Navy and later, the army, where he excelled himself.

Thompson arrived in Sierra Leone on 21 July 1808. He was appalled at the existence of slavery in the Colony; so he decreed that any person dealing in slaves would be severely punished. He also abolished the system of 'apprentices', which he considered another form of slavery. Instead, he established rural villages for the settlement of Recaptives. Leicester was the first settlement established. He allocated lands to those settlers who desired to live there, planning it as a farming district. Other resettlement centres were Congo Town, Kissy, and Portuguese Town. Thompson formed a more effective people's militia and enrolled all males between 15 and 60 years who were capable of bearing arms.

The Governor felt that the name 'Free Town' had been 'perverted to the Purposes of Insubordination and Rebellion', so he changed the Colony's name to Georgetown. The streets were given British names so as to affirm the settlement's close connection with Britain. The Colony's currency of dollars and cents was changed to pounds, shillings and pence, because the former smacked of 'revolutionary American ideas'. Postal services were established between Georgetown, Europe and the West Indies. Sierra Leone's first newspaper – the *Sierra Leone Gazette* – was begun by Governor Thompson.

Laws were passed regulating marriages among the Maroons and declaring children of Maroons, born before December 1808, to be entitled to the privileges of children born in lawful wedlock. Thompson tried to discourage the settlers from worshipping in their own chapels so that he could have one established church for the Colony.

He encouraged many West Indians to emigrate to Sierra Leone. Their numbers further helped to increase the Colony's population. Thompson gave much enouragement to Maroons and Recaptives, who he believed were more active and obedient. He regarded Nova Scotians as a group of insubordinate people. Thompson hoped that Recaptives would be the torchbearers of Western civilization in the interior. They would also farm for the Colony and defend it from attacks from the interior.

Thompson's criticism of the apprenticeship system introduced by the now-defunct Sierra Leone Company did not pass unnoticed. The company still had influential men in London and they fought for his downfall. He was recalled in 1811 and many of his reforms were abolished by his successor. It must be remembered, however, that Thompson devised the most successful and lasting method of rehabilitating Recaptives – that of resettling them in rural communities.

3.5   The era of Governor MacCarthy

Charles MacCarthy was born in 1768 to a French father and an Irish mother, and was brought up in France. He later joined the French and British armies. He served in the Royal African Corps in 1811 and was appointed Governor of Senegal and Goree in 1812. These places were then under British control.

In 1814 Governor Maxwell proceeded on leave, and MacCarthy moved to Sierra Leone to act as Governor. His appointment was confirmed in 1816. MacCarthy was one of the ablest governors in Sierra Leone in the nineteenth century. His successes were many. A far-sighted Governor, he recognized the need to provide some kind of training for the Recaptives so that they could become self-reliant. These Recaptives, torn from their native lands, found nothing familiar in Sierra Leone. They were ridiculed by the older residents, who regarded them as savages. These residents had already set a standard based on Western ideas. Governor MacCarthy strongly felt that through education and religion the Recaptives could be brought within the pale of 'civilization', and, to this end, an appeal was made to the Church Missionary Society (CMS), a Church of England institution. This society, founded in England in 1799, had among its leading members some of the directors of the Sierra Leone Company. William Wilberforce was one of its vice-presidents and Henry Thornton its first treasurer. Zachary Macaulay, the able ex-Governor of the Sierra Leone Colony, was also on its committee. These men had influenced the CMS to choose Sierra Leone as its first sphere of influence. The society sent its first missionaries – Melchior Renner and Perter Hartwig – in 1804. They were Germans, because no Englishman wanted to train as a missionary.

MacCarthy also evolved a kind of local government for the Recaptive villages, which he named the Parish Plan. In 1816 an agreement was effected between the British Government and the CMS. The government was to build churches, schools and parsonages while the CMS took responsibility for staffing Recaptive villages with ministers and school masters. The clergymen's wives were to teach housekeeping and needle-work to Recaptive women.

In 1817 the following eight parishes were established; they were made up of the places mentioned below and their surrounding areas:

St Andrew, Gloucester   St John, Charlotte
St Charles, Regent   St Patrick, Kissy
St George, Freetown   St Paul, Wilberforce
St James, Bathurst   St Peter, Leopold.

In 1819 five more parishes were created:

St Arthur, Wellington   St Michael, Waterloo
St Edward, Kent   St Thomas, Hastings
St Henry, York

CMS personnel took their work very seriously. Recaptives accepted the missionaries' teaching with open hands and began to adopt a Western mode of living. The most remarkable achievement was recorded in Regent village where Rev. William Johnson worked. By 1825, 1079 of the 2 000 residents in Regent were receiving religious instruction; about 150 of that number were communicant members of the church while 710 Regentonians could read and write. Education was highly valued in the Colony because it largely determined one's

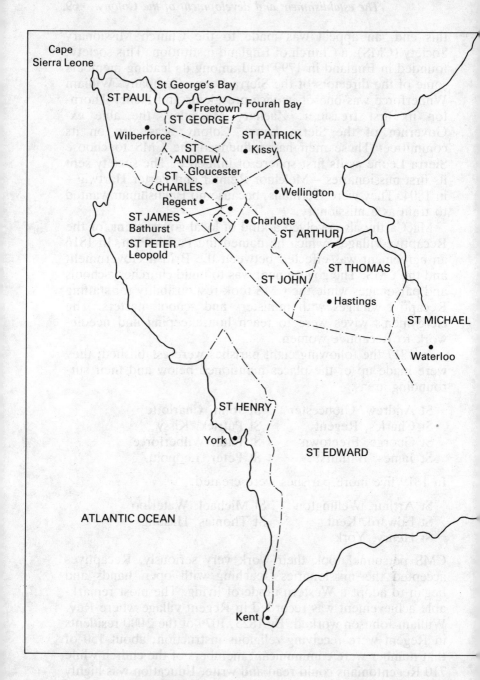

7 *Governor McCarthy's parish plan*

Regent village at the time of the Rev. W.A.B. Johnson

status there. Literate people generally did the lighter work while the more menial jobs were relegated to illiterate citizens.

The CMS had opened the Christian Institution at Leicester in 1814 where Recaptive children were maintained, taught useful trades, and trained as teachers. A plan was then proposed to name a slave child after anyone who gave £5 for its support. This plan, though shortlived, received enthusiastic support in England, and this was how many Colony people acquired well-known European names. The Christian Institution did not flourish and was discontinued. However, by 1824 the CMS were proud of their achievements: 2460 children were then receiving education in their Colony schools; but the overall cost in terms of human and material resources was high. Thirty-eight of the 70 missionaries sent between 1804 and 1824 had died of tropical diseases and the society had spent some £70 000.

MacCarthy's governorship witnessed an increase in the quantity and quality of public buildings in Freetown. The jail was completed in 1816, the foundation stone of St George's Church (later Cathedral) was laid in January 1817, a town hall was built at Water Street (now Wallace-Johnson Street), an officers' mess between Fort Thornton and Pademba Road, a commissariat store at the wharf, and so on.

In 1817 MacCarthy revived the *Sierra Leone Gazette*, which had ceased publication since 1810. He attempted to get the settlers more involved in the community's affairs by appointing a few to municipal office as mayors and sheriffs. Thomas Carew was appointed Mayor in 1818 and John Thorpe was made Sheriff.

The MacCarthian era was also the 'golden age' of the Nova Scotians. MacCarthy healed the old wound between the Nova Scotians and the colonial government and they were reinstated as a favoured administrative class among the black population.

The Court of Mixed Commissions   The initial progress made by the Vice-Admiralty Court encouraged other European nations to establish the West African branch of the Court of Mixed Commissions in Freetown in 1819 to try all foreign slave-dealers. The Freetown court alone freed over 65 000 slaves but most of these were sent out to the West Indian colonies to work in the plantations.

Freetown was also designated the army headquarters and navy supplies depot for British West Africa. An immediate result of these developments was increased commercial activity between the Colony, Britain and the rest of Europe. European ships regularly called at Freetown with foreign goods to supply the local market, while at the same time stimulating markets for local produce. Consequently, the Colony's wealth increased.

Governor MacCarthy also tried to expand the Colony and raise its revenue. He revived British claims to Gambia Island and got the Isles de Los ceded to the Colony. Demobilized African soldiers were sent to found villages such as Wellington, Hastings, Waterloo, York and Kent. They were later joined by Recaptives. MacCarthy also persuaded the Caulkers to lease Banana Islands in 1820 for an annual payment of 250 bars (a kind of currency). In an attempt to stimulate trade with the countries inland, he sent European officers on diplomatic missions to the interior kings. These kings were to convince traders in their territories to sell their goods in Freetown.

Governor MacCarthy went to England on leave in July 1820 and was awarded a knighthood, the first Governor of Sierra Leone to be so honoured. While he was away in

England the British Government decided to unite all its West African colonies with Freetown as the capital. When Sir Charles MacCarthy returned, he was made Governor-General of British West Africa, but he could not control such a wide area, which stretched from the Gambia to the Gold Coast. So the officials in the other colonies did what they liked.

In January 1824 MacCarthy went to Cape Coast to lead a British army in a war against the Asante. He was killed and his army routed. Thereafter, his work in Sierra Leone received a serious setback. The British Government began to cut down drastically on its personnel and expenditure in the Colony. As mortality among the CMS clergymen continued, they asked to be relieved of their administrative functions in the Recaptive villages, so that the few surviving ones could concentrate more on giving religious instruction. This created an acute shortage of qualified staff to effectively run the parishes.

In 1827 the British Government divided the colonies because it was realized that a single individual could not effectively administer the whole of British West Africa.

Recaptives manage their own affairs

The Recaptives were forced to evolve their own institutions in the face of reduced government expenditure on, and little supervision of, their settlements. Between 1825 and 1850 Recaptives were masters of their own destiny.

Because they came from different parts of West Africa, it was felt that they would be able to readjust more quickly to normal life if they settled along ethnic lines. This would also provide for stability in the villages. So in a typical village were found Aku (Yoruba) Town, Ibo Town, Congo Town, and so on.

Communal work became a feature of Recaptive life. It was customary and common for them to share the tasks of planting and harvesting. Recaptives founded welfare and benefit societies which performed services ranging from saving for future investment to burying the dead. One benefit society at Hastings specialized in marriages. A person joined before his marriage and contributed regularly to the society's fund. At the time of the member's wedding, the society bought food and drinks for the marriage party.

Secret societies abounded among the Recaptive population. Many of these were of Yoruba origin. The most widespread of these societies was the *Oje*; its masked devil was called *Egungun*. The spirits of the *Egungun* claimed to know the secrets of the village and their regular performances became a sort of witch-hunt, for local offenders were named, punished or chastised. The society kept the villagers under strict control and provided a means of keeping order in the community. Its influence on the people was therefore considerable. In some places it was the power behind the throne. Its leaders also performed medical services. Hunters' societies were also founded in many of the Recaptive villages. The women's secret society was the Bondo, which served as an educational institution. It provided remedy for bodily diseases such as smallpox. Less important societies included Aro, Agemo and Gelede.

Many Recaptives were Christians, but some, particularly the Aku from Yorubaland, were Muslims. And others stuck to their traditional gods like *Sango* (the god of thunder). Some Recaptive Christians had ably assisted the European missionaries and Settler pastors in preaching the gospel to other Recaptives. These class-leaders, as they were called, continued such good work especially in those villages where there were no missionaries or pastors.

A key factor in the stability of the Recaptive villages was their political organization. Each ethnic group had a headman who acted as chief. In many cases he carried out the colonial superintendent's orders to the people. He was responsible for the prevention and punishment of crimes. Traditional systems of law and order largely prevailed in the villages. In the absence of active government control in many of the villages, certain benefit societies, particularly Sergeant Pott's Society, began to perform political and judicial functions as well. Pott's Society became an extra-legal Colony-wide government which imposed fines on its members for ungentlemanly conduct. A more severe punishment was to 'cut the defaulter off' from the rest of the society by his enduring the silence of all his fellow-members for a specified period of time. In a society that depended heavily on trade for its economic survival, such a punishment could spell financial ruin for the guilty member.

The 'Seventeen Nations' was a 'supra-ethnic organization'. It was the brainchild of the Aku king in Freetown, John

Macauley. In late December 1843, riots broke out in Waterloo between the Aku and the Ibo. After Macauley had made peace he then persuaded the seventeen largest ethnic groups in the town to form a committee which would settle disputes among them. This committee then came to be known as the Seventeen Nations. It gradually spread to other villages.

The Seventeen Nations later became 'a secret government within a government', and was more effective in those areas where government supervision was least effective. It supervised village affairs in the manner of a government, settling disputes, keeping roads and streets open, and preventing social disorder. In York, the Seventeen Nations became the virtual governing body of the town.

The foundations of Recaptive prosperity lay in trade. Recaptives formed commercial companies so that they could have a larger capital, buy more goods and make bigger profits. The companies bought cheap auctioned goods in Freetown from the slave ships and took them into the interior. By the 1830s they were able to underbid the highly competitive European merchants in Freetown. An efficient distribution system through a network of some 400–500 hawkers and traders was developed between Freetown and the interior.

A thrift society, known as the *Osusu*, was formed in several communities. Its members contributed a certain sum each week for the use of a particular member.

As pointed out earlier, many Recaptives quickly adopted Western ways of life. Some began marrying into older settler families, and gradually the distinction between Recaptive and Settler became blurred. Wealthier Recaptives like Emmanuel Cline (after whom Cline Town is named) and John Ezzidio, owned substantial buildings in Freetown. They, too, like the older settlers, began to give their children quality education.

In 1853 the British Parliament declared Recaptives British subjects; they were thus raised to the status of the other settler groups. Ten years later Recaptives succeeded in electing one of their number, John Ezzidio, into the Colony Legislative Council (see 8.1).

Government and the missions

The colonial government was not very pleased with the kind of education provided by the CMS. It viewed the education as being too 'bookish'. The CMS also tended to discriminate against non-Christian children. So after 1824 government decided to take over management of the Colony schools in order to raise academic standards and open the schools to every child. Teachers were forbidden to give religious instruction and clergymen were asked to perform only managerial duties in these schools. This policy adversely affected the CMS, which had relied heavily on teachers for religious instruction.

And the death-rate among the missionaries was increasing alarmingly. The society therefore made a firm determination to establish a Native Agency to train and supply African workers. The Christian Institution was then revived at Fourah Bay in 1827 by Rev. C. L. D. Haensel to train local teachers and missionaries. The CMS also took a firm decision to start and run their own schools. CMS private schools were thus opened at Bathurst, Gloucester and Regent in 1828. And the Sunday School became an important means of instruction for adults as well as children.

A view of Regent, where Samuel Crowther was schoolmaster in 1830

Mrs Hannah Kilham of the Quakers Mission started a girls' school at Charlotte in 1830 and another at Allen Town shortly afterwards. When she left, the Wesleyan Methodist Society (WMS), whose initial work in the Colony had received a serious setback due to financial problems and the rapid death of its missionaries, continued to maintain the girls' schools.

By 1841 the CMS, WMS and Government each had fourteen primary schools to their credit. A total of 8000 pupils out of the Colony population of 40 000 were attending these schools.

The CMS founded the Grammar School in 1845 to provide sound religious and general education for boys. Provision was also made for industrial education. In addition, a separate department was created to train and raise the professional level of primary school teachers. Both the Fourah Bay Institution and the Grammar School were the first of their kinds in sub-Saharan Africa and attracted students from all over West Africa. The Grammar School's female counterpart was also opened in 1845 because the CMS felt the education and training of Christian mothers was essential to the establishment of a native Christian Church. The school was renamed Annie Walsh Memorial School in 1849. The WMS opened the Methodist Boys' High School and the Methodist Girls' High School in 1874 and 1880, respectively.

In 1859 some French priests of the Society of Missions in Africa (SMA) came to Sierra Leone to start active religious and educational work. They were led by Bishop Marion de Bresillac, who was also the founder of the SMA. The priests were soon struck by a yellow-fever epidemic and they all died.

Barely five years later two French priests, Father Blanchet and Father Koeberle, arrived in Freetown to start the Holy Ghost Fathers mission to Sierra Leone. Father Blanchet started St Edward's School for boys at Howe Street soon after his arrival. Another school was later built at Murray Town, on the outskirts of Freetown. Father Koeberle died in 1865. Later, a convent was built for the St Joseph of Cluny Sisters who arrived in Freetown on 12 December 1866. They were led by Mother Marie Theresa who had spent seven years at Cayenne and nine at Goree (in Cape Verde).

More priests and nuns later came out to Sierra Leone. The Roman Catholic missionaries did a lot of good work among the poor.

3.6   Krio society

The early Colony settlers had been encouraged to build an extension of British Christian middle-class life, founded on the church, education and expanding commerce. By the time Recaptives began to arrive in the Colony in 1807, a European culture was already underway there. But the Recaptives never assimilated this culture completely. They made certain cultural selections which eventually produced a new culture – that of the Sierra Leone Krio. This new society, which came into being in the mid-nineteenth century, was a blend of Western and numerous African cultures. It has been suggested that but for the infusion of Recaptives, bringing in their various languages and customs, Krio society would have been similar to Caribbean society. We shall now examine significant aspects of Krio culture.

Language   Many people believe that the Krio language evolved from the Recaptives' earliest contact with the English language. When they arrived in the Colony, they had no prior knowledge of English, and in their struggle to communicate, they used all means at their disposal. The new settlers acquired as much of the new vocabulary as they could, and used these newly-acquired words, while often thinking in the style of their original language – Krio was the result.

But it has also been argued that the present Krio language spoken in Sierra Leone is derived from an earlier West African Creole English which was a trade language along the West Coast during the eighteenth century, when the British dominated the Atlantic slave trade. West African slaves transported the language to the New World. When the ancestors of the Sierra Leone Krio arrived in the Colony at the end of the eighteenth century, they adopted and developed this local Creole (now Krio) as their native speech, enriching it with new expressions reflecting their diverse backgrounds.

While the majority of Krio words have an English origin, the language also has an impressive number of loan words from other languages – chiefly Yoruba and Sierra Leonean languages. From the Portuguese came such words as *pekin*, *sabi*; from French, *boku*; Yoruba, *agidi*, *alakpa*, *beru* (submit); Mandingo, *yuba*, *yabas*; Mende, *bumbu*, *kapu*; Temne, *kofta*, *komra*; Limba, *mampama*.

Krio social and cultural life was a blend of Western European values and African ways of doing things. For instance, the Krio held dinners, balls, fairs and participated in literary, religious and philosophic societies. But they also freely joined African cult societies like *Ojeh*, *Agemo*, *Gelede* and *Hunting*. Many Krio were Christians, though their belief in Christianity did not restrain them from practising ethnic rites and indulging in ancestral customs which often conflicted with orthodox Christianity.

The Krio, like many other people, believed in life after death and that a person's life in this earthly world would affect his position in the hereafter. Elaborate ceremonies and rituals were performed to bid farewell to the dead. These started with a wake and a well-constructed coffin. Then there was the Memorial Service (and here the Christian influence came into an essentially African process) accompanied by a visit to the cemetery. A big feast, *awujoh*, on specific days – the third, seventh and fortieth days and one year after death – was an important follow-up.

There was also the ceremony of *Pul na do* (*komojade*) which introduced a newborn baby to surroundings with which he was expected to be familiar as he grew up. It took place seven days after the baby was born, if it was a girl, or nine days for a boy. The ceremony started with Christian prayers and an invocation, often by a minister of religion. Then the baby was taken out in the streets by an elderly member of the family to be shown those areas familiar to his household.

Krio wedding engagements, too, had elements of African and European cultures. The essence of the Asking Ceremony (Krio *Gej* from English 'engage') was a battle of words between the bridegroom's party and the bride's party, which was essentially African in nature. But the bargaining was done in English of a by-gone idiom. The bride was a 'rose' spotted in her parents' 'garden' which the bridegroom's family wished to possess. The presentation of the 'kalbas ceremony' included African symbols like kola nuts as well as Bibles and rings from another culture.

Western dress apart, there were certain modes of dress which became associated with the Krio. The Yoruba robe (*agbada*) was identified with Krio men. For the women, the cotton print, made in simple but attractive style, and the *kabaslot* represented a sort of ethnic dress.

The independence of Krio women had no parallel either in European or African cultural life. They demonstrated independence of their men by operating as petty traders both in the Colony and in the hinterland. Some owned factories and ventured to trade as far afield as the Gambia. Marriage ties do not appear to have inhibited them in their pursuit of success in commerce.

The Krio adopted Western names, but most did (and still do) carry two names – one European and another African – signifying the coalescence of European and African values in moulding Krio culture. It was therefore not uncommon for a Krio child to be called James Omodele Williams or Francess Ayomi Browne. Thus, the Krio society which provided the pattern of life in the Colony in the nineteenth century was a blend of European influences and vital elements taken from the Recaptives' cultural past.

Krio achievements

The Krio were not satisfied with receiving education only in Freetown. Many entered British universities, often at their families' expense, for higher and professional qualifications. Before long they became easily comparable in their learning to many Europeans. Indeed many of these learned Krio were the 'firsts' of the professional class in West Africa. In 1850 John Thorpe qualified as a barrister. He was followed by Francis Smith and Samuel Lewis. In the field of medicine James Africanus Horton became the first Western-trained doctor; next were William B. Davies, Robert Smith, T. H. Spilsbury and Daniel Taylor. By 1885, 13 had qualified as medical doctors. Samuel Adjai Crowther, the first registered student of Fourah Bay College, qualified as the first Sierra Leonean bishop in 1864. Samuel Lewis (the lawyer) became the first Sierra Leonean knight in 1896, as well as the country's first newspaper editor and owner, and the first to be granted Cambridge and Oxford degrees. Bishop Crowther was noted as an ethnolinguist who had published important works, as had J. C. Taylor and P. J. Williams. Samuel Johnson and A. B. C. Sibthorpe were early historians of Africa along with James Africanus Horton. Johnson was also a noted

Bishop Crowther

authority on tropical medicine, as were J. T. Easmon and Oguntola Sapara.

The period from the 1860s to the 1890s was the heyday of Krio society. Ability, ambition, opportunity and the reluctance of Englishmen to come to what they considered a 'whiteman's grave yard' (as Sierra Leone was then called), combined to give the leading Krio roles in their Colony and throughout West Africa. They soon constituted themselves into an elite class of traders and merchants, lawyers, doctors, teachers, journalists and clergymen. They became the civil servants entrusted with great responsibilities, and their energies and intelligence ran the civil service in Sierra Leone.

Krio traders operated successful businesses in the Colony and in the Sierra Leone hinterland, in Bathurst, Monrovia, Cape Coast, Accra, Lagos and the Cameroons. These enterprising Krio along the coast even called on their mother country to send missionaries and teachers. The Krio responded with vigour and before long they became pioneers of Western education and Christianity in West Africa.

In the Niger Delta a group of Krio pastors led by Bishop Crowther christianized the city-states and created a viable Delta Church. Everywhere they held the prominent church positions: an Anglican bishop, superintendents in Anglican and Methodist churches, a colonial chaplain in the Gambia, archdeacons on the Niger. Krio teachers, like Thomas B. Macaulay, founded schools in many places. By 1875 there were more Krio missionaries and teachers than Europeans in West Africa.

When the British extended their sphere of influence in other West African territories, the Krio were called upon to fill the junior and many of the senior civil service posts in these areas. The Krio sat on the Executive and Legislative Councils of the Gambia, Gold Coast and Nigeria. They also sat in the Supreme Courts in all three countries. In the Gold Coast the Krio served as Colonial Treasurer, Solicitor-General, Postmaster-General, Chief Medical Officer, District Officer, and so on. In Nigeria, the Registrar of the Supreme Court, Colonial Treasurer and Postmaster-General were all Krio. In the Gambia, two successive Chief Justices were Krio. Even outside British areas the Krio made their mark: several became prominent marine engineers in the French African colonies; one became Mayor of Monrovia, Liberia, and another, Charles D. B. King, was elected President of Liberia. In Fernando Po, a Krio prospered as a cocoa plantation owner.

This flow of leaders to the rest of West Africa and the superior educational resources of Freetown caused the Colony to be regarded as the 'Mother of British West Africa' and Freetown the 'Athens of West Africa'. Freetown newspapers, for instance, were read all along the coast, more copies being sold outside than inside Sierra Leone. Between 1850 and

1900, then, Freetown shone with a brilliance and held a place of importance quite out of proportion to its small size. It became the hub of the West African coast. To quote Edward Blyden, 'Freetown was the centre of the African race, the point from which Western civilization spread to illuminate the surrounding areas.'

Thus, the Krio fulfilled in no small measure the aspirations of the founders of the Colony who had hoped that the Colony of Sierra Leone would not only permit the displaced persons of the Atlantic slave trade to evolve a society of their own, but might prove an agency for the social and spiritual regeneration of the whole Negro world.

References

Asiegbu, J. U. J. (1961), *Slavery and the Politics of Liberation 1787–1861* (Longman).

Clifford, Mary L. (1974), *The Land and People of Sierra Leone* (New York).

Foray, C. P. (1977), *Historical Dictionary of Sierra Leone* (Metuchen, New Jersey).

Fryer, Peter (1984), *Staying Power: The History of Black People in Britain* (Longman).

Fyfe, Christopher (1962), *A History of Sierra Leone* (Oxford University Press).

Fyfe, Christopher (1964), *Sierra Leone Inheritance* (Oxford University Press).

Gittens, A. J. (1977), 'Mende and Missionary: Belief, Perception and Enterprise in Sierra Leone', Ph D (Edinburgh).

Jakobsson, Stiv (1972), *Am I Not a Man and a Brother? British Missions and the Abolition of the Slave Trade and Slavery in West Africa and the West Indies 1786–1838* (Uppsala).

Jones, E. and C. Fyfe (eds) (1968), *Freetown, A Symposium* (SLUP).

Peterson, John (1969), *Province of Freedom: A History of Sierra Leone 1787–1870* (Evanston, Northwestern University Press).

Porter, Arthur (1963), *Creoledom* (Oxford University Press).

Spitzer, Leo (1974), *The Creoles of Sierra Leone* (University of Wisconsin Press).

Sumner, D. L. (1962), *Education in Sierra Leone* (Freetown).

Walker, J. S. G. (1976), *The Black Loyalists* (Longman).

Walvin, James (1973), *Black and White: The Negro and British Society* (Longman).

Webster, J. B. et al. (1980), *The Revolutionary Years: West Africa Since 1800* (Longman).

Wilson, Ellen G. (1976), *The Loyal Blacks* (New York).

Wyse, A. J. G. (1989), *The Krio of Sierra Leone* (London, Hurst for the International Institute).

Wyse, A. J. G. and C. Magbaily Fyle (1979), 'Kriodom: A Maligned Culture', JHSSL, Vol. III, nos 1 and 2.

Questions PART A

1 Why was the Colony of Sierra Leone founded in 1787?
2 Discuss the contributions of either Governor John Clarkson or Governor Zachary Macaulay towards the development of the Colony.
3 Describe the settlers of the Sierra Leone Colony between 1787 and 1800 and briefly state the problems they encountered.
4 Why did the British Government take over the Colony in 1808?
5 Describe the institutions of the Nova Scotian settlers.
6 What contributions did Governor T. P. Thompson or Sir Charles MacCarthy make towards the development of the Colony?
7 Describe the economic and social organizations of the Recaptives.
8 What was the importance of the Recaptives in Sierra Leone up to the mid-nineteenth century?
9 What were the main features of Krio society during the second half of the nineteenth century?
10 Discuss the achievements of the Krio from about 1850 to 1900.
11 Why has it been said that the Krio were leaders of West African society from about 1850 to 1900?
12 How did the Christian missionaries contribute to the development of the Sierra Leone Colony in the nineteenth century?

Questions PART B

1 'Granville Sharp's "Province of Freedom" was not intended to be a colony of the traditional type.' Discuss.
2 Was the Sierra Leone Company a missionary society?
3 Discuss the significance of the Nova Scotian rebellion for the history of Sierra Leone.
4 'The Nova Scotians gave a new meaning to Sharp's original dream of a province of freedom in Sierra Leone.' Discuss.
5 How did the abolition of the trans-Atlantic slave trade contribute to the development of the Sierra Leone Colony?
6 Explain how Sierra Leone came to be called the 'mother' and Freetown 'the Athens' of British West Africa.

4 Commercial exchanges in the hinterland

The earliest form of trade in the interior began at the village-level when the inhabitants exchanged things among themselves. As social contacts widened, goods were exchanged with peoples of adjacent villages, and this process was facilitated by the establishment of fixed marketplaces and market-days. Gradually, in the nineteenth century, trade spread over very large areas and some villages possessing an important strategic site, or an abundant supply of particularly desirable products, grew into great commercial centres. The barter system gradually gave way to the use of currencies.

4.1 Indigenous trade

Two main types of commercial systems evolved in the Sierra Leone hinterland – regional trade and long-distance (trans-regional) trade. The hinterland then extended to Kankan and Futa Jallon.

Regional trade involved commercial transactions among groups of people or various political organizations within a particular region. For example, in the Solima Yalunka state there was some form of regional trade in which all the countries bordering the state participated. This trade may have started in about the seventeenth century as the Solima travelled towards the Samu area (close to the Scarcies) to procure salt. Salt was exchanged for gold and country cloths from Sankara. When the Solima state was created in the late eighteenth century, Falaba, its capital, soon became the

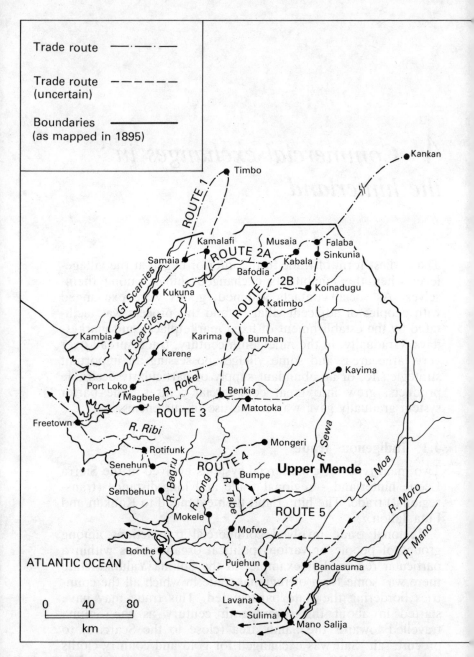

Legend

Trade route ——————

Trade route - - - - - - -
(uncertain)

Boundaries ————————
(as mapped in 1895)

Map labels

Kankan

Timbo

Kamalafi

ROUTE 1

ROUTE 2A

Musaia Falaba
Samaia Sinkunia
Bafodia Kabala
ROUTE 2B
Koinadugu
Gt Scarcies Katimbo
Kukuna
Lt Scarcies
Kambia Karima Bumban
Karene
Kayima
Port Loko Benkia
Magbele R. Rokel Matotoka
ROUTE 3
Freetown
R. Ribi Mongeri
Rotifunk R. Sewa
Senehun ROUTE 4 Upper Mende
Sembehun R. Bagru Bumpe
R. Jong R. Tabe R. Moa
Mokele ROUTE 5 R. Moro
Bonthe Mofwe R. Mano
ATLANTIC OCEAN Pujehun Bandasuma

0   40   80
km

Lavana
Sulima Mano Salija

8   *Trade routes and trade centres in the hinterland, seventeenth to nineteenth
centuries*

[86]

major centre where most of these exchanges were effected. Locally-grown agricultural products were exchanged for country cloths, soap, iron goods and gold.

In the south, certain towns located at the heads of navigable rivers, became centres of regional trade. Such towns were Senehun and Bumpe on the Tabe, Mokele on the Jong, Sembehun on the Bagru, Mofwe on the Bum and Rotifunk on the Bumpe.

Long-distance trade went across several regions. And it was carried along well-established routes. There were three main routes in the north and north-east. One started from Timbo and moved through Samaia, Kukuna and terminated at Kambia. Another started from Kankan and went through Falaba, Kabala, Katimbo, Bumban and then to Port Loko. A third route passed through Sando Kono country, Konike country, Matotoka, Benkia and Magbele. Trade items along these routes included gold, cattle, ivory, hides, some rubber, shea butter, beeswax, calabashes, *kenda* (a condiment), kola nuts, groundnuts and cotton. Occasionally European manufactured goods such as textiles, matchets, mirrors and guns, found their way into this network. Colony traders stationed at Kambia, Port Loko and Magbele often bought wholesale from the interior traders. They later took the goods to Freetown.

Certain interior traders moved to Freetown with such products as dried peppers, guinea corn, cassava, egusi (seasoning) and other things for urban consumption. Some traders came from faraway Futa with gold and hides. Some, like the Fula and Mandingo, settled in the east end of Freetown and they gave rise to Fula Town. They often acted as hosts or landlords to other interior traders and assisted them in selling their goods in Freetown. Dala Modu was one such landlord.

The southern region had two main routes. The first route passed through Mongheri, Senehun and on to Freetown. The second started from near the upper Mende countries and radiated to Mofwe, Pujehun and Bandasuma, then by waterways to Bonthe, Lavana, Sulima and Mano Salija. Trade items included camwood, slaves, iron goods, country cloths, rice, groundnuts and kola nuts. Colony and European traders on the coast and headwaters participated in the trade as middlemen. They brought various European merchandise in exchange for local products. In the process, they helped to spread Western influence in these areas.

As trade developed and increased in volume, international markets were established at strategic places. There were at least two such markets: at Falaba in Yalunka country and Katimbo in Biriwa Limba country. Rulers through whose countries the trade routes passed became wealthy. They participated in the trade and also collected duties from the traders. They in turn provided adequate security along the trade routes.

4.2　Overseas trade

Some of the goods involved in indigenous trade such as ivory, kola nuts and camwood, found their way into European countries. After the abolition of the British slave trade, the Freetown Colony administration began to encourage Africans to trade in new products that would bring them greater benefits, so that they would forget about the slave traffic.

But, ironically, this legitimate trade caused an increase in the trade in slaves within Sierra Leone. Chiefs and other big men who came to control the trade needed abundant cheap labour for producing the new crops, then in demand in Europe, and for transporting these crops and other products to buying centres. Moreover, the trade served as an excuse, though an unconvincing one, for the Freetown colonial administration to openly interfere in the politics of certain areas. The trade also became a major cause of wars in the interior.

The first major new export after abolition was timber. Cutting began in 1816 along the Sierra Leone River and gradually spread to the more northerly and southerly rivers. An Irish merchant, John McCormack, who had extensive business in Freetown, dominated overseas sales. But as exporting became more competitive there were greater opportunities for local chiefs and big men to cut and sell logs. Often, there were clashes between local competitors.

About 22 000 logs worth over £60 000 were sent down the Sierra Leone River in 1825. Timber was the single most valuable export officially recorded during most years from the 1820s to the 1840s, and shipments continued until the 1860s.

The trade robbed Sierra Leone of an important natural resource; its forest timber, wastefully felled, was never replaced, which caused deforestation. This may have contributed to the spread of tsetse flies. These insects do not breed in high forests, but in areas where there is shade close to the ground. Moreover, trypanosomiasis (which is spread by tsetse flies) only began to attack horses in Freetown in the late 1850s, just at the period when the surrounding country had been denuded of trees by the timber traders.

The major export crops during the nineteenth century included groundnuts, benniseed, kola nuts, palm oil and kernels. The period also saw a substantial growth of such imports as tobacco, alcoholic drink, tools and other manufactures.

Indigenous commerce and industry suffered a severe setback and visible decline following the Protectorate proclamation of 1896. The railway was perhaps the most important agency that precipitated this destruction. For it became the vehicle for flooding the interior with cheap European mass-produced goods. But, moreover, with the delineation of the Sierra Leone/Guinea border in 1895, trade from the Sankaran region (including Kankan and Futa Jallon) hardly found its way into Sierra Leone again. These areas now belonged to the French who imposed prohibitively high tariffs on goods going across the border.

4.3 Sherbro Island

Sherbro Island lies to the south-east of Freetown. The Island comprises Bonthe town and a number of little islands which form a small archipelago. Bonthe is 90 miles (145 km) from Freetown by sea. Other important centres are Bendu, Victoria and York Island.

Sherbro Island was of great economic importance to the Colony administration, foreign and local traders, as well as to the hinterland peoples. It was an area of immense potential wealth in natural resources, an *entrepôt* and trading centre and a gateway into the rich interior.

European ships began calling at the Island in the early seventeenth century to buy camwood and ivory, which were in plentiful supply. As time went on, Europeans began establishing trading posts on the Island. These traders eventually opened up branches up the numerous rivers that ran down from the interior into the Sherbro River. These rivers were the natural highways of commerce to and from the interior.

From the mid-nineteenth century foreign merchants, principally German, French and the British, began to compete for control of the Island. In 1858 a French gunboat forced the chief of Bendu to sign a treaty, but the chief would rather give his lands to the British (see page 115).

The major products from the Sherbro were palm products, piassava and kola nuts. By the second half of the nineteenth century, trade in palm products had surpassed that in all other commodities. Palm kernels were in great demand in Europe to feed European chemical industries. The Island was also a world-leader in the export of piassava.

Some notable traders in the Island in the last few decades of the nineteenth century included a German, Otto, who had one of the major streets in Bonthe named after him; Charles Heddle, probably the first to export kernels from the region; and S. B. A. Macfoy, a Krio businessman who owned a cargo steamer – *Sherbro Monarch*. By 1880 Macfoy's imports from a Manchester firm in England were valued at £40000 per annum. The great depressions of the 1870s and 1880s, however, had an adverse effect on trade in the Island.

Colonial political control was gradually extended to Sherbro Island. Bendu was designated the seat of government. Direct taxation was introduced but limited to the main centres. English law was administered in these centres. Beyond, save for an occasional policeman, rule by chiefs was allowed to continue as long as open violence was avoided. Towards the end of the nineteenth century, Bonthe had, however, become the seat of government. Bonthe was essentially a trading centre.

4.4 Gallinas country

Gallinas, the country of the Vai, was originally part of the Kuoja kingdom, which was ruled by a king who lived near Cape Mount. Gallinas country today lies in the southern coastline between the Kerefe, Moa and Mano rivers. It extends some miles inland and covers an area of roughly 1100 square miles (2860 sq km). The country is now divided into three chiefdoms – Kpaka, Gallinas Perri and Soro-Gbema. Until the late nineteenth century, European influence was mainly confined to towns on the waterways, which offered virtually the only means of penetrating the interior.

There was much internal trade in local products – rice, country cloths, slaves, and so on. The Europeans bought some ivory, gold, pepper and camwood, but Gallinas was subordinate to Sherbro in terms of trade. European unions with Africans in the region gave rise to powerful families such as the Rogers.

King Siaka

The Gallinas kingdom was founded by King Siaka, who was head of the Massaquoi family. His capital was at Gendema. Through warfare and kinship links Siaka was able to extend his influence far inland. He derived a lot of wealth from the slave trade.

The greatest social upheaval during Siaka's reign was the Zawo (Jao) slave revolt. In 1825 slaves at Zawo took up arms against the free people. Some traditions maintain that the revolt was a response to material hardship – the slaves were finding it extremely difficult to get their living. Others view the revolt as resulting from tensions between social strata. Many of the slaves had been converted to Islam which angered many free people, because it would make the slaves see themselves 'equal with the free people before God'. It is significant that Muslim students and criminals wanting to escape punishment joined the slaves in their revolt. Later, however, the free people appeared to have returned the situation to normal.

King Siaka became blind and bedridden by 1840 and in 1843 he passed away.

The reign of Prince Mana

Mana, who had on many occasions deputized for his father Siaka, easily became king after him. But during the early years of his reign he shared power with the leading Rogers. It was during his reign that the British intensified their efforts to stamp out the slave traffic in the Gallinas and other areas. Naval officers would land and destroy slave factories. They would then block the river mouths, thereby preventing any slave vessel from going in or out. Afterwards, they would force the chiefs to sign treaties giving up the slave trade. Such was the case in the Gallinas. The abolition did not, however, seem to have adversely affected the political economy of the region. Most people had been engaged in legitimate trade and this continued to flourish. Export of palm products from the area also effectively replaced the slave trade.

By the 1850s, Mana began cultivating the friendship of some foreign rulers. In 1854 he visited Thomas Stephen Caulker of Shenge, Dala Modu and Governor Kennedy of Freetown. Kennedy welcomed him with a royal salute and a guard of honour, and he was presented with the King George III Medal. The foundations were thus laid for the close relationship between Mana and the colonial government which lasted until his death.

Mana also had his own share of political problems. In a dispute between himself and the Tewo chiefs in 1850, his own subjects joined the enemies' side because 'he was taking too many women as his wives or because of his extravagance in building and furnishing houses'.

Mana also fought a trade war with another coastal chief, William Tucker of the Bum Kittam. His forces invaded the Bum Kittam in 1862 and 1863, causing consternation among the traders there.

Mana no doubt invested his gains from slave trading in such a way as to ensure his survival when the export of slaves ceased. It is Mana not Siaka who is commemorated in Mende proverbs for his affluence: '*Bi wova wovangò wa sia Mana wili kpatehun*' ('Your age is as great as the number of years for which Mana remained rich'). His wealth consisted not only of goods (both European and African) and fine houses, but also of human beings whose services he controlled. As the supreme political authority, he owned the largest number of slaves and he was widely thought to have about 500 wives.

Mana died in 1872.

Succession disputes

Following Mana's death, the politics of the Gallinas area became mixed up with trade due to powerful influences from the coast. Mana was succeeded by his brother Jaia, who was old and blind. In this situation, two rivals then determined to supplant him. One was Boakei Gomna and the other was Francis Fawundu. Gomna lived in Gomna Jembehun, some 15 miles (24 km) north of Gendema and three miles (5 km) south of his father's town Kpasambu. Through his Islamic knowledge and his close connection with the Kòò Mende, he was able to play an important role in Prince Mana's reign, sometimes acting as his deputy and settling disputes in the interior on his behalf. He later called himself a 'servant of the House of Massaquoi'.

Francis Fawundu, a leading Krim chief, had also enjoyed close relationship with Mana, whose mother is said to have been Fawundu's mother's sister. He had been entrusted by Mana with the supervision of the area between Kasi and the Kerefe River. He helped to protect Mana from external threats; he assisted him in the war against William Tucker. When Mana died, Fawundu regarded himself as one of his heirs.

Gomna, in alliance with some inland Mende chiefs, seized the Massaquoi (Gallinas) Crown and is believed to have murdered Jaia. Fawundu demanded that Gomna be exiled, executed, or be made to pay a fine of £4000 (an impossible sum for any chief to raise) for killing 'our King whom all of us put confidence upon'.

S. B. A. Macfoy went to the Gallinas in 1886. Macfoy was able to persuade the combatants to stop fighting, but he proceeded to advance Gomna £100 to start trading. Fawundu and his allied coastal chiefs were alarmed, fearing that if Gomna had Macfoy supporting him he would soon dominate the trade in the whole Gallinas country, which might have been detrimental to their interests. Led by Makaya, they constantly attacked Gomna's territory; and this led them to attack Sulima where the British had a customs post. Makaya was defeated and as a result he withdrew inland. He then decided to give up war for trade. But his attempts to gain access to the coastal trade which was bringing so much wealth and prosperity to some of his fellow chiefs, proved unsuccessful. Therefore he again resorted to war. His activities diverted trade, particularly produce, from the Mano and Moa rivers to the Kittam. He and his allies continued to obstruct British trade in the Sulima area.

A British force led by Captain Copland Crawford attacked and conquered Makaya in 1888. Makaya was subsequently deported to the Gold Coast. The Gallinas problem was then amicably settled by the Governor.

4.5 Trade wars

Interior trade was affected by all kinds of hazards, the most prominent of which were wars. Wars and hostile relations between ruling authorities in neighbouring or competitive central places might lead to blockages of trade routes. But the blockages were often temporary, for the people responsible also had an interest in the continuation of the trade. Because warriors and agriculturalists were distinct professionals, agriculture and related trades were likely to proceed even during wars.

These wars have incorrectly been called tribal wars. The protagonists in these wars were not tribes but individual rulers and their followers. It was not uncommon for chiefs of the same ethnic group to fight against each other. We shall now examine some of the major nineteenth-century trade wars in the Sierra Leone hinterland.

The Masimera–Loko wars

The quarrel between the Masimera Temne and the Loko emanated largely from the attempt by the Masimera king, Bei Simera, to dislodge Gombu Smart from his strategic position on the trade route from Fula country to Freetown.

A Loko slave at Bunce Island, Gombu Smart had proved himself so capable and intelligent that he was given his freedom in the 1780s. He then acted as agent for slave traders in the Rokel. There he raised a large private army of his own people, which he used to help the Masimera Temne in war. Bei Simera showed his gratitude by allowing Smart and his followers to settle at Rokon on the Rokel River. Smart turned Rokon into a large well-laid-out town, and he soon became the most powerful chief in the area. As a wealthy chief, he gave large presents to his overlord Bei Simera, who was very happy.

When Smart died he was succeeded by his son, also called Gombu Smart. But with the end of the legal slave trade the fortunes of the Smart family were steadily declining. The young Smart could therefore not afford to shower large presents on Bei Simera, who then became angry. Bei Simera therefore sought to eject Smart from Rokon, which had become an important town on the Futa–Freetown trade route. Consequently they quarrelled. But if these parties went to war the Fula trade would be adversely affected and this would not be in the interest of the Colony. Two leading Maroons were then despatched from the Colony in 1825 to mediate. But neither Bei Simera nor Gombu Smart could give in. The dispute was finally submitted to the *Alikali* of Port Loko, Fatima Braima, who upheld Bei Simera. But the Loko rejected the *Alikali's* decision. So all the neighbouring Temne united against the Loko and attacked them. Smart was killed but the struggle continued.

William Savage, a Colony trader with Temne connections, prevailed upon the colonial administration to send the *Alikali* ammunition, ostensibly to protect the timber traders. The Temne sacked Loko towns and many Loko took refuge in the Colony.

Governor Findlay sent the Colonial Secretary with Savage and John McCormack in 1831 to settle the dispute. The Loko submitted and the *Alikali* and his allies signed a treaty of friendship with the Freetown government, promising not to make war without first asking the Governor to mediate. They in turn were promised an annual stipend. But this 1831 treaty only brought temporary truce as war between the Temne and Loko continued. Colony traders often took sides in the war and when their trading interests were endangered, they appealed to the Governor for help. Some Colony farmers, mostly Mende Recaptives, had settled in Koya, which was beyond British control. They, in alliance with their countrymen inland, began to support the Loko. This made for an uneasy relationship between them and the Koya Temne.

Dala Modu travelled to Magbele in 1836 in a final attempt to end the Temne–Loko conflict. He assembled most of the influential Temne and Loko chiefs. He was later joined by Governor Henry D. Campbell. A new peace treaty was signed and the chiefs received more stipends. Dala Modu was formally made the regent of Loko Masama and he remained at Magbele as the Governor's agent, with wide powers which made him predominant over others in the Rokel.

By 1840, however, Temne country was full of pocket armies

who were helping the Temne. These armies suddenly began to attack Colony immigrants at Koya, killing or enslaving them. John McCormack again went to mediate and was fairly successful. But the final onslaught on the Loko began after the coronation of Namina Modu as *Alikali* of Port Loko in 1841. Kasona, the Loko stronghold, was taken and Loko power was broken. Having at last defeated the Loko, the Temne established complete hegemony as far as the Mabole River. The Loko were pushed into small chiefdoms beyond the Mabole. But the Smart family was allowed to stay at Mahera. Some Loko took refuge in the Colony at Russel; another group led by a warrior, Suri Kesebeh, went to fight for Chief Caulker of Bumpe country. Kesebeh was rewarded with land at Rotifunk. The end of the Temne–Loko wars made it possible for the Fula to revive the gold trade with the Colony.

The Caulker wars

In 1684 an Englishman, Thomas Corker, came to the Sherbro as an employee of the BRAC, and eventually rose to be Chief Agent at York Island. He married a woman of the Ya Kumba family which ruled the shores of Yawri Bay between the Sierra Leone peninsula and the Sherbro estuary. Their descendants kept the paternal name (later spelt Caulker) but established their claim to rule the maternal province, which they extended to include the Plantain and Banana Islands. These areas were important slave centres. The Caulkers grew rich and powerful through trade.

Nineteenth-century Sherbro politics were in the hands of two Caulker families – those at Bumpe and those at the Plantain Island. These families quarrelled often for the acquisition of more territory, independence of one another, and for wealth. We shall examine the quarrels between Thomas Stephen Caulker of the Plantain Island and Canreba Caulker of Bumpe.

Since the 1820s the trade in timber had been gradually replacing the slave trade in the Sherbro. By the 1840s timber was being exported on a large scale in Bumpe country. Thomas Stephen Caulker, who was crowned after his brother's (George Stephen Caulker's) death in 1832, determined to participate actively in the timber trade. The Plantain Island was then losing its importance very fast as a result of the abolition of the slave trade. But Thomas could not get a foothold on the mainland and take part in the trade without annoying the Bumpe Caulkers.

The coronation of Canreba Caulker in 1842 as king of Bumpe seemed to provide Thomas with a *causus belli* (cause of war). Canreba had been brought up by his uncle at Gbang-baya in Imperi country, his motherland. When he came to Bumpe to be crowned, Thomas questioned his parentage. This suspicion led to a bitter quarrel between Canreba and Thomas. A fierce battle ensued, mercenaries were hired and new alliances made. It is important to note, however, that the main reason for the quarrel was the attempt by Thomas to possess part of the mainland and participate in the timber trade, and the attempt by Canreba to resist such expansionist moves.

Canreba went on the offensive and succeeded in driving Thomas off to Bendu. While there, Thomas enlisted the support of Jong and Bagru chiefs and hired Mende mercenaries. He was also greatly assisted with arms by his son George, who had spent several years in England. Canreba, in league with Thomas Kugba Caulker (who was a nephew and a ward of Thomas Stephen), regrouped their forces at Bonthe and advanced on Bendu, but they were beaten off. Thomas then made several unsuccessful attempts to recapture the Plantain Island.

Thereafter, he went to Freetown to appeal to the Governor to mediate between them. The Acting Governor went to the Sherbro in a naval ship in July 1849 and made the two chiefs agree to divide the Sherbro. Canreba took what lay north, Thomas Stephen what lay south, off the Cockboro Creek. Thus Thomas secured part of the mainland and was able to engage in the timber trade. Thomas, now established on the mainland, founded a new town at Shenge, opposite the Plantain Island.

The Yoni wars

The Yoni Temne quarrelled with their neighbours several times between the 1860s and 1880s in their attempt to control some important centres.

The Yoni Temne were the most southerly of the Temne

groups. They lived inland, away from the important trading centres. Their nearest centre was on the Rokel which was controlled by the Masimera and the Marampa Temne. They denied the Yoni access to the Rokel trade. The Masimera and Marampa Temne were also in a more advantageous position to buy arms from the Colony traders, and grew prosperous through trade, while the Yoni remained poor.

The Yoni then determined to secure a foothold on the Rokel. They therefore waged wars on the Masimera and Marampa several times in the second half of the nineteenth century. In 1860 the Yoni, in alliance with some Koya chiefs and Mende mercenaries, raided Magbele and plundered the traders' factories, including the WMS Mission House, which they thought was a store. The Yoni did not, however, hold Magbele. But they persisted in their attempts to get a trading centre.

Fighting broke out again in 1876 when the Masimera invaded the Yoni. They retaliated the following year. Bei Simera was forced to go into exile. The Yoni also attacked the Marampa and sacked Magbele. By the end of 1878 this important commercial town, which had had a population of nearly 6000, was reduced to a hamlet of three or four huts.

Governor Sir Samuel Rowe invited the Yoni ruler, Bei Sherbro, to Freetown in 1879 in an attempt to settle their dispute, but Bei Sherbro could only go as far as Foredugu, for it was feared that any Yoni king who visited Rokamp (Freetown) would die. Some Koya people attacked Bei Sherbro at Foredugu and he sought refuge in Rotifunk where he died. The Yoni were so bitter about this incident that they avenged their king's death. Peace between the Yoni and their north-western neighbours was finally negotiated in 1883. The Yoni agreed to the peace mainly because the Rokel timber trade had dwindled and the traders were now moving further south in the palm-producing areas.

The Yoni therefore diverted their attention to the south-west where they hoped to gain access to the Bumpe and Ribbi rivers. This would enable them to trade directly with the Colony. But the Bumpe and Ribbi people would also not allow the Yoni free access to their riverheads. So they decided to capture some riverhead towns by force. The nearest big centre the Yoni could attack was Rotifunk, which was in Bumpe country. But the Bumpe and Ribbi areas had been brought under the Colony's influence. The Yoni invaded Ribbi country early in 1884 and plundered the factories there. The Wesleyan Mission at Mabang was also looted. Governor A. E. Havelock tried to mediate. While Havelock was on leave, the Yoni attacked Rotifunk. Chief Suri Kesebeh of Rotifunk was fully prepared for the Yoni invasion, his own Loko being reinforced by 200 Fula residents. And as Bumpe was under British influence, Acting Governor F. F. Pinkett felt justified in sending police reinforcements to Rotifunk. The police helped to protect the other towns near Rotifunk. The Yoni raided and looted Songo town in November 1885.

In the meantime, relations between the Yoni and their southern neighbours were assuming very dangerous proportions. The Mende of Taiama, who also refused the Yoni access to their trading centres, took the offensive against the Yoni in 1887. While Police Inspector Revington was restraining the Mende, the Yoni attacked Senehun, alleging that the Inspector was favouring the Mende. Several Krio traders were killed in Senehun. When the Colonial Office was informed of this attack, it decided to send a military expedition to stop these wars. Since the Yoni were the latest aggressors, the expedition was against them.

Two hundred soldiers marched out of the Colony and were joined by several hundred Mende, Loko, Fula and Koya Temne allies. In the expedition against the Yoni, little fighting took place. Rockets were fired at Robari, a stockaded Yoni town. The defenders retreated. Soldiers were stationed at Robari to forestall further Yoni invasion. So Yoni hopes of gaining a trading centre were again frustrated. The Yoni expedition of 1887 was a landmark in the history of the Temne people, for it marked the end of almost half-a-century of continuous warfare in Temne country.

References

Abraham, Arthur (1978), *Mende Government and Politics Under Colonial Rule* (Sierra Leone and Oxford University Press).

Foray, C. P. (1977), *Historical Dictionary of Sierra Leone* (Metuchen, New Jersey).

Fyfe, Christopher (1962), *A History of Sierra Leone* (Oxford University Press).

Fyfe, Christopher (1979), *A Short History of Sierra Leone* (Longman).

Fyfe, Christopher (1964), *Sierra Leone Inheritance* (Oxford University Press).

Fyle, C. Magbaily (1979), *Solima Yalunka Kingdom* (Nyakon, Freetown).

Howard, Allen (1979), 'Production, Exchange and Society in Northern Coastal Sierra Leone during the Nineteenth Century', in Vernon Dorjahn and Isaac Barry (eds), *Essays on the Economic Anthropology of Liberia and Sierra Leone* (Institute of Liberian Studies, USA).

Ijagbemi, E. A. (1972), *Gbanka of Yoni* (Ahmadu Bello University).

Jones, Adam (1983), *From Slaves to Palm Kernels – A History of the Gallinas Country (West Africa) 1730–1890* (Frantz Steiner Verlag, Weisbaden).

Mitchell, P. K. (1962), 'Trade Routes of the Early Sierra Leone Protectorate', SLS (ns), no. 16.

Skinner, David (1980), *Thomas George Lawson* (Hoover Institution Press).

Questions PART A

1   Describe the main types of commercial systems that evolved in the hinterland in the nineteenth century.

2   What incentives were provided to reduce the economic attractiveness of the slave trade following its abolition in 1807?

3   Why was Sherbro Island important in the nineteenth century? (See 5.3, The Mendi Mission.)

4   What were the achievements of either King Siaka or Prince Mana of the Gallinas kingdom?

5   Why did the Masimera Temne fight against the Loko in the nineteenth century?

6   Why did the two branches of the Caulker family fight against each other in the 1840s?

7   What were the causes of the Yoni wars of the 1860s to the 1880s?

Questions PART B

1   How far did the political systems in the interior facilitate or hinder the development of trade in the nineteenth century?

2   Examine the nature of the conflict between Boakei Gomna and Francis Fawundu of the Gallinas.

3   'The Yoni expedition of 1887 was a landmark in the history of the Yoni people.' Discuss this statement.

4   'Legitimate trade, far from bringing peace and security, was a major cause of wars in nineteenth century Sierra Leone hinterland.' Discuss.

5 Christian missions in the hinterland (c1600–1900)

European Christian missionary activity in the present area of Sierra Leone started in the early seventeenth century. The early missionaries encountered many difficulties. Missionaries were few in number; they had limited funds at their disposal and lacked experience. The preparations they made were inadequate. The climate constituted a major problem, as did the tropical diseases and the high death rate. The influence of traditional religions and Islam too added to their problems.

5.1 The early missions

During the fifteenth and sixteenth centuries Portuguese seamen visited many lands that had not been visited before by Europeans. After these voyages of exploration, the Portuguese and Spanish monarchs became interested in spreading Christianity in these new-found lands. One such area was Sierra Leone. In 1596 King Philip of the Iberian Peninsula (Spain and Portugal) appealed to the Jesuits (an Order of the Roman Catholic Church) of Portugal to send missionaries to the Guinea Coast to propagate the Christian faith. Thus Father Balthasar Barreira, who was an elderly priest with several years' experience in the Congo, was sent to Sierra Leone in September 1605. He was the first Christian missionary in Sierra Leone, though he was not the first priest to visit the country. Some resident Portuguese traders, inspired by real Christian zeal, had also begun planting Christianity among the local peoples.

Father Barreira succeeded in baptizing the ruler of the Sierra Leone peninsula, Bei Farma, who took the name Philip Leonis – 'Philip' in honour of the king of the Iberian Peninsula, and 'Leonis' in honour of Farma's kingdom. Another prominent king, Tora, who lived on the north bank of the Sierra Leone River, also received baptism. He had been impressed by the conversion of Leonis, who was his brother-in-law. Tora took the name Peter. Other kings in the neighbourhood of the peninsula also became Christians. These local dignitaries gave Barreira some of their sons to be instructed in Western education and religion. These youths became constant companions of the priest.

Father Barreira's missionary activities were, however, partly frustrated by the work of certain Muslim clergymen. He bitterly commented that 'one of the greatest obstacles to conversion is that there are already in this region Africans from other parts, who take upon themselves to spread the teaching of Mohammed'.

Father Barreira was later joined by another Jesuit missionary, Father Manuel Alvares. The two systematically trained a group of local people as leaders to service the small Christian community that had grown up in north-western Sierra Leone.

Spanish missionaries (Capuchins) took over the work of the Portuguese missionaries in the north-western hinterland, but by 1680 the last of the Spanish priests had died, and no other resident priests arrived until the 1860s. But these were based in Freetown (see 3.5). During this period religious rivalry and jealousies were strong, and the Catholics felt that the Protestant missionaries had stolen the march on them.

The Protestants began missionary work at the end of the eighteenth century, after they had overcome most of their basic problems. The Baptists were the first to found a missionary society (the Baptist Missionary Society, BMS) in England in 1792. The BMS became actively involved in the fight for the abolition of the slave trade. It showed great interest in working in Sierra Leone where there were many Baptists among the Nova Scotian population. The BMS sent its first two missionaries, Jacob Grigg and James Rodway, to Sierra Leone in 1795. Rodway was to work in the Banana Islands, under the patronage of Chief Cleveland, while Grigg was to go to Port Loko. Rodway fell ill in 1796 and he returned to England without achieving much success. Grigg went to Port Loko with a member of the Baptist Church in Freetown, John Kizzel. The latter was to build a factory and engage in trade on behalf of the Sierra Leone Company. The Port Loko mission failed mainly because certain European slave-traders in the town incited the people to rise against Kizzel and Grigg. It was feared that the activities of these two people would seriously endanger their trading interests.

The Glasgow Missionary Society sent two laymen, Duncan Campbell and Robert Henderson, to start a school and a church at Rokon on the Rokel in 1797. But their mission was a failure also. The two men were not qualified for missionary work, and, in addition, their work was adversely affected by the slave trade.

Some London Missionary Society clergymen were sent to the Bullom shore in 1797, but they returned disappointed. The local people were not too keen on having their children educated in the mission school for fear that they might abandon their relatives and take to the ways of the white man. However, Edinburgh Missionary Society personnel who worked in the Rio Pongas scored some minimal success.

The CMS was to be the dominant agent of education and evangelization in the northern Sierra Leone hinterland in the nineteenth century, just as it was in the Colony.

In March 1808 Rev. Melchior Renner was asked to lead a party to the Rio Pongas to preach among the Soso. They were heartily received by Chief Fantimane. He and a slave-trader called Curtis gave the missionaries some land at Bashia. They were also given a house to be used as a school. Later, a new missionary station was established at Canoffee, some miles from Bashia. From 1808 to 1812 this was the only work of the CMS in the area. By 1812 there were 120 pupils in the mission school. In that same year three lay missionaries came to impart industrial training. Some Africans, such as Richard Wilkinson and Jellorum Harrison, who had spent some years in England, helped to teach in the school. It was later proposed that books be published in the Soso language and that some of the older boys who had excelled themselves be trained as catechists and teachers to assist the missionaries.

Missionary work in the Rio Pongas area was, however, greatly affected by the renewed activities of the slave-traders.

Between January and June 1813, for instance, more than a thousand slaves were taken from the Rio Pongas. Governor Maxwell's attempts to clamp down on the slave-factories angered many slavers, and these became hostile to the missionaries. These people felt that the missionaries were agents of the Freetown government. Consequently, their stations were attacked and burnt. By early 1818 the missionaries were forced to abandon the area. Renner took 60 children with him to England.

Another missionary, Gustav Nylander, went up the Bullom shore to preach at the end of 1812. He later produced a grammar and translations of part of St Matthew's Gospel in the Bullom language. His work was also affected by the slave trade.

After these initial failures, the CMS was asked to temporarily abandon missionary work in the interior and concentrate on the Recaptives in the Colony.

5.2 Later missions

Despite certain setbacks, the missions that were opened in the hinterland from the 1830s were more successful than the earlier ones. The missionaries were better prepared for their arduous task and they had more funds.

In July 1833 the CMS sent Rev. C. L. Haensel to Port Loko to re-establish their mission, but he received very litle cooperation from the chiefs. Haensel therefore moved to Magbele where he had some support from the chiefs and Recaptive traders. But the mission failed to grow after Haensel's departure.

In October 1840, Rev. C. F. Schlenker led a party to Port Loko. A school was opened, but some prominent people in the town were strongly opposed to the school system. They feared that once their children had acquired Western education, they would abandon them completely. After ten years of hard work, the CMS failed to make much impact on the people of Port Loko.

After the failure of the Port Loko mission, another attempt was made by Rev. John S. Wiltshire to refound the Magbele station in 1855. Rev. Wiltshire was a Jamaican who was ready to work in Africa. He got on very well with the chiefs and the people. He opened an industrial school which was largely successful. Rev. Wiltshire's station was, however, attacked and destroyed in 1860 by the Yoni Temne during a war with their neighbours. Wiltshire survived the attack, but he later died in Freetown. And this brought to an end the Magbele experiment.

In 1873 the Roman Catholics attempted to extend their activities in Port Loko, but they were bitterly opposed by the CMS, who regarded Port Loko as one of their spheres of influence. It was also felt in official circles that if the Roman Catholic priests (who were French) established a foothold in Port Loko, the area would eventually fall into French hands. CMS missionaries and Thomas G. Lawson, the Government Interpreter, were quickly despatched to Port Loko to persuade the chiefs not to accept Roman Catholicism, on the grounds that the priests were agents of the French. Towards the end of 1878 Rev. John Alley from England went to revive the Port Loko mission. He was assisted from time to time by other missionaries, white and black alike. These made occasional visits to places like Kambia, Mange, Ro-Kilma, and so on. The Roman Catholic priests moved to the Rio Pongas and Mellacourie where the French were more sympathetic to their cause.

In the early 1890s there was a scarcity of CMS missionaries. As a result, Rev. W. J. Humphrey, Principal of Fourah Bay College, appealed to Colony young men in 1895 to come forward and be trained as missionaries. This was the start of the Forward Movement Plan, and the students selected were known as the Short-Course Men. They were required to have gone through their full primary course before being admitted to the college. There they went through an intensive course of study for one year, and were then sent to the mission field. They worked under the supervision of European missionaries. They were sent into the northern interior. Thus Rogbere, Rosanta, Magburaka, Makeni, Musaia, Kabala, etc. came to be open to religious and educational influence.

5.3 The Mendi Mission

This mission was established by Mende and Sherbro Recaptives and American missionaries in rather unusual circumstances. In March 1839 a slave vessel with about 200 Mende and Sherbro slaves sailed from Domboko in the Sherbro for the West Indies. Three months later, the ship arrived in Havana, Cuba, where forty-nine of the slaves were bought by two Spaniards, who put them on board the schooner *Amistad* (in Spanish *amistad* means 'friendship'). They hoped to resell the slaves in the United States of America.

As a result of the inhuman conduct of the ship's crew, the slaves, led by one Sengbe Pieh, revolted and killed some of their captors. The slaves then forced the crewmen to steer the ship back to Sierra Leone. But the ship finally landed on Long Island, New York, where American officials took the ship and the slaves into custody. Sengbe made desperate attempts to escape, saying they had only one chance for death and none for liberty. 'You had better be killed than live many moons in misery', he told his countrymen.

An American newspaper, the *New York Sun*, reported that had he lived in the days of Greece or Rome, the name Sengbe 'would have been handed down to posterity as one who practised those most sublime of all virtues – disinterested patriotism and unshrinking courage'.

The slaves were charged with murder and piracy, but their case was taken up by prominent citizens, such as Lewis Tappan, who was a businessman and founder of the New York Anti-Slavery Society, and John Quincy Adams, a former United States President. The case dragged on for several months, but in the end the slaves were set free.

As the United States Government showed no interest in repatriating these blacks, the Amistad Committee, which had been formed to provide legal and other forms of relief for the accused slaves, again took up their cause. Through the services of a Mende freed slave working in America, James Covey, the committee was able to locate the exact homeland of the ex-slaves. During their stay in America, the slaves had been introduced to Christianity. Nearly half of them had died.

On 25 November 1841, the ex-slaves boarded the barque *Gentleman*, chartered by the Amistad Committee, for their return journey to Sierra Leone. They were accompanied by two black American teachers, Mr and Mrs Henry Wilson, and three white missionaries, Rev. William Raymond and his wife and the Rev. James Steele. The missionaries were instructed to open a 'Mendi Mission' near Sengbe's home town, Mani in upper Mende country, which was about 200 miles from the Gallinas coast.

The ship arrived in Sierra Leone in mid-January, 1842. The missionaries and the returnees could not travel to Sengbe's town because the area was politically unstable. Some of the returnees then decided to go back to their homes.

The missionaries and the few freed men that remained behind (ten adults and four youths) later travelled to the Sherbro where they negotiated for land with Chief Harry Tucker at Komende on the Jong River. They were granted 400 acres of land on which to start the Mendi Mission. The missionaries built their first school which they fittingly called 'Amistad Memorial School'.

Four years later the American Missionary Association of the United States Congregational Church assumed responsibility for the Mendi Mission. They established schools and churches at Mo-Tappan on the Sewa River (the settlement was named in honour of Lewis Tappan), and also at a place just a few miles above Mano on the Bagru River which they called 'Avery Station'. A sawmill was later built at the latter station, which was renamed Moseilolo. By 1856 the Mission had established three stations, two churches with a membership of 153 and two schools with an attendance of 80 pupils. The Mendi Mission was later handed to the United Brethren in Christ (UBC) Mission, another American religious organization.

The first UBC missionaries in Africa were the Revs W. J. Shuez, D. C. Kumler and D. K. Flickinger. They landed in Sierra Leone on 1 March 1855, and a few days later they sailed down to the headquarters of the Mendi Mission in Bonthe which by mutual consent became their temporary home until they established themselves. They later met Chief Caulker of Shenge at Bendu who gave a good ear to their request to start work among the Sherbro. In 1857 these missionaries were established at Shenge, and for 26 years they ran schools and churches in the Shenge area. Their work branched into Rotifunk in 1877. Later Moyamba, Kwelu, Ronietta, Yonibana and Taiama came under their influence.

The UBC educational system had an industrial bias. The boarders in the boarding schools worked four hours a day in farms and gardens in addition to their normal manual work during school hours. UBC's campaign for evangelization and

The main gate to the Harford School with the Intermediate building in the background

education was so vigorous that by 1900 they managed two-thirds of the schools in the southern region. Three of their largest schools were at Rotifunk with an enrolment of 183, Shenge 140 and Moyamba 93.

5.4 Further advance inland

By the second half of the nineteenth century, WMS missionaries working in the Colony were satisfied that they had made much progress there. They then extended inland. Between 1877 and 1881 three missions were started in three different language areas – Sherbro mission (Bonthe), Limba mission (Fourecaria) and Temne mission (Mabang).

A catechist was sent to Bonthe in 1877 to start a mission among the Methodists who resided in the town. It was also suggested that Bonthe should be the centre of operations from which fieldworkers should be trained and sent to the neighbouring Sherbro and Temne countries. The following year a catechist was sent to Mokelleh, 50 miles (80 km) from Bonthe. And by 1899 WMS stations had been opened at Moseley, York Island, Bandajuma, Mofwe, Bumpe and Kateri.

The first attempt by an English missionary to open a mission in Limba country in 1878 failed due to ill health. The following year two WMS missionaries, Rev. Matthew Godman and Rev. Jope, were despatched to Tonko Limba to explore the possibility of establishing a mission there.

In March 1880 Rev. James Booth, lately arrived from England, began work in Fourecaria where he got the full cooperation of the Tonko Limba king and his sub-chiefs. Booth made great efforts to learn Limba, Soso and Temne, and by mid-1884 he had succeeded in translating parts of the Bible into Limba. One of the king's sons was given to Booth for training and performed so well that he was sent to England for further studies. He became known as James Lahai Booth. He later served as a missionary among his people.

Other people, such as the Krio catechist, Philip Johnson, and the new converts, were also instrumental in spreading the Christian religion in the neighbourhood of Fourecaria. Although only a small minority of the Tonko Limba population embraced Christianity, their influence on the majority was considerable. For instance, James Lahai Booth got the chiefs to decree that anyone found working on the Sabbath should be severely punished.

Rev. James Booth later married a Temne woman in the traditional manner. As a result, he fell out with his superiors. He then resigned and became a trader. Nevertheless, missionary work continued in the Tonko Limba areas.

A Krio catechist opened a station at Mabang (Ribbi) in 1880. From there his work began to extend gradually into the surrounding areas, such as Masanke. WMS pastors also made great efforts to preach among the Colony residents in Koya.

Other Protestant missionary bodies that operated in the hinterland in the nineteenth century were the United Methodist Free Church, African Methodist Episcopal, Sierra Leone Church Missions, Christian Alliance, and the American Wesleyan Methodists. The operations of these bodies were, however, minimal.

Roman Catholic missionary activity in the southern hinterland started in 1871, when Father Kayser made a preliminary survey in the Sherbro. A rich Jewish merchant on York Island, Mr Harris, who was married to a Catholic woman, expressed an earnest wish for a mission and a school and promised land and some money. Later, Father Blanchet acquired land and built a house in 1890. A church was built the following year. Father Fegel became the first resident priest in the area and he was visited from time to time by priests from the Colony.

The spread of Christianity in the hinterland, as we have observed, was not just the work of European missionaries. It was a cooperative enterprise in which Africans played an essential part.

Conclusion

At the close of the nineteenth century, many people in the hinterland had become Christians, but not the majority. This was for many reasons.

(a) Islam was firmly entrenched in many areas in the interior, particularly in the north. And Islam was able to present itself, though also an immigrant religion, as an African religion, whereas Christianity always suffered from being 'the whiteman's religion'.

(b) Christianity was not adapted to African society and it made heavy demands on the convert. For instance, admission into the Christian church involved arduous teaching and spiritual preparation of the catechist, who was also required to abandon completely his old religion.

(c) In addition to making conversion more difficult, Christianity also attacked the African way of life. For example, polygamy, slavery, magic, use of charms and initiation ceremonies were all vehemently condemned.

(d) Many people regarded Christianity as a disruptive force; this was largely why many missionaries were killed and their churches destroyed during the hut tax rising of 1898 (see 7.2).

A great expansion of Christianity, however, took place in the twentieth century.

References

Abraham, Arthur (1987), *The Amistad Revolt* (USIS, Freetown, Sierra Leone).

Crowder, Michael (1968), *West Africa Under Colonial Rule* (Hutchinson).

Gittens, A. J. 'Mende and Missionary: Belief, Perception and Enterprise in Sierra Leone', Ph D (Edinburgh).

Government Information Services (1976), *Partners for Progress* (Freetown).

Hamelberg, E. (1964), 'The Jesuits in Sierra Leone 1605–17: A Whirlwind of Grace', SLBR Vol. 6, no 1, June.

Jakobsson, Stiv, *Am I Not a Man and a Brother? British Missions and the Abolition of the Slave Trade and Slavery in West Africa and the West Indies 1786–1838* (Uppsala).

Olson, G. W. (1969), *Church Growth in Sierra Leone* (Williams Eerdman, USA).

Sumner, D. L. *Education in Sierra Leone* (Freetown).

Turay, Amadu E. (1977), 'Missionary Work and African Society: James Booth in Tonko Limba', ARB, Vol. VII, no. 2, March.

Questions PART A

1 What were the chief difficulties facing Christian missionaries in the hinterland up to the early nineteenth century?
2 Give an account of the growth of Christianity in the interior up to the end of the nineteenth century.
3 How was the Mendi Mission established in the Sherbro in 1842?
4 Outline the activities of *one* of the following missionary bodies in the spread of Christianity and education in the Sierra Leone hinterland.
   (a) Church Missionary Society
   (b) United Brethren in Christ
   (c) Wesleyan Methodist Society
5 Why did many people in the interior refuse to adopt Christianity in the nineteenth century?

Questions PART B

1 Evaluate the impact of the Amistad Revolt on Sierra Leone.
2 Discuss the role of Colony Africans in the spread of Christianity in the hinterland.
3 To what extent was Christianity a disruptive force in the interior?
4 Discuss the similarities and differences between Christianity and traditional religions in Sierra Leone.

6 The declaration of the Protectorate

Britain assumed control of the Colony settlement in 1808, but it was only in 1896 that a British Protectorate was proclaimed over the Sierra Leone hinterland. Why did it take the British so long to establish formal control over the hinterland? For an answer, we need to examine British policy towards West Africa in the nineteenth century.

6.1 Non-annexation policy

For most of the nineteenth century, the British showed little interest in acquiring colonies in West Africa, mainly because it was expensive to maintain such colonies. Where trade between a particular area on the coast and Britain was considered substantial enough to warrant some administrative control, a company of merchants could be permitted to govern such an area. The British Government gave the company an annual grant to offset costs.

When the British Government took over the Colony of Sierra Leone, it showed no interest in extending the Colony's frontiers. And it insisted that the Colony must pay for its administration. Government revenue was obtained largely from duties, but these did not amount to much, for the Colony's trade with Britain was never large. Thus extra revenue-collecting areas had to be explored.

The Sierra Leone governors were also faced with the difficult task of stopping or controlling the slave trade in the hinterland. Attempts by the governors to deal with these problems – raising money for the Colony administration and suppressing the slave trade – led them to effect closer relations with, and gain a measure of influence over, the coastal and interior kings.

The governors used a variety of methods to extend their influence inland. These included sending diplomatic missions in the hinterland, signing friendship treaties with the interior kings, the use of force and the offer of material assistance to the kings.

Government-sponsored missions were sent into the interior to convince traders there to send their products to Freetown. Sometimes, these missions were to report on the political and economic situation in certain areas. William Cooper Thomson went to Timbo in 1814 with instructions to find out the major causes of conflict which interrupted trade in the area, and to examine the best means for the expansion of trade with the interior. Between 1817 and 1822 four major expeditions were sent. Major Gordon Laing, for instance, went to Falaba in 1822 on a trade mission. He attracted much attention as he was the first white man to visit the town. These expeditions enhanced the Colony's trade position in the interior and provided valuable information about ruling families, potential alliances, and products available for trade. John McCormack and Dala Modu also acted as ambassadors and mediators to the colonial administration.

Certain governors also tried to take over some territories. Governor MacCarthy had tried to raise the revenue of the Colony by expanding its frontiers. His successor, Charles Turner, continued in a similar vein. He used the suppression of the slave trade as a smoke-screen to justify his expansionist policies. He tried to convince the British Government that the most effective way of stopping the slave trade in the coastal areas was to annex these areas.

In Sherbro country the Caulkers and Clevelands were at war and in 1825 one of the combatants, Chief George Caulker, asked Governor Turner to mediate. The Governor could not let this opportunity slip from his hands. When he arrived at the Plantain Island, where all the Sherbro chiefs had assembled, he made it quite clear that he would do nothing unless the rulers agreed to give up their countries to the British Crown. In return they were to receive British protection and become British subjects. The chiefs agreed out of politeness.

Governor Turner also took advantage of an election dispute in Port Loko to force the chiefs there to give up their territories. He led colonial troops to support the Colony's candidate, Fatima Braima, in the disputed succession at Port Loko in 1825. Braima's brother was agent for a rich businessman in Freetown, Kenneth Macauley. Macauley was in fact a member of the Governor's Council, which was the governing body of the Colony. He had told Governor Turner that if Fatima Braima was not crowned *Alikali* of Port Loko, there would be war which would adversely affect trade.

The Secretary of State for the Colonies, Earl Bathurst, refused to sanction Governor Turner's annexations. He made it quite clear that the British Government would not 'consent to any arrangement which might be construed into a desire for territorial aggrandisement'. Earl Bathurst therefore instructed the Governor to return the chiefs' lands back to them. Turner, however, deliberately ignored the Secretary of State's instructions.

Governor Alexander Findlay was more diplomatic. He inaugurated in 1831 a policy of extending indirect influence by signing treaties of friendship with the interior rulers. These treaties generally required African rulers to stop the slave trade, permit European and Colony traders to move freely in their towns, allow missionaries to settle and spread the gospel without hindrance, keep roads open for commercial transit, and avoid war. In return for their cooperation the hinterland kings were given an annual fixed sum called stipends. However, both parties did not always honour the terms of the treaties. Successive governors extended the treaty area and by the mid-nineteenth century, it stretched along the coast to Rio Nunez, inland to the Mende and Limba countries.

More annexations were made during the governorship of S. J. Hill. He was an army colonel. Hill made several attempts to capture new lands and interfere in the internal affairs of the countries bordering the Colony. He interfered in the Port Loko election of 1857 and led colonial troops to attack Maligia in Kambia. He also fraudulently brought western Koya under British rule in 1866. A Recaptive, trading in Koya, was plundered after he had abducted a Temne man's wife. An officer sent to investigate the matter returned to say that he had been molested. Governor Hill then asked the Koya king,

Bei Kanta, to either pay £300 or lease his country to the British. The king agreed to lease his lands, but the treaty he signed declared it annexed. The annexed lands included Robaga and Robana, two sacred towns which for centuries had been the home of the Koya kings.

Later that year Governor Hill annexed parts of the Sherbro. The French were increasing their influence in the Sherbro and were determined to use force if necessary. In 1858 French warships attacked Bendu, ostensibly because a French trader had been insulted. The French then forced Thomas Caulker, chief of Bendu, to sign a treaty by which he would undertake to protect French interests. Chief Caulker knew that the French aimed to take over Bendu. He therefore decided to cede his country to the British with whom he had historical connections.

Chief Caulker then requested Governor Hill to take over Bendu. The Governor was delighted, for the Sherbro was a major trading centre and a potential revenue-collecting area. He therefore grasped at the offer. Hill even got the other Sherbro chiefs to give up their territories to the British in November 1861. Thus, the Colony was extended over a large area on the Sherbro.

The British Government ratified Hill's treaties with the Sherbro kings. The British had thus accepted the threat of a foreign power as a partial reason for sidestepping their former policy of non-annexation. The rest of the Sherbro was ceded to the British for fiscal purposes in 1887.

6.2 The Native Affairs Department

As British relations with the hinterland grew, there arose the need to establish a foreign affairs system, whose job would be to promote the Colony's interests in the interior (such as signing treaties with interior rulers), and to seek the welfare of important local dignitaries and traders who visited Freetown. The purpose of extending hospitality to these people was threefold: to encourage the traders to return, to build up a good reputation for the Colony among the people of the interior, and to obtain information about trade routes, trade prospects, and the political situation generally. A fund was set aside for this purpose.

A department was thus created to liaise between the Freetown administration and the interior rulers. This was the Aborigines Branch of the Secretariat, which later became known as the Native Affairs Department. It was centred on Thomas George Lawson. Lawson, who was born probably in 1814 to a chiefly family in Little Popo (in what is now the Republic of Togo), left his home in 1825 for further studies in England. He broke his journey in Freetown, where he stayed until his death in 1891. An Irish trader, John McCormack, who was also a government agent, became Lawson's patron and teacher in Freetown. Lawson regularly accompanied McCormack into the interior on trade and peace missions on behalf of the colonial administration. In time, Lawson learnt several of the indigenous languages and he developed friendly relations with many interior rulers. He later married a Temne woman from Koya.

In 1846 Lawson became Governor Macdonald's emissary and six years later was appointed Native Interpreter and Government Messenger. He was in effect the unofficial foreign minister of the administration.

His duties as a Government Interpreter, which also combined the functions of a police inspector, were many and various. He interpreted between the colonial officials and the indigenous rulers at meetings as well as in the law courts.

As Messenger, Lawson saw to it that government policies and demands were understood and executed by the chiefs. It was also his responsibility to pay stipends to those chiefs who had signed treaties with the colonial government. When these chiefs and other local dignitaries visited Freetown, Lawson entertained them in his home. He even arranged for the education of chiefs' sons in Freetown schools. He regularly acquainted government with developments in the interior. Lawson's original salary was £100 per annum but, as his official duties increased, this sum was progressively raised to £350 per annum.

For a very long time Lawson's informal ministry was a one-person ministry. This was largely because the administration wanted to reduce its expenditure to the barest minimum. But as contact with the interior became wider and more permanent, more officials were appointed into the ministry. Winwood Reade, an English explorer, was appointed agent in 1869, while Dr E. W. Blyden was appointed to a similar post in 1872. Blyden did not, however, hold on to the job. He resigned, apparently due to ill health. Two Africans later joined the staff of the Aborigines Department. James C. E. Parkes was made assistant to Lawson, while Mohamed Sanusi became the Government Arabic Letter Writer. Many of the hinterland kings communicated with the Freetown colonial administration in Arabic.

The Resolutions of 1865

The desires of the Sierra Leone governors to enlarge the country's physical borders were partly frustrated by the Resolutions of the Select Committee of the British House of Commons. This committee was set up in March 1865 to determine whether the British colonies in West Africa were worth keeping. Britain lost some soldiers in 1863–4 during a war with the Asante (Gold Coast) and this incident had angered many British people who demanded that Britain withdraw entirely from the West Coast.

The committee recommended that the British Government should not acquire new territories in West Africa or offer protection to the local peoples, and that steps should be taken to prepare colonial West Africans for self-government. It also recommended eventual British withdrawal from West Africa except Sierra Leone (which had an important naval base). In the interim, the British West African colonies were to be united under a Governor-in-Chief, resident in Freetown.

Although the British Government failed to implement all of the committee's recommendations because of new developments in West Africa and Europe, the policy had important consequences for Sierra Leone. When, for example, Governor Blackall sought authority in late 1865 to make small extensions along the Mellacourie River, which was an important groundnut trading centre, permission was rejected immediately. The French eventually took over the area. In February 1866 Governor Blackall was appointed Governor-in-Chief of West Africa and so Freetown again became the administrative headquarters of the coast. The policy also allowed the Sierra Leone Colony people to hope that they would take over the administration of Sierra Leone when the British left – whenever that would be.

6.3   Pressures for the declaration of a Protectorate

The Colony governors were not the only advocates of an extension of the Colony's frontier, although they had taken the initiative in the early nineteenth century. In the last quarter of that century Colony businessmen with their counterparts in Britain, and some local colonial officials, such as J. C. E. Parkes, began to exert more pressure on the Colonial Office to take over the hinterland. Certain developments in the hinterland and on the international market seem to have precipitated this move.

The expansion of legitimate trade in the interior had created rivalries among kings and other big men which often resulted in wars. The world trade depressions of the 1870s and 1880s had an adverse effect on the economy of the Colony. There was an increase in trade between Freetown and Europe during this period, but commodity prices fell drastically in Europe. This in turn drastically reduced the profit-margin of the traders. Government revenue also depreciated. Consequently, there was not enough money to pay for the administration of the Colony.

The traders wrongly believed that the trade-wars in the hinterland were solely responsible for their declining profits and thus called on the administration to annex the hinterland and put a stop to these wars so that trade would prosper once again.

In an effort to salvage the economy, Governor John Pope Hennessy abolished the house tax in the Colony in 1873 and, instead, increased customs duties, because some people complained that they were too poor to pay the house tax. High tariffs brought the Colony more revenue, but drove trade away. Many traders moved into areas that were not under British control and therefore paid no taxes to the Freetown administration. Because they paid no taxes they sold their goods cheap, which attracted many customers. Freetown traders, who were subject to customs, got annoyed. One prominent trader, William Grant, mobilized other Freetown traders to petition the British Government to annex all the coastal regions and collect taxes there as a way of solving the Colony's financial problems. Calls were also made to decentralize the administrative unit of British West Africa so that Sierra

Leone would be relieved of the administrative burden imposed on it by the fact that it was the headquarters of British West Africa. A dismantling of this unified structure would then enable Sierra Leonean officials to concentrate more on domestic issues.

The Colonial Office, unenthusiastic about territorial acquisition but concerned about the Colony's financial problems, suggested that British influence should be extended only along the coastal areas, where it was possible to place customs officials and collect duties.

As the trade-wars in the Sherbro and Gallinas continued, attempts were made to recall a former governor of the Colony, Sir Samuel Rowe, to deal with the situation. It was felt especially in the Colony that Rowe was the only man capable of handling the situation. In his efforts to increase the revenue of the Colony and at the same time satisfy the wishes of Colony traders, Rowe had in the mid-1870s embarked on an aggressive policy towards the interior. His first major attack had been in the Sherbro where he led two expeditions. He succeeded in putting down the trade wars in the Bagru and Mongray river basins.

Rowe accepted an invitation to return to Sierra Leone in 1885. On arrival he concluded that unless a protectorate was declared and officers posted in the hinterland who would quickly deal with disturbances there, the region would know no peace. Some officials in the Colonial Office also shared this view, as did most of the members of the African Association. This association, formed in Freetown in 1885, had its members drawn from the wealthier Krio and European business and professional men. A leading member of the group, the Honourable Samuel Lewis, got his colleagues to send a memorandum to the British Government requesting the enlargement of the Colony by a policy of peaceful annexation. Rowe gave his blessing to the memorandum and emphasized that its proposals should be seriously considered if the Colony was to continue to be economically viable.

While the Colonial Office was adopting a rather slow approach to the political problems in the southern hinterland, a more serious threat was appearing to the north of the Colony, which was to force British colonial officials to take a more decisive step in proclaiming a Protectorate over the Sierra Leone hinterland.

6.4   Samori Toure and European imperialism

Samori Toure was a Muslim Mandingo military ruler who resisted several attempts by the French to take over his vast commercial empire, which included parts of modern Guinea, Sierra Leone and the Ivory Coast. His Sofa warriors had brought these areas under his control through a series of *jihad*s waged between the 1870s and 1880s. Samori's army depended very heavily on Sierra Leone for weapons and in order to guarantee the smooth flow of these weapons, an attempt was made to control the important Kankan–Freetown trade route, which was regularly used by Samori's kinsmen, the Jula traders. This route was often blocked by trade wars.

Governor Havelock warned Samori in 1884 not to attack any towns on this route as these places were part of Britain's informal empire. Samori ignored the warning. He despatched one of his generals, Nfa Ali, to subdue Falaba, which was an important commercial centre and capital of the Solima state. Ali, in alliance with some of Falaba's enemies, attacked Falaba in April 1884. This attack brought a lot of hardships to the people. But rather than accept defeat, the king of the Solima state, Manga Sewa, with many of his elders, war-leaders and senior wife committed suicide in his armoury. The Sofa warriors completely destroyed the Solima state.

The warriors then moved southwards to attack the Biriwa Limba. The Biriwa Limba king, Suluku, put up some resistance, but his army was no match for the Sofa, who captured many of his towns. Suluku gave up in November 1884 and he became a Muslim. Having occupied Biriwa, the Sofa now diverted trade away from Bumban through the Mandingo town of Karina. They wanted to ruin Suluku economically so that the Mandingo of Biriwa would prosper. But Suluku, being an astute politician, got the assistance of the Colony government to put a halt to Sofa occupation of Biriwa. Since Freetown was the source of arms for the Sofa, the Freetown government had an edge over them. It successfully persuaded them to leave Biriwa.

The Colony government's intervention prevented the Sofa from advancing southwards any further. But they moved to Soso country and captured the Soso trading-town of Samaya.

Next they captured many of the Koranko towns, and by 1886 northern Sierra Leone, save Temneland, had become part of Samori's empire.

Sofa successes created panic among the Colony nationals who feared that they would be the next victims of the Sofa raids. They vehemently protested to Governor Rowe, who then appealed to the Sofa warriors to moderate their activities. Samori complied and even asked that the British take over his empire, if only to prevent the French from annexing it.

But the Colonial Office could not sanction such a move. Samori had recently concluded a treaty with the French, and Britain did not want to be involved in a diplomatic or military entanglement with another European power. This was against the spirit of the partition of Africa.

In the meantime, the French were busy claiming vast areas to the north of the Sierra Leone Colony. In 1865 and 1866 they had signed treaties with chiefs along the Mellacourie, Rio Pongas and Rio Nunez rivers. Chiefs in these areas had earlier signed friendship treaties with the Freetown administration. But as the British showed no sign of bringing the region under their rule, the French stepped in.

In 1882 the British and French governments, without consulting the traditional rulers, had agreed that the Great Scarcies River would mark the northward limits of Sierra Leone. Four years later, the southern limit was settled with Liberia.

The French still wanted more territories, so they continued to pursue Samori southwards and to claim all his lands as theirs by right of conquest. The British began to fear that the French might hem-in on the Colony and eventually capture Freetown. Humanitarian, economic and strategic considerations prompted the British to act quickly.

Britain had a strong affinity with the Colony, which she regarded as her brainchild. To relinquish it was to dishonour the achievements of the philanthropists. The Colony's survival was dependent on trade with and taxes from the interior; so if the interior fell into French hands, Britain would be compelled to shoulder the burden of the Colony. Then there was the strategic importance of the Freetown port. It was the only port suitable for coaling British naval vessels in West Africa. Its bays also provided anchorage for warships, where they would lie hidden from enemy view. At a time when Germany was threatening Britain's seapower, she could not afford to lose Freetown.

Britain then embarked on several courses of action, one of which was to create 'a barrier to Samori's further progress towards the coast by forming a confederation of friendly tribes'. An emissary was also despatched to Samori so that friendly relations would be re-established between his empire and Freetown. Major Festing set out on this mission in January 1888. He met Samori at Heremakono on 19 May. Samori made it quite clear to Festing that he would surrender his empire to the British if the latter would assist him in crushing his enemy in Sikasso (in northern Ivory Coast). But Festing could not commit the British Government to action. He left with merely a promise of a treaty.

The French viewed Festing's mission as a piece of British treachery. The French therefore quickly signed another agreement with Samori. Unfortunately for Samori, he was defeated in Sikasso and there was a general uprising in his empire which was in part inspired by the French. They took advantage of Samori's misfortunes to inflict a crushing defeat on him. The French captured most of his territory.

Standard treaties   At such a time of intense European rivalry, Britain realized that the friendship treaties she had signed with the interior rulers were ineffective. For nothing could prevent these rulers from giving away their lands to the French if they wanted to. British colonial officials therefore resolved to sign more 'effective' treaties, called standard treaties, as from 1890. Among other things, the treaties forbade chiefs from entering into negotiations with any foreign power without the consent of the British. British subjects (Krio) in the interior were to be protected and chiefs were to keep the peace and promote trade.

Two Travelling Commissioners – G. H. Garrett and T. J. Alldridge – were appointed to sign these treaties with the chiefs. Garrett went to the north, while Alldridge went to the south and east. The Commissioners were instructed by the Colonial Office 'to extend the sphere of British influence as far as possible'. But this was a very late move, for the French had already taken possession of many fertile areas in the northern hinterland, such as the Futa Jallon area.

While trekking through the north, Garrett met Kemoko

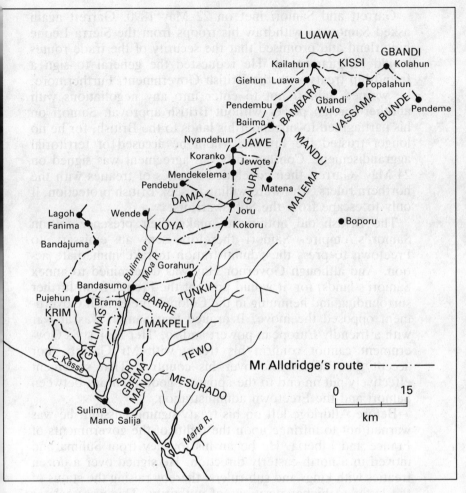

9 *Standard treaty-signing missions in the hinterland, showing T.J. Alldridge's route*

Bilali, a Sofa war leader, at Kaliere on 28 April 1890. Garrett advised Bilali to put a halt to Sofa activities in the northern region, but Bilali appeared unwilling to do so. Garrett continued his journey to Bisandugu, Samori's capital, where he hoped to meet with the general. On his way he was struck by the ravages of the Sofa warriors. Burnt houses and human carcases littered the ground in practically every village he passed through.

Garrett and Samori met on 22 May 1890. Garrett again asked Samori to withdraw his troops from the Sierra Leone hinterland and promised that the security of the trade routes would be guaranteed. He requested the general to sign a friendship treaty with the British Government. Furthermore, he warned Samori not to enter into any negotiations with another foreign power without British approval. Samori on his part agreed to surrender his lands to the British, for he no longer trusted the French, whom he accused of territorial aggrandisement. Consequently, an agreement was signed on 24 May. Garrett then concluded a series of treaties with the northern rulers, who were willing to seek British protection, if only to escape from the Sofa warriors.

The British did nothing to make their presence felt in Samori's empire. Samori therefore sent an emissary to Freetown to press the administration to take immediate action. And although Governor Hay was determined to annex Samori's lands, for 'it would prevent the French from further surrounding and hemming in the Colony', the British Government opposed the move. It argued that Samori was at war with a friendly European power; and so, 'Her Majesty's Government cannot confirm his treaty with Mr Garrett, nor accept the Protectorate over his country.' That statement effectively put an end to the apparent good relations between Samori and the Freetown administration.

Before Alldridge left on his treaty-signing mission, he was warned not to infringe upon the rights of the governments of France and Liberia. He began his journey from Sulima and moved in a north-easterly direction. He signed over a dozen treaties with kings and sub-rulers, thereby raising the status of the latter to higher positions of authority. This was to later create serious political problems in the interior. In the meantime Governor Hay himself was busy concluding a series of treaties with chiefs in the middle Mende belt. Many chiefs still regarded these new treaties as treaties of friendship, so they signed them. Little did they know that they were giving away their sovereignty.

The Frontier Police

On 15 January 1890, the British inaugurated the Frontier Police Force, in an attempt to ensure peace and stability and protect trade routes in the hinterland. At its inception the authorized strength of the force was one Inspector-General, three Inspectors, four local Sub-Inspectors, and 280 other ranks. The rank and file of the force was recruited from practically every ethnic group in the country. At first, the bulk of this force was stationed along or to the south of a road which ran from Kambia to Mano Salija by way of the heads of navigation on the rivers. The hinterland was divided into five police districts and manned by Frontier Police Inspectors.

The officers were advised not to meddle in local politics. They were not to behave as administrators; further, they were to give maximum respect to the chiefs. However, barely three years after the establishment of the force, numerous reports began to pour in about Frontier Police brutality. Taking advantage of their being far away from headquarters, many of these policemen constituted themselves into judges and little despots, molesting and maltreating the people at will. Some insulted and imprisoned chiefs. One officer even had the impudence to install his mistress as chief of Bagru. By and large, the colonial government tended to dismiss the many complaints against these officers.

The Waima incident

Following the failure of the British to take over Samori's territories, the French stepped up their campaign to eliminate him completely. They succeeded in cutting off the Sofa route to Freetown in 1893. This forced the Sofa army to move into Kono country to establish a new route. But the Colonial Office now regarded the Sofa as a menace in the interior. This view was shared by Colonel Ellis, commander of the Freetown garrison, and Captain E. A. W. Lendy, the Inspector-General of Police. Anxious to achieve military glory, both men stirred the British Government to take strong action against the Sofa, who were causing considerable destruction in Kono country. The Sofa had also attacked King Nyagua, who had signed a treaty with the colonial administration, and sacked one of his towns. The expedition, which consisted of some 470 officers and men of the West India Regiment and the Frontier Police, left Freetown on 27 November 1893 under the command of Captain Lendy.

During the expedition the so-called Waima Incident occurred. A French army officer, Lieutenant Gaston Maritz, with a small party of soldiers, was in Kono country making treaties with the chiefs. He was told that there was a large encampment of troops at Waima. Not having been warned of the British expedition, he assumed they were the Sofa and attacked them. The battle started at about 6 a.m. on 22 December, during heavy rain. Maritz and Lendy and many of their soldiers were killed. A smaller force sent later from Freetown was able to overcome the Sofa, who suffered many casualties. The Waima Incident was the only time during the whole European scramble for Africa that Europeans fired on one another.

The British, thinking that the French were the aggressors, asked for compensation and £9 000 was later paid to them. The Waima affair made it all the more necessary to demarcate proper boundaries between the French and British 'spheres of influence'. This was effected in 1895. It also speeded up the Protectorate proclamation of 1896.

6.5   The Protectorate is proclaimed

When Frederic Cardew became Governor of Sierra Leone in 1894, he was entrusted with the responsibility of declaring a Protectorate over the British sphere of influence. He immediately set out to accomplish his task. During his six years in Sierra Leone he made three extensive tours of the hinterland.

During these tours Cardew attempted to explain his policies and plans to the interior chiefs. These policies and plans included the declaration of a Protectorate, taxation and the construction of a railway. Cardew's plans for a Protectorate were to a large extent incomprehensible to the majority, if not all, of the chiefs he met.

An Order of the Queen-in-Council made on 24 August 1895, under the Foreign Jurisdiction Act, gave the legislature of Sierra Leone the power to make laws for the adjoining Protectorate as it had for the Colony. A series of Ordinances passed by the Legislative Council between 1896 and 1897 established British jurisdiction over, and made provisions for the administration of, the Protectorate. These raised protests from certain quarters. Sir Samuel Lewis, for example, argued in the Legislative Council that the legislations were improper, because the Protectorate had not been acquired by conquest and there was not enough evidence that the chiefs had willingly given up their lands. Despite these protests, a Protectorate was proclaimed over the Sierra Leone hinterland on 31 August 1896. The proclamation was only issued in the Colony, not in the Protectorate it established. The British tried to justify their action by saying that the proclamation was 'best for the interests of the people.'

6.6 Notes on some Colony personalities

There were some Colony people who in the nineteenth century either helped to shape British policy in Sierra Leone or influenced the British mode of thinking. One such personality, T. G. Lawson, was briefly discussed earlier. Lawson retired from government service in 1886 and was awarded a personal decoration by Governor Rowe in appreciation of his invaluable services. He was also put on an annual pension of £210. Two other important dignitaries were Sir Samuel Lewis and James C. E. Parkes.

Sir Samuel Lewis

Samuel Lewis was born on 13 November 1843. His parents were Egba Recaptives from Nigeria who had settled at Murray Town in western Freetown in 1828. His father, William Lewis, was a successful businessman.

Lewis attended the CMS Grammar School, and on completion assisted in his father's business until 1866 when he proceeded to England to read law. He was called to the Bar of the Middle Temple in 1871. The following year he returned to Sierra Leone and worked as acting Queen's Advocate (Attorney-General) for fifteen months. He was a successful private lawyer and declined offers for a permanent government job, though he temporarily acted as Chief Justice on two occasions. He had clients all along the British West African coast. Lewis was a firm believer in justice.

As acting Queen's Advocate in 1872, Lewis was appointed one of the *ex-officio* members in the Legislative Council. In

Sir Samuel Lewis

1882, he became a permanent unofficial member and worked to develop the limited means by which such members could try to check abuses of power by the Governor. Through his untiring efforts councillors gained the right to receive information, debate legislation, propose amendments and even appeal to the Colonial Office.

He was also instrumental in the re-establishment of the Freetown municipal council in 1893 which he regarded as a means of training in self-government. In that same year he was awarded the CMG. Lewis became Mayor of Freetown in 1895 and was re-elected the following year. In 1896 also, he was made Knight Commander of Saint Michael and Saint George (KCMG), the first African to be thus honoured by a British monarch.

Sir Samuel Lewis was a staunch supporter of British imperial expansion and strongly believed in the many values that the British stood for. But he opposed the fraudulent manner in which a Protectorate was proclaimed over the Sierra Leone hinterland.

Sir Samuel Lewis was always willing to advise the interior chiefs and to secure justice for them in their dealings with the colonial authorities. His vigorous pursuit of a land case in 1896 (the Mokasi land case) aggravated the already strained relationship between him and Governor Cardew. Cardew went so far as to call Lewis a 'pettyfogging lawyer'.

After the hut tax insurrection of 1898, Sir Samuel Lewis and other prominent Krio were held responsible for stirring up trouble in the Protectorate. It then became clear that many of Lewis's hopes for the place of acculturated Africans within the British African empire were not to be realized. But Sir Samuel Lewis remained a respectable person in Freetown until his death from cancer in 1903.

James C. E. Parkes

J. C. E. Parkes was born in Freetown in 1861. His father was a disbanded West Indian soldier and his mother part-Nova Scotian. Parkes was educated at the Grammar School and worked in the Queen's Advocate Department before leaving for Britain to study law. A serious illness forced him to abandon his course and he returned to Sierra Leone in 1882. He was then appointed clerk to the Commandant of Sherbro, but was transferred to the Aborigines Department in 1884 where he worked under Lawson. When Lawson retired in 1886 Parkes was appointed Superintendent of the Aborigines Department. His salary was increased to £150 a year.

Parkes was given added responsibilities. He had to formulate and implement new policies of treaty-making, and in addition he was responsible for the construction of a frontier road which connected important produce-growing areas in the interior. The Aborigines Department was renamed the Department of Native Affairs in 1891, and Parkes became Secretary of the Department. His salary was again increased to £250 with an annual increment of £20.

Parkes suggested in 1892 that a Protectorate be declared over the Sierra Leone hinterland and that five Krio 'Political Agents' be appointed to administer the different districts there. These agents would advise and direct chiefs on such matters as clearing roads, implementing new agricultural schemes, and settling disputes. They would further prevent the imposition of severe punishment and see that treaty provisions were honoured. His aim was to reduce the influence of the Frontier Police in the Protectorate. The colonial administration rejected his proposals. The administration not only increased the role of the force, but also cut down drastically on the activities of the Department of Native Affairs, much to Parkes's embarrassment.

Parkes and Governor Cardew also held different views on taxation in the Protectorate. Parkes proposed a poll tax of two shillings while Cardew preferred a house tax, arguing that a poll tax could be easily evaded. Cardew's suggestion was implemented and thereafter, Parkes's influence began to decline steadily. He became ill in 1899 and died on 10 August that same year at the age of 38.

References

Abraham, Arthur (1976), *Topics in Sierra Leone History* (Leone Publishers, Freetown).

Abraham, Arthur (1978), *Mende Government and Politics Under Colonial Rule* (Sierra Leone and Oxford University Press).

Crowder, Michael (1968), *West Africa Under Colonial Rule* (Hutchinson).

Deveneaux, Gustav (1979), 'Trade Routes and Colonial Policy in Sierra Leone', JHSSL, III 1 and 2.

Encyclopaedia Africana – Dictionary of African Biography, Vol. 2, Sierra Leone – Zaire (Reference Publications, USA, 1979).

Foray, C. P. (1977), *Historical Dictionary of Sierra Leone* (Metuchen, New Jersey).

Fyfe, Christopher (1964), *Sierra Leone Inheritance* (Oxford University Press).

Fyfe, Christopher (1979), *A Short History of Sierra Leone* (Longman).

Fyle, C. Magbaily (1979), *The Solima Yalunka Kingdom* (Nyakon, Freetown).

Hargreaves, J. D. (1954), 'The Evolution of the Native Affairs Department', SLS (ns), no. 3, December.

Hargreaves, J. D. (1963), *Prelude to the Partition of West Africa* (Macmillan).

Hargreaves, J. D. (1958), *Sir Samuel Lewis* (Oxford University Press).

Koroma, Abdul Karim (1977), 'Samori Toure and the Colony and Hinterland of Sierra Leone: Diplomatic and Military Contacts, 1880–1892', JHSSL, Vol. 1, no 2, July.

Lasite, A. J. (1974), 'The Native Affairs Department and the Development of British Policy in the Northern Interior of Sierra Leone 1850–1900', MA (USL).

Newbury, C. W. (1965), *British Policy Towards West Africa, 1786–1874*, Oxford.

Skinner, David (1980), *Thomas George Lawson* (Hoover Institution Press).

Questions PART A

1 How did the Sierra Leone Colony governors extend their influence in the hinterland in the nineteenth century?
2 What were the functions of the Native Affairs Department?
3 Why did Samori Toure invade the Sierra Leone hinterland?
4 Why was a Protectorate declared over the Sierra Leone hinterland in 1896?
5 Write notes on the career of *one* of the following people:
   (a) T. G. Lawson
   (b) Sir Samuel Lewis
   (c) J. C. E. Parkes

Questions PART B

1 'They were perhaps less important as a guide for the Colonial Office (which ignored them when convenient) than as a public statement of

British policy in West Africa.' Discuss this assessment of the Resolutions of the 1865 Select Committee of the House of Commons.

2 What was the attitude of (a) the French and (b) the Krio to the 1865 Resolutions of the Select Committee of the House of Commons?

3 Discuss the evolution and functions of the Native Affairs Department.

4 Examine the view that, for a greater part of the nineteenth century, British policy in Sierra Leone was aimed at providing extra revenue without incurring extra expense or responsibility. Illustrate your answer by special reference to one area in Sierra Leone.

5 Comment on the remedies suggested by the Hon. William Grant in 1874 for the economic problems of the Colony of Sierra Leone.

6 How did Samori Toure and his Sofa warriors influence the politics of Sierra Leone in the 1880s and 1890s?

7 In what circumstances did the Colonial Office in the 1890s sanction a policy of expansion in Sierra Leone?

8 'Anglo-French rivalry in West Africa in the late nineteenth century led to the proclamation of a British Protectorate over the Sierra Leone hinterland.' Discuss.

7 The structure and operation of local government

A system of local government based on the British model was introduced in the Colony at the end of the eighteenth century. After the Protectorate proclamation a new type of local government structure was introduced in the Protectorate which was very different from that of the Colony. This was the indirect rule system.

In Sierra Leone the inhabitants of the Colony had had a much longer exposure to British customs, values and institutions than the people of the Protectorate. As a result, Governor Cardew was reluctant to introduce Colony laws in the Protectorate; if he did, 'there would be an abrupt subversion of Protectorate laws and customs'. The laws would also deprive the chiefs of their authority and their traditional sources of revenue. Indirect rule was also introduced as an economic necessity. If the British adopted direct rule in the Protectorate, a large number of European officials would be needed to administer the region, who would be paid a great deal of money. It was better therefore to make use of the indigenous political leaders for the purposes of local government, as these leaders would be given only a small remuneration for their work.

The use of traditional institutions, however, required certain modifications. For instance, those aspects of traditional government that were distasteful to the British, such as ritual murder, were to be eliminated. In addition, traditional institutions were to be moulded in a way that would ensure peace and stability, thereby enabling the colonizers to live a quiet

[133]

life. It was hoped that these institutions, under the guidance of the resident European District Commissioner, would be continually developing into more efficient units of administration, responding to and adapting themselves to the new situations created by colonial rule. Let us now examine how the indirect rule system was put into practice in Sierra Leone.

7.1   Early Protectorate administration

For administrative purposes the Protectorate was initially divided into five districts – Karene, Ronietta, Bandajuma, Panguma and Koinadugu – and each was placed in the charge of a British District Commissioner. Chiefdoms were carved out of the districts and headed by principal local rulers who became known as Paramount Chiefs. The chiefs were responsible to the District Commissioner who in turn was responsible to the central government. The Governor had powers to depose a Paramount Chief and could appoint another, while the District Commissioner could banish any individual.

Three types of courts were established – the Court of Native Chiefs, the Court of the District Commissioner and Native Chiefs, and the Court of the District Commissioner. The District Commissioner's court decided all cases between non-natives or between a native and a non-native, all land cases and all criminal cases that were considered inimical to modern development, such as witchcraft, slave-raiding and trading. Other criminal offences such as murder, rape and ritual murder connected with secret societies, such as the Human Leopard Society, the Alligator Society and the Poro Society, were decided by the Court of the District Commissioner and Native Chiefs (the chiefs acted as assessors). The Court of the Native Chiefs (native court) dealt with civil cases (including commercial disputes) within the indigenous population.

Once the Protectorate was declared, a number of important questions arose, among which was how to finance the Protectorate administration, which was estimated to cost £5 000 for a start, plus an additional £19 000 for policing its frontiers. Governor Cardew's request for a British government grant was turned down. Being a forceful Governor, Cardew was anxious to develop the Protectorate. He felt strongly that if money was not raised in the Protectorate for its administration, slavery would continue to flourish there, chiefs would continue to fleece their subjects through exorbitant taxation and the Protectorate would be a profitable field for smuggling operations by the French and Liberian authorities.

Cardew also believed that the Protectorate's people had a moral and legal obligation to pay for their administration and protection (though they had not asked for them). To defray the costs of administering the Protectorate, he imposed a tax on people's houses. He called it the 'hut tax' because he felt most people in the Protectorate lived in huts. Owners of houses with four or more rooms were to pay ten shillings, and those with fewer than four rooms, five shillings. The tax was to be first implemented in the three districts nearest the Colony – Karene, Ronietta and Bandajuma, where he felt a lot of money would be in circulation due mainly to government activities such as the proposed railway works. The tax was to come into effect on 1 January 1898. In the last two districts – Koinadugu and Panguma – where there was little money in circulation, the tax would be later paid in kind, and mostly with rice, which could either be consumed by government officials working there or sold to traders, or both.

Cardew's enthusiasm for directly taxing the Protectorate at that stage was not shared by the Colonial Office in London. The Colonial Office feared that the tax issue might lead to open resistance in the Protectorate. In spite of these fears Cardew was still allowed to go ahead with his policies. J. C. E. Parkes had also expressed his reservations, but Cardew did not listen to him.

7.2 Protectorate grievances

The people of the Protectorate in general did not like to be taxed by a foreign administration, especially one that had not conquered them. They believed that taxation on their houses implied rent, which therefore denied them ownership rights. In December 1896 some Temne chiefs sent a petition to the District Commissioner of Karene, Captain Wilfred Sharpe, in which they complained generally about the new administration. They also called for a repeal of the new laws and exemption from the house tax. While Cardew was on leave in 1897, a similar petition was sent to the Acting Governor. But

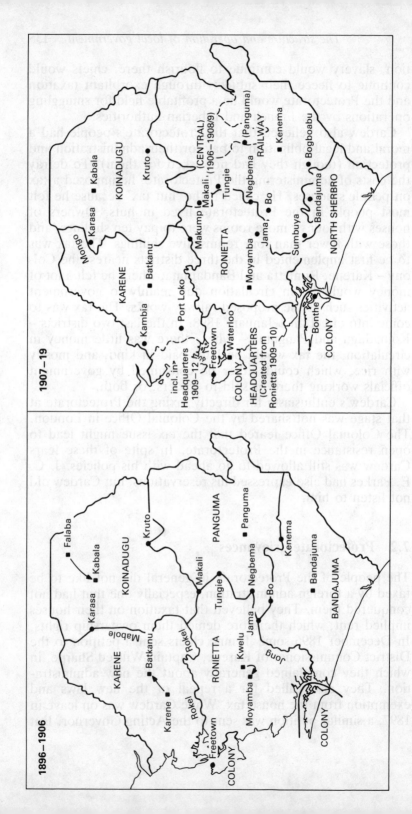

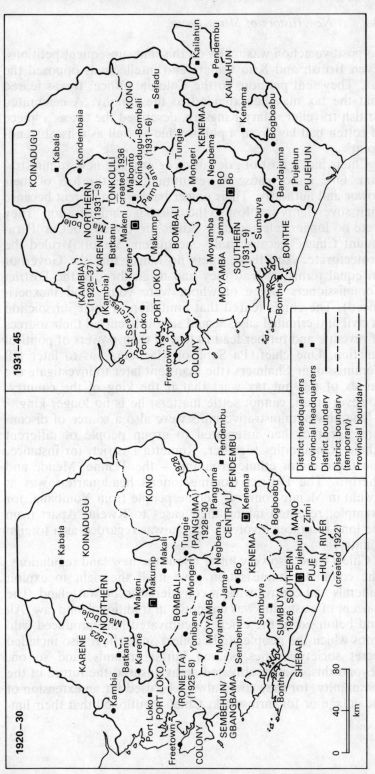

10 Administrative boundary changes, 1896–1945

no positive action was taken on this and subsequent petitions. Even British and Krio traders and intellectuals opposed the tax. They sent petitions to the Colonial Office. It was feared that the tax may be extended to the Colony. A celebrated British traveller, Mary Kingsley, described the tax as a 'piece of rotten bad law from a philosophic as well as a fiscal standpoint'.

Chiefs had a host of grievances against the new administration. One major cause of resentment was the loss of their power and authority. Their power base was undercut because their sovereignty was lost to the colonial administration. They were no longer referred to as 'kings' or 'queens' but as 'Paramount Chiefs' because only one queen (Victoria) ruled the Protectorate. And these rulers no longer met the Governor on equal terms; instead they had to go through the District Commissioners (some of whom were young and inexperienced). The chiefs feared that limitation of their jurisdiction in civil and criminal cases would seriously curtail their sources of revenue and further lead to loss of their powers of political sanction. One chief, Pa Suba of Magbele, was to later tell Commissioner Chalmers (the man sent later to investigate the causes of the hut tax war) that if the king of the country, however small, cannot settle matters, he is no longer king.

The new administrative units were also a source of discontent, for they had attempted to group people of different ethnic communities together. Ronietta District, for instance, had three major ethnic groupings – the Temne, Mende and Sherbro. The District Commissioner's headquarters was at Kwelu in Mende country. Temne people from Yonibana, for example, resented taking their cases to Kwelu. Apart from the long distances involved, Kwelu was regarded as a foreign country.

Chiefs were also very bitter about the new land regulations. The colonial administration gave itself the right to exploit minerals and control what it considered to be wasteland. The concept of wasteland was unknown in traditional land law. All land belonged to the chief. Uncultivated land produced wild crops which the people could collect and sell. It also included secret society bushes, sacred burial grounds, and so on. Beyond this, the uncultivated areas ensured the future of the community, for they could always be used for an extension of the village or for farm-work. Chiefs petitioned that their limited jurisdiction in court cases and the new land laws were 'nothing short of the total dispossession of their country'. The Colonial Office later repealed the land laws. But the chiefs were already convinced that the colonial administration intended their ruin.

The abolition of the slave trade tended to upset the economy as chiefs had relied heavily on slave labour for farm work and for transportation of their produce to buying-centres. Dishonesty on the part of certain traders was another source of grievance. Some Colony traders cheated the people by paying less for their produce and labour. Farmers and porters were normally paid in kind but with far less than what they were due. These traders paid porters two pieces of cloth worth about two shillings and sixpence for carrying a load from Freetown to Panguma. The official rate was 21 shillings. The traders also extended the measures for a bushel and a gallon when buying from the people. Even chiefs complained about the prevailing low prices for their produce.

Missionary activity played a part in fomenting trouble in the Protectorate. Apart from their opposition to native customs of sacrifice, fetish and polygamy, some missionaries identified themselves with the colonialists by asking the people to pay the house tax. And so many people began to hate them.

Frontier Police brutality was another source of annoyance. Many of these policemen were runaway slaves and ex-convicts. These now returned into the interior to lord it over the chiefs and their subjects. Rather than protect the people, they constituted themselves into 'little judges and governors' extorting and oppressing the people at will. They raped women and deflowered young girls. They even beat up and imprisoned chiefs.

From the above, it could be seen that the people really had genuine grievances against the government and its collaborators. The people were therefore anxious to get rid of the white man and regain their independence.

Governor Cardew returned from leave with full determination to carry out his fiscal policy. He wrongly felt that the chiefs would not combine forcibly to resist the tax because they lacked cohesion and powers of organization. The point, however, is that the Governor was determined to use force in the event of an opposition. He relied on the Frontier Police.

Cardew modified his original plan of assessment towards

the end of 1897. He now imposed a flat rate of five shillings per house irrespective of the number of rooms. The chiefs were to collect the tax in their areas and pay the money over to the District Commissioners and police officers. Some District Commissioners (for example, Captain Sharpe) began to bully people into paying. Chiefs who would not collect the tax were arrested and imprisoned. Thinking that a famous warrior, Bai Bureh, was the strongman behind the opposition in the north, Captain Sharpe ordered his arrest.

The hut (house) tax war

While the colonial forces were moving towards Kasseh to arrest Bai Bureh, local armed warriors jeered at them. The commander ordered that the colonial forces open fire. The warriors decided to resist and this began the hut tax war in Februry 1898.

Bai Bureh became the undisputed leader in the north. As a former ally of the British, he knew their fighting techniques. He and his men organized an effective guerrilla warfare.

By 19 February Bai Bureh's forces had severed the British line of communication between Karene and Port Loko and seriously hampered communications with Freetown through

A carving of Bai Bureh

successful guerrilla raids. They controlled the road and blocked the river routes. The colonial forces commander, Major Buck, attempted punitive expeditions against many northern towns, but he was not always successful. Mahera was attacked on 14 March, followed by onslaughts on Kagbantama, Romaron, Kateri, Magbolonta and Matiti. Meanwhile, the British were getting reinforcements and they eventually took control of the Port Loko–Karene road. The Temne put up their last strongest defence at Mafouri on 25 April, but by then companies of the West African Regiment had overrun Kasseh, though Bai Bureh and his allied leaders were still at large. Governor Cardew then offered £100 reward for the capture of Bai Bureh. Bai Bureh reciprocated in more general terms by offering £500 for the Governor's head. He and his allies, however, finally surrendered on 11 November. The colonial forces' victory had been achieved at the cost of the complete destruction of Kasseh country.

Meanwhile, the southern communities planned an uprising on 27 April at Bumpe. The war-planners used the Poro as a cover to ensure secrecy, swearing their supporters on a 'one-word' (in Mende, *ngo-yila*) oath, which gave one choice – obey or be killed. As Christopher Fyfe puts it,

the accumulated grievances against Government, Creole traders and unpopular chiefs, broke in a wave of fury, to sweep forever all taint of alien influence. Every wrong was recalled, even the memory of Mende labourers recruited for the Congo, who never returned. Captured Creoles awaiting their death were mockingly told they were being sent to the Congo.

The body of a frontier officer buried at Bandasuma was dug up and burnt, as if to rid the soil of pollution.

As the warriors rushed from town to town offering the alternatives of joining them or being killed, they gathered support from those eager to plunder. Some warriors directed their anger against missionaries. Missions at Mano Bagru, Rotifunk, Taiama, Yele and in the Sherbro, to name but a few places, were destroyed and the missionaries killed. In Mofwe (attacked on 29 May) children attending the Methodist school were burnt alive after the warriors had set fire to a house in which frontier policemen and some Krio traders had barricaded themselves. At Sembehun the frontier policemen and Krio traders escaped by boat down the Bagru. Chief Nancy Tucker was sent to Kwelu to seek protection.

Two British columns, reinforced by local allies, went out after the freedom fighters. One started from Songo and another from Bonthe. The first column advanced through Rotifunk and overran Taiama. The second column met with fierce resistance in Bumpe, but elsewhere there was little fighting.

The Chalmers Commission   The Colonial Office appointed a Royal Commissioner, Sir David Chalmers, to investigate the cause of the war and to make recommendations in a general way on how the country should be administered and financed.

Chalmers, who had worked in Sierra Leone before, as Queen's Advocate, arrived in the country on 18 July 1898. He was warmly received by the Freetown community. But Cardew mistrusted him on sight. Chalmers was a lawyer and Cardew mistrusted lawyers. Chalmers's inquiry lasted for about four months and during this period he took evidence from a lot of people in Freetown (including Sir Samuel Lewis and other Krio critics of the Governor) and in the Protectorate. His final report was submitted on 21 January 1899, and it was highly critical of the Cardew administration. Chalmers too did not like Cardew.

Chalmers attributed the causes of the rising to the imposition of the house tax and put the blame on Cardew's rashness. He warned that though people with military background could be useful as Governors and District Commissioners, 'there is danger in allowing their influence and ideas to be paramount'. Most often, they would resort to the use of force rather than persuasion to put down even the least resistance to their rule, he further remarked.

He also recommended a general amnesty and proposed the abolition of the tax, a drastic reduction or, if possible, disbandment of the Frontier Police Force, restoration of the powers and authority of chiefs, a modification of the duties of the District Commissioners, and government financial assistance to missionaries.

Governor Cardew, in reply to the Commissioner's report, stoutly defended his policies. He again argued that he needed money to develop the Protectorate. Besides, abolition of the tax would imply a victory of the chiefs over his administration. He also pointed out that Chalmers had overstated his case which in certain instances was not supported by adequate evidence. It is important to note that Chalmers relied heavily on the evidence of the Krio critics of the Governor for his conclusions.

The Colonial Office was impressed by Cardew's counter-arguments. So it upheld Cardew's submissions and rejected its own Commissioner's report. At any rate the Colonial Office was not still prepared to give substantial grants to Cardew.

Immediately after the war four columns of colonial forces marched through the Protectorate to instil fear into the people and to make it clear that the British now effectively ruled them. Many of the freedom fighters were executed for murder and three prominent leaders – Bai Bureh, Bei Sherbro and Nyagua – were deported to the Gold Coast.

The British had learnt a bitter lesson from the war and for a number of years they were preoccupied with maintaining law and order and forestalling any further unrest. One way in which they tried to accomplish their goal was to break up large political entities into small chiefdoms. This was how many petty chiefdoms appeared in the early twentieth century. War-towns were ordered to dismantle their stockades so that they would be very vulnerable to attack by colonial forces. In addition, Paramount Chiefs who would be amenable to the British were appointed. For example, Rev. D. F. Wilberforce was made Paramount Chief of Imperi when his predecessor died in prison. Madam Nancy Tucker was confirmed Paramount Chief of Bagru, while Bangali Margai was made chief of Banta. The powers of the chiefs were further eroded until they were reduced to the status of 'colonial civil servants'. The Krio, who were accused of stirring up trouble in the Protectorate, were now heavily discriminated against. In 1901 the Frontier Police Force was amalgamated into the West African Frontier Force which became a purely military body. The soldiers now lived in barracks under strict discipline. So they no longer went about the countryside molesting people. The hated house tax was in 1900 reintroduced in the Colony, outside the municipality of Freetown, at a minimum rate of three shillings.

7.3 Some Protectorate leaders

Let us briefly examine the careers of certain leaders who made history in the hinterland in the late nineteenth and early twentieth centuries. All of these leaders followed the same political process; they organized small groups of people into large states.

Madam Yoko

Madam Yoko is reputed to be the only woman in Sierra Leone to have attained supreme rule over an area as extensive as the Kpaa Mende Confederacy, which was roughly equivalent in territory to the present Moyamba District.

Yoko, whose original name was Soma, was born in the late 1840s in Gbograma in present-day Gbo Chiefdom, Bo District. Her family later moved to Taiama where she was initiated into the Sande society, through which she acquired fame as a great and beautiful dancer. She then took the name Yoko. Her first marriage was to a warrior, Gongoima, but the marriage was short-lived. Then she married the chief of Taiama, Gbenjei. She eventually won her husband's confidence and became his senior wife. When Gbenjei died, Yoko married the Kpaa Mende king, Gbanya, and moved to Senehun west, her new husband's home.

Yoko established her own Sande bush to which she attracted girls from all over Kpaa Mende country. Young girls from most ruling houses were trained by her, who then ensured their marriage to the leading and contemporary chiefs and warriors, thereby procuring the friendship and gratitude of those who mattered.

Yoko's position as senior wife of the Kpaa Mende leader further helped to increase her fame. As kings thought it unwise and unsafe in those days to travel out of their kingdoms, Gbanya sent Yoko on a number of diplomatic and political missions in the Colony. In the process she became well-known in official circles.

Gbanya died in July 1878. Before his death he had asked his closest relatives and Governor Rowe to help Yoko to succeed him. After Gbanya's death Yoko became more involved with British officialdom. She exploited this connection to extend and consolidate her power. When Gbanya's successor, Movee, died in 1884 the colonial administration sought to get a dependable ally in Kpaa Mendeland by installing Yoko as the principal ruler of the Kpaa Mende.

Madam Yoko's installation was vehemently protested

against by many Kpaa Mende warriors and chiefs. They believed that Yoko was a usurper. The Kpaa Mende state had been created by war and cemented by the powerful Wonde society and could thus be ruled only by Wonde warriors and leaders. Many of Yoko's sub-chiefs therefore ignored her authority and went their separate ways.

Yoko became one of the stipendiary chiefs. As a loyal friend of the administration, she willingly agreed to collect the house tax when it was levied in 1898. This angered many of her subjects, who planned to kill her. The secret was leaked, however, and Yoko took refuge in the Frontier Police barracks. She was later instrumental in the arrest of those chiefs who had taken part in the hut tax war.

After the war Yoko was recognized as Paramount Chief. She then moved over to Moyamba because her headquarters, Kwelu, had been destroyed during the war. Yoko died in August 1906.

Bai Bureh

Bai Bureh was the resilient general, military strategist and warleader of the Temne in the war against the British in 1898. He was born probably in the 1840s in Rothkene, near Makeni. He trained as a warrior at Gbendembu Gowahun where he acquired the nickname 'Kebalai' ('he whose basket is never full of dead enemies'). Kebalai had by means of military prowess and great organizing ability acquired the chieftaincy in Kasseh and had assumed the title of Bai Bureh.

As a stipendiary chief Bai Bureh honoured his obligations and on occasions referred disputes with his neighbours to the Governor for arbitration and mediation. He had helped the Soso in their war with their neighbours, but resented the fact that peace was made in his absence. He therefore declared his intention to continue the war. He was then arrested but he escaped. In 1892, however, he served with distinction with the British expedition against Tambi.

In 1895 the French alleged that Bai Bureh's warriors had assisted a Soso chief, Surakata, to attack areas under their sphere of influence. Governor Cardew, who was anxious to prevent a conflict with the French, attempted to arrest Bai Bureh, 'and put a stop altogether to his warlike propensities'. When he finally met Bai Bureh in Port Loko, the Governor ordered him to pay a fine of fifty guns for assisting Surakata and for forcibly resisting the police. Bai Bureh paid the fine, but thereafter maintained a safe distance from the Colony. When the house tax was levied, Bai Bureh was in the vanguard of opposition to the tax. The District Commissioner of Karene then determined to arrest Bai Bureh and make an example of him. While his troops were moving towards Kasseh where Bai Bureh resided, they clashed with local warriors and this started the hut tax war. Bai Bureh and his men waged successful guerrilla warfare, though they refrained from killing anyone who was not directly connected with the colonial administration. Between February and March 1898, attempts to capture Bai Bureh or force him to comply with the tax proposals cost the British heavy casualties.

Lieutenant-Colonel Marshal, who took command at Port Loko on 1 April 1898, described the operations against Bai Bureh as 'some of the most stubborn fighting that has been seen in West Africa'. In a desperate attempt to end the fighting, the British forces burnt all the villages in and around Kasseh. Bai Bureh's warriors were consequently left high and dry, and on 11 November 1898, nine mouths after the fighting had begun, Bai Bureh surrendered. He was quickly taken to Freetown and subsequently deported to the Gold Coast. He returned to Sierra Leone in 1905 and was reinstated as chief of Kasseh the following year. Bai Bureh died in 1908.

Nyagua

Nyagua was born in the 1840s and was the son of Faba Kpovoma, ruler of Dodo Chiefdom in present-day Kenema District. He grew up to become a famous warrior and during his father's reign succeeded in extending Dodo's political influence in Kono country south of the Baffin River, in Nongowa, as well as in lower Bambara. When Nyagua succeeded his father in 1889, he immediately tried to consolidate his rule over this vast empire in upper Mende country. He built a new capital at Kpanguma (Panguma). Nyagua then installed Matturi, a great Kono warrior and trusted friend, over the southern Kono, while he allowed two of his father's reputable warriors to rule in Dodo and Nongowa.

Nyagua signed a treaty of friendship with the British on 25 May 1889, and was granted an annual stipend of £10. In the same year he surrendered Makaya, a notorious warrior, to the British. He then asked that his son, Gbanyeh, be educated in Freetown. The government agreed to pay the boy's fees, and the boy was admitted to the Grammar School. Nyagua, as a friend of the British, contributed soldiers as part of an expeditionary force sent against the Sofa in 1893.

But he soon fell out with his British friends, largely because of his independent outlook. He was one of those held responsible for the hut tax rising, although his district had been exempt from the tax. The District Commissioner of Panguma had reported that Nyagua was holding secret meetings with chiefs and piling up ammunition in Kenema for an intended attack. Nyagua's arrest was ordered and he was immediately brought to Freetown.

Pleas for Nyagua's release went unheeded and though he had done nothing that in his judgement would be construed as rebellious or inconsistent with justice and truth, he was deported to the Gold Coast along with Bai Bureh and Bei Sherbro, where he died in 1906. Nyagua, the great empire-builder in upper Mende country, became another victim of colonial repression.

Kai Londo

Kai Londo was a great Kissi warrior who succeeded in creating what became known as the Luawa state, from several independent townships in the late nineteenth century. He was born in Komalu (now in the Republic of Guinea) where he was trained as a warrior. He began to make his mark as a warrior during a war between Mendekelema and Nongowa. On his return to Luawa after the war, Kai Londo built a small town which he named Mofindoh, after a town in Njaluahun country where he had been hospitably received on his homeward journey.

Kai was initially on good terms with Ndawaa. They jointly took part in the 'Kpo-veh wars' of the 1880s. The two warriors, however, later fell out because Kai complained that Ndawaa's men maltreated his slaves. But the main reason for Kai's grievance was that he and Ndawaa could not agree on a proper distribution of the spoils of war. Kai assembled his war-boys and set off for Mofindoh, destroying all the bridges behind them. This angered Ndawaa, who vowed to teach Kai better manners. He used another route and arrived at Ngieyehun in Luawa, where he allied with some chiefs.

News of Ndawaa's arrival threw the Luawa rulers into confusion and terror. An emergency meeting was convened at Gbondu to discuss the threat posed by Ndawaa. It was at this meeting that Kai volunteered to rid Luawa of the Ndawaa menace if the rulers would agree to abrogate their sovereignty over Luawa and make him their king. The rulers agreed. In the ensuing encounter between Kai and Ndawaa, the former emerged victorious. And true to their promise, the Luawa rulers made Kai, a Kissi man, their king.

Kai's first task was the internal reconstruction of his state. He built a new town at the site of old Sakambu and called it Kai Lahun (Kai's town). Other towns destroyed by the war were rebuilt, but they were much larger than their former sizes in order to ensure greater security. Roads were constructed to link strategic places and these were closely guarded. Kai encouraged the growing of food crops and did not entertain laziness. Weekly markets flourished all over the state.

His next move was to expand his state's borders. He conquered many lands including Vaahun, Kissi Tongea, Gbele country and all lands east of the Mafessa River. These he annexed to his state. He then extended his authority to Gbandi country. He succeeded in putting down a rebellion organized by three sub-chiefs, Faagbandi, Manjakewai and Jobo, who had again collaborated with Ndawaa and one of his lieutenants, Mbawulomeh, to destroy the new Luawa. Another rebel chief who had called in Sofa warriors was defeated.

Kai Londo signed a treaty of friendship with the British in 1890. He died in 1895 in another campaign against Mbawulomeh.

Almamy Suluku

Almamy Suluku, a descendant of the Konde (Conteh) clan from Sankaran in Guinea, was born in the 1820s. He became a famous warrior, and his father Sankailay, who was *Gbaku* (king) of Biriwa country, made him *kurugba* (general) and stationed him at the state's capital, Bumban. In recognition of his incredible strength and destruction in warfare, Almamy was nicknamed 'Suluku' meaning 'wolf'. As *kurugba*, he was largely responsible for extending Biriwa political influence to parts of Loko and Saffroko countries. Suluku's frequent military successes made him increasingly important in the state and by the end of the 1860s he had thoroughly eclipsed his father, Sankailay, in Biriwa. He succeeded his father in 1873. His immediate task was to consolidate the political and economic situation in Biriwa.

He put his sons as heads of towns and further appointed governors for the provinces. He made his son, Kpebe, *kurugba* and *gbaku bamet* (town chief) of Boumbadi, a strategic town. He did not wish to retain the *kurugba* in the capital as this would predetermine succession. All towns managed their own internal affairs but paid customary tributes and supplied troops as and when necessary. Suluku ruled at the capital with a governing council.

He kept a firm hand on the internal distribution of essential food items. He encouraged agriculture and trade in his empire.

His relations with the colonial government offer a vivid example of subtle diplomacy. Suluku maintained cooperation with the British while judiciously seeking his own interests, some of which were inimical to British interests. He encouraged internal slave-trading, which the British were trying to abolish, and he participated in warfare. His men plundered Jula traders and prevented these traders from carrying arms through Biriwa country. This tended to disrupt trade. When the British asked him to moderate his activities, he conveniently ignored the request.

He was always very friendly and generous to colonial officials who visited his kingdom. They in turn wrote favourable reports about him. When the hut tax war broke out, he offered his services as mediator between Bai Bureh and the British, though it was rumoured that he was secretly sending troops to aid Bai Bureh. Suluku died in June 1906.

7.4 Consolidation of Protectorate administration

The system of local government established in the Protectorate in 1896 remained essentially the same until 1937. Each chiefdom (there were some 200 of them) remained substantially a 'native state'. The British were happy to preserve the chief as head of ethnic life with respect to domestic and customary matters, while they kept overall authority for the maintenance of law and security.

Chiefs were made to realize that they now held their positions at their colonial masters' pleasure and not on any former traditional principle of acceptance by their people. This, in effect, meant that they were now required, first and foremost, to promote the interests of their masters, not those of their subjects. This inevitably put the chiefs in a totally different position in relation to their people. Many maltreated their subjects because they knew they had the backing of the colonial government.

One such ruler was Madam Humonya who became Paramount Chief of Nongowa Chiefdom, Kenema District in 1908, following the death of her mother Matolo. Humonya, like her mother, had been elevated to the Paramount Chieftaincy because the colonial administration was anxious to get a dependable ally in the eastern region after the 1898 house tax crisis. She received special support from the Governor and, using this to her personal advantage, before long won a reputation for petty tyranny. Complaints against Humonya's arbitrary rule fell on deaf ears. Attempts by the egalitarian District Commissioner of Kenema, W. D. Bowen, to investigate the charges against her led to Bowen's transfer.

But as opposition to Humonya's rule mounted, the Governor was forced to look into the allegations against her. The outcome of the inquiry was that Humonya's private councillors were banished; a Speaker and five Section Chiefs were elected by the people; Madam Humonya was ordered to accept a tax of rice in lieu of her 'state farms'; stocking and improper punishments were banned; and 25 policemen and a clerk were dismissed. She was later voted out of office.

In order to make chiefs dependable allies in the indirect rule system, they were given financial incentives. These included a five per cent rebate on collection of the house tax, incidental gifts, entertainment allowances and tributes from sub-chiefs and headmen. Economically, the chiefs made capital of the tribute paid them in goods and services to enhance their standing in the community. Some chiefs amassed wealth from ground rents paid to them by mining companies and by non-natives.

*

The slave trade was finally abolished in Sierra Leone after the Protectorate proclamation of 1896. But this did not put an end to slavery. Slaves were closely tied to the economic system – they worked the chiefs' farms and transported produce to buying centres. An immediate legislation against slavery was therefore bound to seriously disrupt the economy of the Protectorate. The initial attempts to outlaw slave-raiding and slave-dealing had induced a widespread feeling of dissatisfaction and resentment, and the grievance felt by the chiefs, owing to the interference of the government with slavery, was a material factor in the house tax rising. A rather slow and cautious approach was thus adopted to end slavery in Sierra Leone. Laws were passed which stipulated that a slave could be redeemed on the payment of a fixed sum (£4 for adults, £2 for children). But redemption by this method was very slow.

In 1905 a new law made it unlawful to harbour or assist any native who left his chiefdom without authority. Despite the law, many slaves continued to escape from their masters. The question of runaway slaves kept recurring in one form or another.

The existence of slavery in Sierra Leone became an embarrassment to the administration after the First World War when the issue of slavery began to be discussed in the League of Nations and elsewhere (France had repudiated all forms of slavery in her colonies). The other British West African colonies had also abolished slavery. The British Government therefore took a definite step to end slavery in Sierra Leone. In 1926 it was decreed that any person born in the Protectorate in or after that year was a free man and that when a master died his slaves automatically became free. Two years later slavery was abolished altogether in Sierra Leone.

Socio-economic changes By the 1930s a lot of socio-economic changes were taking place in the Protectorate. Educational facilities were expanding in the Protectorate and education helped to widen the people's horizon. Mining, agriculture and trade led to increased commercial activity in many towns. Construction of the railway and rudimentary road systems facilitated the flow of ideas and movement of people within the Protectorate.

These changes brought new problems in the chiefdoms. For example, many town-dwellers now began to question the right of the chiefs to demand customary labour and tributes. This caused some political tension which worried the central administration. An attempt was therefore made to reform and re-organize certain institutions in the Protectorate. New courts were established; for example, the Magistrates' Courts, to try more serious cases and the police arm of the District Commissioner, called the Court Messenger Force, was upgraded by new methods of recruitment.

The Native Administration system

This system, which was based on the Nigerian model, was formally introduced in the Protectorate in 1937 in order to put the chiefdom administration on a sound footing. It had three main principles. These were:

(a) the establishment of separate financial institutions, known as Chiefdom Treasuries, for each unit of the administration;
(b) the grant of tax authority to each chiefdom unit; and
(c) authorization of Paramount Chiefs and other Tribal Authorities to enact by-laws and issue orders in pursuance of social services and development functions.

Under the new system the chiefdom unit of the administration was designated 'Tribal Authority' which was defined to mean 'the Paramount Chief, the Chiefs, the Councillors and men of note elected by the people according to native law and custom'. The Paramount Chief was the head of the Native Administration and was to be paid a regular salary in place of the traditional dues he formerly collected.

The Native Administration raised revenue from the following sources:

(1) The chiefdom tax.
(2) A block grant from the government at the rate of 20 per cent of the house tax collected. (This was in addition to the rebate of five per cent which chiefs received for collecting the government house tax.)
(3) Specific grants from government for the maintenance of feeder roads and primary education, and capital grants of 50 per cent of the cost of new Native Administration school buildings.
(4) Court fines and fees.

The Chiefdom Treasury received Native Administration revenue, kept accounts of revenue and expenditure and maintained an inventory of Native Administration property.

The main functions of Native Administrations
(a) They were responsible for justice, law and order in their chiefdoms.
(b) They exercised control over the land in their chiefdoms.
(c) Tribal Authorities of the Native Administrations were responsible for the assessment of the house tax and the chiefdom tax and for their payment. (The District Commissioners directed the assessment of the house tax. This tax later became known as local tax.)
(d) They were responsible for the provision of such local services as primary education, local sanitation, the employment of midwives and dispensing staff and the construction and maintenance of feeder roads.
(e) Some Native Administrations spent money on minor agricultural projects like seed or demonstration farms or loans to farmers, or on protected forests.

Certain chiefdoms were too small to constitute a viable Native Administration unit. As a result, the government encouraged the amalgamation of such units into larger ones. At first, many chiefs were not willing to join the Native Administration system because the salary of Native Administration chiefs was not attractive. Steps were later taken to raise salaries so as to attact more chiefs into the system. In spite of this, many chiefs continued to exploit their subjects in order to augment their income.

In 1937 18 out of 202 chiefdoms were in the Native Administration system; by 1947 some 121 out of 211 chiefdoms had joined the system. By the late 1950s practically every chiefdom in the Protectorate was a member of the Native Administration.

Evaluation of the Native Administration system
Successes
The Native Administrations succeeded in maintaining law and order in their chiefdoms. They also provided essential services like schools, clinics and maternity centres. They brought large tracts of land under cultivation and gave loans to farmers to cultivate swamp rice. They also assisted in forest protection schemes.

Failures

Many chiefs were authoritarian. They ran the Native Administration as if it was their personal property. Many of the top personnel were dishonest, incompetent and poorly educated. Certain chiefdoms were either too large and poor (for example, Tambakha in Bombali District and most chiefdoms in Koinadugu and Kailahun Districts), or too small (for example, Toli in Kono District and Gbo in Bo District) to effectively manage their own affairs. The Native Administrations were poorly supervised by the District Commissioners, many of whom were inexperienced and ill-equipped for the job.

Because of the above flaws and weaknesses in the functioning of Native Administrations, the colonial authorities decided to have them operate side by side with a more efficient system of local government, namely District Councils. The central government had formed an unholy alliance with the chiefs; to abandon them completely would have proved disastrous for both parties.

Changes in provincial administration

In 1986 the towns of Karene, Panguma, Bandajuma, Falaba and Kwelu were designated the district headquarters of Karene, Panguma, Bandajuma, Koinadugu and Ronietta, respectively. Five years later three of the headquarters were transferred to more convenient locations – from Falaba to Kabala, from Karene to Batkanu and from Kwelu to Moyamba.

In 1907 Panguma and Bandajuma districts were amalgamated to form a new Railway District, with Kenema as the headquarters. The changing pattern and volume of trade in the area following the completion of the main railway line with its feeder roads was the main reason for the reorganization. A Central District was created to the north of the Railway District, but was incorporated into the latter in 1909. North Sherbro District, which was administered from Bonthe, was also formed from the southern chiefdoms of the old Bandajuma District and several from Ronietta District. The western part of Ronietta District was named Headquarters District, with Waterloo as the headquarters. Karene and Koinadugu remained unaltered. However, between 1907 and 1920 some sub-districts were created in the Railway, Karene and North Sherbro districts, and the headquarters of the North Sherbro District was moved to Bandajuma in 1911 and to Pujehun in 1913.

As the colonial administrators gained more knowledge of the Protectorate and as the communication system improved, especially in the northern region, some alterations were again made. In 1920 the districts were dissolved and the entire Protectorate was divided into three provinces each with four districts. Minor corrections were made in 1922 and 1927. A shortlived Mano River District was created from the eastern part of Pujehun District in 1922; Kambia and Ronietta districts were included in the Northern Province; Sefadu became the headquarters of Kono District, and a new Panguma District came into existence in 1927.

Another major reorganization took place in 1931. It was occasioned again by socio-economic changes in the Protectorate. The Central Province was absorbed into the Southern Province and the number of districts in the enlarged Southern Province was reduced from ten to seven. The Northern Province was unaffected by the changes.

Except for a few minor alterations the system remained the same until 1940 when the administrative organization reverted to the old district and sub-district systems. Six years later the Protectorate was redivided into three provinces – Northern, Southern and Eastern – and this system survived the colonial era.

Until 1946 there was no senior official who supervised the activities of the District and Provincial Commissioners. The Secretary for Protectorate Affairs, who was their administrative head, had no executive authority and remained part of the establishment in Freetown. In 1946, however, the Secretary for Protectorate Affairs became the Chief Commissioner of the Protectorate, with headquarters in Bo. He was now responsible for coordinating government policy in the Protectorate and measures were also taken to locate at Bo or its neighbourhood senior representatives of those departments which were directly concerned with the development of the Protectorate, namely, agriculture, education, public works and health. The first Chief Commissioner was J. S. Fenton. He was succeeded by Hubert Childs, who remained in office until 1959 when the post of Chief Commissioner was abolished.

District Councils

District Councils evolved from conferences of chiefs that took place during the early and mid-1940s. These conferences were initiated by Paramount Chief Julius Gulama of Kaiyamba Chiefdom, Moyamba District, to seek Protectorate and chiefs' interests. Amidst the postwar spirit of reform that enveloped the British Empire, the government decided to formalize these conferences, giving them legal status under the Protectorate Ordinance of 1946. Thus District Councils were set up in all the provincial districts to perform the following functions:

(a) to advise government on any matter brought before it;
(b) to make recommendations to government or the Protectorate Assembly on matters affecting the people of the district as a whole;
(c) to make rules altering or modifying native customary law in the district;
(d) to act as commissions of enquiry into local matters such as boundary disputes and complaints against chiefs.

Although the councils were intended to later replace the Native Administrations in the sphere of local government services, the colonial authorities were reluctant to let them develop outside the scope of the latter's influence. Consequently, Paramount Chiefs were made *ex-officio* members of the councils. Other members (one from each chiefdom) were selected by the Tribal Authorities to represent the commoners' interests. The District Commissioner was made President of Council. In 1950 more literate members were appointed.

The councils were then charged with welfare and development functions in addition to their advisory capacity. It was hoped that eventually they would assume most of the District Commssioners' tasks in supervising the chiefdoms.

Local public works, community development, social welfare and town planning became the sole responsibility of the concils. Agriculture, forestry, education and medical health were to come under their auspices but with professional personnel seconded from the central government.

And indeed the councils quickly took over most of these functions. They constructed and maintained inter-chiefdom roads serving important economic areas, built and ran many primary schools, health centres, and established agricultural holdings.

Each District Council was entitled to a certain percentage of the local tax paid in the district. It also received grants for specific projects.

In 1954 chiefs secured the right to elect one of their number President of the Council. Popular representation through direct election was extended to District Councils in the late 1950s.

A building scheme which aimed at lending money or loaning building materials to people who wanted to put up dwelling houses ran into difficulties as many of the beneficiaries failed to pay back their loans. Some councils were also inefficient and hardly followed laid-out policies. Funds remitted by the central government for agricultural development, for instance, were either spent on schools or used to erect costly council offices. The Native Administrations too shifted much of their social responsibility to District Councils without granting them a corresponding share of their local finance.

By 1962 there were many complaints of corruption and mismanagement by the District Councils, and investigations in that year confirmed these allegations. Government accordingly suspended most of the councils and appointed Committees of Management in their place. Following popular requests, however, the councils were reinstituted in 1965 only to be suspended again in 1967 by a military junta. District Councils have again been reactivated in principle.

7.5 Local government in the Colony

The Colony consisted of the Sierra Leone peninsula, Sherbro Island, the Tasso, Banana, Turtle, Plantain and York Islands, other islets, and some areas of territory inland. Of these areas only the Sierra Leone peninsula, Tasso Island, Banana Island, York Island and the town of Bonthe, Sherbro, were administered as part of the Colony, the other areas being administered in every respect as if they were within the Protectorate.

The Colony was administered by the following authorities:

(a) The Freetown City Council;
(b) Rural Area Councils;
(c) The Sherbro Urban District Council.

Freetown City Council

Local government in the city of Freetown was based on the English pattern. Freetown was first constituted a municipality in 1799 by a Royal Charter. It provided for a Mayor, Aldermen and Sheriff, who were chosen by the Governor and Council. But these officials became redundant after 1821 when the colonial administration assumed full responsibility for running the city.

The second municipality was constituted under the provisions of the Freetown Municipality Ordinance of 1893. The city, with a population of 128 000, was constituted a corporation, consisting of a Mayor, 12 elected and three nominated councillors, and citizens of Freetown, working through the Freetown City Council. Some difficulties were experienced by the council and in 1927 a new Ordinance replaced it by a council of eight members (later nine): a President, four nominated and four elected members. A fresh Ordinance, to restore democratic government to the city, was introduced in 1945, but did not come into force until 1948, when an amending Ordinance was passed.

For purposes of representation the city was divided into three wards. Four councillors were elected by ballot from each ward who served for a period of three years each. The Governor had power to appoint six councillors of whom at least two must be Africans. They also served for three years and they, like the elected councillors, could be reappointed.

A candidate for the councillorship had to fulfil certain conditions. He must be a Sierra Leonean, a registered elector and be literate in the English language. He was banned (except in the case of the Mayor) from taking up any form of appointment or contract with the council. Up to 1955 there used to be property qualification as well. A councillor's seat became vacant upon his death, resignation, continuous absence for six consecutive months from the meetings of the council, or upon disqualification.

Six Aldermen were elected from the elected councillors to represent the three wards at the annual meeting of the council held in November every third year. They too held office for three years and were eligible for re-election. The Mayor was elected at this meeting. He did not necessarily have to be a councillor. The Mayor held office for one year and was eligible for re-election. He received an allowance, which was determined by the council. He served as chairman and re-presented council at various organizations and attended a number of ceremonial functions. In like manner the Alder-men had no specific function and their office was purely ceremonial.

The duties of the council were laid down in Sections 64 to 67 of the Freetown Municipality Act. It was expected to:

(1) provide and maintain such public places as markets, slaughterhouses, cemeteries, public gardens and parks and vehicle parks;

(2) name all roads, streets, parks and public places in the city;

(3) fix and collect rents and fees for the use of these places and to issue licences where necessary;

(4) fix and collect rates and taxes for houses and water supplies;

(5) provide relief for the poor;

(6) provide and maintain schools and a fire service;

(7) dispose of refuse.

The day-to-day work of the council was done under the super-vision of various officials who headed different departments. The Town Clerk was responsible for the general administra-tion, correspondence, and coordination of the council's activi-ties. He served as council secretary, and as secretary to the various committees that helped council officials to carry out their functions more effectively. He was the link between the central government, other local organizations, the general public and the council. The City Treasury was responsible for finances, while the Engineering Department took charge of public works. The Valuation Department fixed rates, while the Education Department looked after municipal schools. There was also the Fire Brigade.

The council's main source of revenue was a property rating system. It also received grants from the central government. Although this local body usually operated on a low budget, its contribution to the socio-economic development of the city was considerable. For it was largely able to carry out the functions outlined above. The council was, however, not free of malpractices. Successive reports on it by the Government

Audit Department before and after independence always indicated serious financial anomalies.

Rural Area Councils

The rural area of the Colony comprised the whole of the Colony peninsula including Banana and Tasso Islands. Up to 1936 this entire area was administered by a European District Commissioner who was assisted by a President and twelve persons nominated by the Governor. Thereafter, the region was divided into four administrative areas – Wilberforce, York, Kissy and Waterloo, including British Koya. Each was placed in the charge of a Rural Commissioner. He governed with a Rural Area Council of which he was the head. The council derived revenue mainly from house taxes and licence fees.

In 1950 the area was again divided into six rural districts – Kissy, Waterloo, British Koya, Wilberforce, Mountain and York. A three-tier system of local government was then introduced. The villages in each district were ruled by Village Area Committees. The committees elected six members to the Rural District Council. These councils performed the main executive duties of local government. These included the construction and maintenance of secondary roads, provision of water supplies, parks, gardens and other public places of recreation and regulation of markets, slaughterhouses and cemeteries. Each District Council elected one of its members to the Rural Area Council. This council acted as the link between the central government and the Rural District Councils. It also assisted, coordinated and supervised the Rural District Councils and Village Area Committees in the performance of their duties. Each Village Area Committee and District Council elected its own chairman. For the first three years of its existence, the President of the Rural Area Council was an officer in the public service. Thereafter, the council elected one of its members president.

The Rural Area Council had power to levy rates and village improvement taxes. With the help of funds from the central government for community development some Village Area Committees were able to provide community centres and improved water supplies in their respective areas. An annual inter-village competition for the best-kept village was begun in 1951 and was carried out with much enthusiasm.

A Five Year Plan for Economic Development of the Area came into effect in 1952. The plan made provision for the improvement of road communications, for increased production of oil palm, fruits, vegetables and fish and for other measures designed to bring about a general rise in the standard of living of the people in the area.

Tribal Headmen in Freetown

The Tribal Headmen constituted an important group of local government officials in Freetown and later in the rural areas. They came into being in the late nineteenth century. Tribal Headmen were elected by the adult males of their respective groups. They continued to function in an informal capacity until 1905 when they were given legal recognition. The Tribal Headmen usually held office for five years and were eligible for re-election. They were ably assisted by section chiefs and sub-chiefs.

Duties of the Tribal Headman   He assisted the police and the Justices of the Peace in the discharge of their duties. He was empowered to make rules for the benefit of the members of his group on such matters as the relief of the poor and sick; the burial of the dead and the administration of the estates of such deceased persons (not exceeding £5); the registration of births and deaths, and so on. He enforced discipline among his ethnic group and could convict offenders.

The Tribal Headman also had a socio-political importance. He was the political centre of his ethnic group. For he was the only official with authority to represent his people in Freetown and he served as a liaison between the provincial chiefs and their people in Freetown.

He was also the authority who played the chief's role in ethnic life. He usually provided the initiative for most of his group's social activities. For instance, he organized companies for building mosques, houses, etc. Many of the cases in his court concerned marital problems, such as disputes arising from seduction, desertion, a woman's ill-treatment by her husband, and so on.

The Tribal Headman assigned duties to his section chiefs. Such duties included the general superintendence of the affairs of the members in their sections, settling disputes and the location of wanted persons. The section chiefs also stood bail in court for any respectable member of their ethnic group who got into trouble.

The Tribal Headmen often gave direct assistance to the central government. During the Second World War, for instance, they recruited labour and arranged shows for war charities. They were also requested to use their influence to frustrate sabotage and quieten the people during the 1955–6 riots. Finally, the institution of Tribal Headmen made it possible for the provincial migrant to orientate himself to life in Freetown as it helped him to adjust more readily to the strange surroundings.

Sherbro Urban District Council

A Sherbro Judicial District Board was set up in 1923 to administer the town of Bonthe, York Island and some islets adjacent to Bonthe. The rest of Bonthe District was administered by the District Commissioner, Bonthe District. He was also *ex-efficio* President of the Sherbro Judicial District Board. This board consisted of the President, the Medical Officer, Bonthe, and four unofficial members, of whom two were appointed by the Governor, and two were elected by adult male taxpayers. A new and more effective body, the Sherbro Urban District Council, replaced the Sherbro Judicial District Board in January 1952. The new council now comprised eight councillors: six elected, one nominated by the Governor and *ex-officio* the Medical Officer, Bonthe. The council chose one of its elected members to be president and exercised the normal functions of local government similar to those exercised by the Freetown City Council and by the Rural Area Councils.

*

Bo, the chief town of the Protectorate and headquarters of the provincial administration had its own town council. It was established in 1954. Council members were elected by ballot and the chairman was chosen from among the members. The Bo Town Council performed functions similar to those exercised by the Freetown City Council.

References

Abraham, Arthur (1976), *Topics in Sierra Leone History* (Leone Publishers, Freetown).

Abraham, Arthur (1978), *Mende Government and Politics Under Colonial Rule* (Sierra Leone and Oxford University Press).

Barrows, Walter (1971), 'Local Level Politics: Alliances in Kenema', PhD, (Yale).

Collier, Gershon (1970), *Sierra Leone: Experiment in Democracy in an African Nation* (New York).

Crowder, Michael (1968), *West Africa Under Colonial Rule* (Hutchinson).

Denzer, La Ray and Michael Crowder (1978), 'Bai Bureh and the Sierra Leone Hut Tax War of 1898', in Michael Crowder (ed.) (1978), *Colonial West Africa* (Frank Cass).

Encyclopaedia Africana – Dictionary of African Biography, Vol. 2, Sierra Leone–Zaire (Reference Publications, USA, 1979).

Foray, C. P. (1977) *Historical Dictionary of Sierra Leone* (Metuchen, New Jersey).

Fyfe, Christopher (1962), *A History of Sierra Leone* (Oxford University Press).

Fyfe, Christopher (1979), *Sierra Leone Inheritance* (Oxford University Press).

Fyle, C. Magbaily (1977), 'Collaboration, Co-operation and Resistance – The Case of Almamy Suluku and the British', JHSSL, Vol. 1, no. 1.

Hargreaves, J. D. (1956), 'The Establishment of the Sierra Leone Protectorate and the Insurrection of 1898', Cambridge Historical Journal, Vol. 12.

Hargreaves, J. D. (1958), *A Life of Sir Samuel Lewis* (Oxford University Press).

Harrel-Bond, Barbara et al. (1978), *Community Leadership and the Transformation of Freetown* (The Hague, Mouton).

Kilson, Martin (1966), *Political Change in a West African State – A Study of the Modernization Process in Sierra Leone* (Harvard).

Lenga-Kroma, J. S. (1973), 'District Councils and the Evolution of Local Government in Sierra Leone 1896–1971', MA (USL).

Pratt, S. A. J. (1968), 'The Government of Freetown' in Jones, E. and C. Fyfe (eds, 1968), *Freetown: A Symposium* (Sierra Leone University Press).

Protectorate Ordinance, 1896.

Protectorate Ordinance, 1946.

Questions PART A

1 Why did Governor Cardew impose the house tax?
2 What were the main causes of the hut (house) tax war?
3 How did Madam Yoko rise to prominence in Kpaa Mendeland during the last three decades of the nineteenth century?
4 Examine the career of Bai Bureh.

5   Write notes on the career of *two* of the following:
    (a) Nyagua of Panguma
    (b) Kai Londo of Luawa
    (c) Almamy Suluku of the Biriwa Limba.
6   How was the Protectorate administered from 1896 to 1936?
7   Why was the Native Administration system introduced in the Protectorate?
8   Describe the composition and functions of *one* of the following local government bodies during the colonial period.
    (a) District Councils
    (b) Freetown City Council
    (c) Rural Area Councils
    (d) Sherbro Urban District Council
9   What were the functions of the Tribal Headmen in Freetown?

Questions PART B

1   How did the Protectorate proclamation of 1896 affect the fortunes of the interior rulers?
2   What significant parallels can one draw between the quit-rents (imposed in the Colony in the 1790s) and the house tax of 1898?
3   How far were economic factors responsible for producing a rebellion in the hinterland in 1898?
4   'Governor Cardew and the Colonial Office must share blame for the hut tax war.' Do you agree?
5   Describe the course and results of the hut tax war.
6   How important is Bai Bureh in the history of Sierra Leone?
7   Why did it become necessary to diversify Protectorate administration from the 1930s?
8   How effective were District Councils as modern local government institutions during the colonial period?

8 Constitutional and political developments 1863–1945

When the British Crown took over the management of the Colony in 1808, no African was included in the Colony's administration. The Governor with a few white officials ruled the Colony. By the mid-nineteenth century, however, the Krio were becoming increasingly anxious and determined to have a say in the government. A 'Committee of Correspondence', comprising a powerful group of Krio businessmen, was formed in 1853 with the primary objective of securing the right of political representation for Colony citizens. Petitions were sent to the Secretary of State for the Colonies, and newspapers critical of the government, like the *New Era*, began to appear. An inter-racial body, the Mercantile Association, superseded the Committee of Correspondence in 1858. It petitioned against abuses over taxes and duties and called for a new constitution for Sierra Leone. This association, together with other politically-minded groups, also asked for an elected assembly.

8.1 The 1863 Constitution

The response came in 1863 though it was discouraging to the Krio cause. The legislature was reorganized, but no provision was made for popular representation.

The constitution established two councils – the Executive Council and the Legislative Council – to replace the Governor's Advisory Council. The Executive Council comprised the Governor, the Chief Justice, the Queen's Advocate (Attorney-General), the Colonial Secretary and Officer Commanding the Troops. These were known as the Official members. The Legislative Council consisted of all the Official members and other Nominated (Unofficial) members. Two such members were appointed in 1863 – Charles Heddle, a European-African and John Ezzidio, a Sierra Leonean. Ezzidio was nominated by the Mercantile Association. The Legislative Council was responsible for enacting laws for the Colony. The Executive Council was simply an advisory body which the Governor was bound to consult except in specified cases, but advice given was not binding on him in arriving at his decisions on any matter.

The 1863 constitution, like the previous charters used to

Peace talks between kings, queens, chiefs and Europeans at Freetown in the 1880s

administer the Colony, conferred excessive powers on the Governor.

The Krio were bitterly disappointed when the constitution failed to meet their expectations; for they had hoped to take over the Colony administration from the British. Yet they did not take the law into their own hands, but worked within the framework of the constitution.

In 1887 Krio intellectuals and professionals arranged an elaborate programme to celebrate the Golden Jubilee of the reign of Queen Victoria. This event coincided with the centenary of the founding of the Colony. The Krio used the occasion to express their gratitude to the British for their beneficence. They welcomed 'the day with feelings far beyond that which can find expression in mere words'. In the end a beautiful park was created in central Freetown and named 'Victoria Park' in honour of Queen Victoria.

By this time, however, some people were beginning to discern some cracks in the relationship between the British and the Krio. Because the Krio were being denied much political say in the affairs of the Colony, more pressure groups emerged which began to exercise varying degrees of influence in the colonial system. These groups included the Rate Payers' Association (1895), the Civil Servants' Association (1907–9), the Aborigines Rights' Protection Society (1919) and the Sierra Leone Bar Association (1919). The Rate Payers' Association attempted to organize the election of candidates into the Freetown Municipal Council.

The newspapers also became another effective constitutional weapon for airing the grievances of the colonized people. The most important newspapers included *The West African Reporter* (1874–84), the *Sierra Leone Weekly News* (1884–1951), *The Artisan* (1884–8) and *The Sierra Leone Times* (1890–1912). *The Sierra Leone Weekly News*, which was owned by the May family, became famous for its balanced editorials and presentation of views. By the 1920s it was described as the 'best newspaper in West Africa'. Although the colonial officials were often not pleased with the kinds of articles carried by some of the papers, little attempt was made to silence the press, at least until the mid-1930s.

Relations between the Krio and the British were very poor by the time the First World War broke out in 1914. One would have thought, therefore, that the Krio would not only refuse to support Britain in her war with Germany, but would take advantage of the war situation to assert their independence, even if temporarily. On the contrary, the Krio loyally supported their colonial master. A call was even made in the Colony for the formation of a regiment, to be called the King's Own Creole Boys', 'to fight, and if possible die, for our Gracious King and good old England'. Some Krio professionals even worked with British imperial troops in such places as the Cameroons. These subjects supported Britain in the hope that they would be given a greater say in the management of their own affairs after the end of the war. This hope was heightened by the principles of liberal democracy and self-determination propounded by President Woodrow Wilson of the USA and Prime Minister David Lloyd George of Britain. After the war, however, the British Government put political questions aside and instead concentrated on the economic exploitation of the African colonies.

8.2   The railway workers' strike and anti-Syrian riots

The frustration of the educated and working classes, the African traders and the unemployed in the big towns was given expression in the 1919 railway workers' strike and anti-Syrian (Lebanese) riots. These events occurred simultaneously and were sparked off by economic, social and political factors.

During the war many young male farmers had been conscripted into the army. This subsequently led to food shortages. Prices of basic commodities rose considerably, while wages remained at the prewar levels. For instance, a cup of rice usually sold at one penny was now sold at fivepence. Bread was sixpence per pound and fish one shilling and sixpence. When the war ended, many workers including soldiers, were laid off. The situation was aggravated by an influenza epidemic in September 1918 and a famine in that same year.

The foreign companies in Freetown ordered rice but railed it to the Protectorate where they hoped to sell for higher prices. The government had insisted that rice should be sold at the control price. Government also ordered rice mainly for the Colony, but unfortunately ordered too little and too late.

Salary bonuses were also granted to government workers, but these were not immediately effected. The daily-wage workers in the Railway Department went on strike on 15 July 1919 for their unpaid bonuses. The strike was well coordinated. Europeans and Africans who remained loyal were prevented from going to work by the strikers. And all operations including train services were suspended from 16 to 22 July.

The strike soon turned into a populist riot on the night of 18 July, as the returning soldiers were celebrating the end of the war. The riots were directed against the Syrians, whose shops were attacked and looted. The riots then spread to the provinces, mainly in the railway towns of Bauya, Moyamba, Mano and Bo. Syrians in these towns had to flee for their lives and many took refuge in the Wilberforce Memorial Hall in Freetown.

The riots were suppressed within a few days and about 245 people were arrested. One Syrian died from injuries sustained during the riots and two others died of other causes. Over £500 000 worth of property was destroyed. The railway men resumed work on 23 July. They and other workers who had not received the bonus were paid in full.

Many people in Freetown blamed the Syrians for the riots, because they had hoarded rice and sold at inflated prices. But that was not all. Syrians were hated mainly because they had replaced the Krio in business. The government, however, accused the Krio of instigating the riots and many Krio were heavily punished. The Freetown City Council was also fined £5 000. The money was to go towards the general improvement of the city.

Some Syrians were compensated. Martial law was declared in Freetown and policemen were brought from the Gold Coast who temporarily transformed the Protectorate into a police state. Some laws were strengthened which made it impossible to expel Syrians from the country. Police officers were brought from Britain to rejuvenate the Sierra Leone Police Force.

8.3   Congress politics

In 1920 some educated British West Africans decided to form a regional congress to fight some of the injustices in the

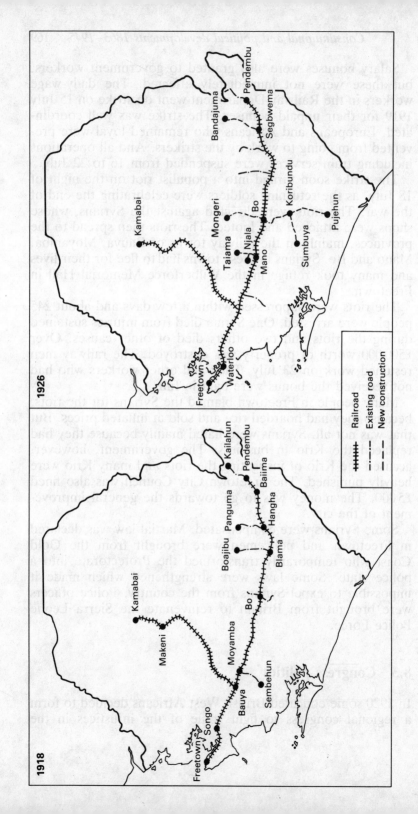

1926

Kamabai
Bandajuma
Pendembu
Segbwema
Koribundu
Mongeri
Bo
Pujehun
Taiama
Njala
Sumbuya
Mano
Waterloo
Freetown

Railroad
Existing road
New construction

1918

Kamabai
Makeni
Kailahun
Pendembu
Panguma
Baiima
Boajibu
Hangha
Blama
Bo
Moyamba
Bauya
Sembehun
Songo
Freetown

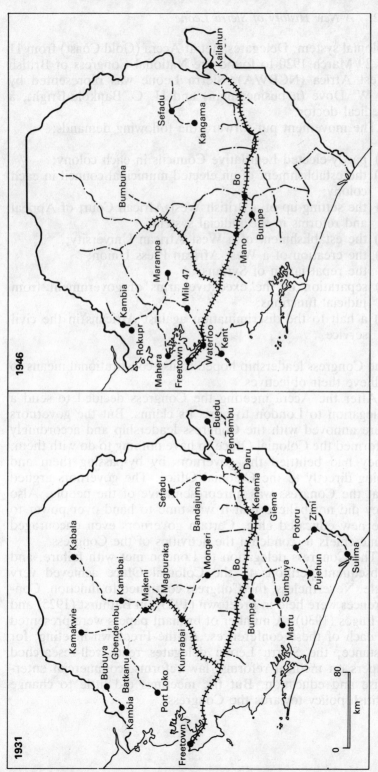

11 Evolution of the transport network, 1918–46

1946

Kailahun
Sefadu
Kangama
Bumbuna
Bo
Bumpe
Mano
Marampa
Mile 47
Kambia
Rokupr
Mahera
Freetown
Waterloo
Kent

1931

Kabala
Buedu
Pendembu
Daru
Kamakwie
Sefadu
Bandajuma
Kenema
Giema
Zimi
Kamabai
Makeni
Mongeri
Bo
Potoru
Bubuya
Gbendembu
Magburaka
Bumpe
Sumbuya
Pujehun
Batkanu
Kambia
Port Loko
Kumrabai
Matru
Sumbuya
Sulima

km
0   80

colonial system. Delegates met at Accra (Gold Coast) from 11 to 29 March 1920 to found the National Congress of British West Africa (NCBWA). Sierra Leone was represented by F. W. Dove (a businessman) and H. C. Bankole-Bright, a medical doctor.

The movement put forward the following demands:

(a) partly-elected Legislative Councils in each colony;
(b) the establishment of an elected municipal council in each colony;
(c) the setting-up of a British West African Court of Appeal and reforms in the judicial system;
(d) the establishment of a West African University;
(e) the creation of a West African Press Union;
(f) the repatriation of Syrians;
(g) separation of the executive arms of government from judicial functions;
(h) a halt to the discrimination against Africans in the civil service.

The Congress leadership hoped to use constitutional means to achieve their objectives.

After the Accra meeting the Congress decided to send a delegation to London to press its claims. But the governors were annoyed with the Congress leadership and accordingly informed the Colonial Office to have nothing to do with them. They had belittled the governors by by-passing them and going directly to the Colonial Office. The governors argued that the Congress was unrepresentative of the people. Also they did not believe that it was time to hand over power to the new educated elite. Certain governors even encouraged some chiefs to condemn the activities of the Congress.

The Congress delegation to London met with failure, and subsequent petitions to the Colonial Office achieved very little. Nevertheless, the Congress continued to function. Conferences were held in Freetown (1923), in Bathurst (1925) and in Lagos (1930). A number of brilliant papers were presented at each of these conferences. At the Freetown meeting, for instance, the Sierra Leone delegates read well-researched papers on medical reforms, law reforms, commercial enterprise and education. But the meetings did little to change British policy towards the Congress.

Sierra Leone branch

In Sierra Leone the activities of the Congress were confined largely to the Colony, mainly because the Protectorate was still legally regarded as foreign country.

While the Congress was busy agitating for reforms in the colonial system, a new Governor was appointed to Sierra Leone who initially appeared willing to further African interests. He was Sir Ransford Slater, formerly Colonial Secretary in the Gold Coast. Slater was a determined and forceful Governor. Shortly after his arrival he was formally welcomed by the Sierra Leone branch of the NCBWA. In their Address of Welcome the Congress officials called on the new Governor to introduce 'popular representation and elective franchise' in the Colony. The Governor was prepared to concede this demand, but he made it known that it was absurd to have a legislature for both the Colony and the Protectorate, which had no Protectorate member on it.

Members of the Committee of Educated Aborigines (CEA) also called for direct Protectorate representation in the Legislative Council and more development for the Protectorate. The CEA had been formed in 1922 to seek Protectorate interests. Its leaders were H. Kabia Williams (President), John Karefa-Smart (Vice-President), S. E. Carew Kamara (Secretary) and W. Carenba Caulker (Assistant Secretary).

Governor Slater sought to satisfy some of the demands of Sierra Leoneans by appointing a few Krio to junior positions in the civil service. He also planned a new constitution which conceded the elective principle for the Colony and with provision made for some Protectorate representation in the projected legislature. But the Governor insisted that the Protectorate would be represented by chiefs only, because 'under the tribal system no others would have adequate title to speak with authority'.

Some Krio opposed the idea of Protectorate representation in the Legislative Council on three main grounds. Krio politicians argued that since the chiefs would be nominated rather than elected, they would not be the true representatives of the people. The chiefs were also considered to be puppets of the colonial administration. As such they could not become effective representatives. The third argument, which was of a legal nature, carried the greatest weight: that since the Legislative

Council was originally intended to legislate for the Colony whose inhabitants were British subjects, it was illegal to appoint any African from the Protectorate (who would be considered a foreigner) to sit in such a legislature and legislate on behalf of British subjects.

One Krio politician, the Hon. Shorunkeh Sawyerr, suggested in the Legislative Council that the Protectorate be annexed to the Colony and its inhabitants declared British subjects. Thereafter, they would be eligible for membership into the Legislative Council. But the Governor refused.

The 1924 Constitution

In November 1924 Governor Slater promulgated a new constitution which revoked the 1863 Constitution (which had been slightly amended). The constitution also provided for a Governor, a Legislative Council, and an Executive Council, but with the councils differently constituted.

The new Legislative Council was to have 12 Official and ten Unofficial members. The Official members included all heads of principal departments of government. The Unofficial members were made up as follows: two European representatives, three elected and two nominated Colony representatives, three Paramount Chiefs, nominated by the Governor – one from the north and two from the south and east.

The Executive Council was composed of the Governor as president and senior government officials. It had an exclusively colonial membership without any African representation. The Council was still an advisory body.

The franchise for the Colony seats restricted the vote to the commercial and educated elite. The qualification in the urban area – Freetown (which was given two seats) – was an income of £100 or property of taxable value of £10 a year, and in the Rural Area (one seat) an income of £60 or property of £6 value. The average wage of a semi-skilled worker at that time was less than £20 per annum.

Important features of the constitution
(a) It showed a compromise between the desire to extend indirect rule and the demands of the Colony elite for elective representation.

(b) The only African groups represented were Colony professionals and Paramount Chiefs.
(c) The Legislative Council had an Official majority and the agenda was set by the Governor.
(d) By the joint administration of both parts of the country, an attempt was being made to merge the Colony and the Protectorate together.
(e) The Constitution denied the educated Protectorate elite the right to represent their areas. The Protectorate was also grossly under-represented. The constitution was therefore not fully responsive to the demands of the local population.

8.4   The 1926 strike

Barely a year after the introduction of the 1924 constitution, serious political problems again erupted between the Krio and the Freetown colonial administration. These resulted from a strike organized by the Railway Workers' Union (formed in 1925). The strike began on 14 January 1926.

The junior railway workers were objecting to certain measures instituted by the railway management, such as their having to take special tests before they could be promoted. Europeans were excluded from such examinations.

As the strike gained momentum, troops were called in and the strikers and their supporters were fired on. The Freetown community, however, gave their full support to the strikers. This was understandable, for the community already had many complaints against the colonial government. A Strikers' Relief Fund was created which generated over £500 for the striking workers. Governor Slater was hurt by this show of solidarity. He now saw the strike as a 'political fight to the death between Government and the Creoles'. The Colonial Office in London gave its full support to whatever decision the Governor took to end the strike.

The railway men returned to work on 26 February, on the conditions laid down by the Government. Pensionable employees who had joined the strike were dismissed and the salaries of many workers were reduced. The Railway Workers' Union was banned.

When it was found out that two of the elected Colony

members of the Legislative Council – Dr Bankole-Bright and Mr E. S. Beoku-Betts – had assisted and encouraged the railway workers, the Colonial Secretary proposed suspending the constitution as far as it provided for elected members. The Governor disagreed on the grounds that this would be too harsh and dangerous. He suggested instead that government should proceed 'at a much slower pace with Africanization of the Service' and temporarily halt further constitutional developments.

The Freetown City Council was dissolved after the strike. The official reasons given for the Council's dissolution were lack of experience on the part of Council workers, financial irregularities, lack of funds and general neglect of Council affairs by its elected members. But the Freetown community were of the opinion that the dissolution of the Council was a calculated attempt on the part of the colonial administration to punish the Krio for supporting the railway workers during their strike. Even Governor Slater admitted that in abolishing the Council he had turned the clock back fifty years as far as the political advance of the Krio was concerned.

8.5 The Haidara rebellion

Haidara Kontorfili was a Soso Muslim 'missionary' from Guinea who attempted to set up a power-base in Kambia in the early 1930s. His fanaticism, healing powers, and ability to perform miracles had won him a considerable following. He was obeyed even by chiefs. In January 1931 he wrote a letter to the District Commissioner of Kambia threatening to kill all those who did not convert to Islam or practise it according to his own principles. He also asked his devotees not to pay the house tax.

The administration considered these threats as a danger to peaceful and orderly living. So on 9 February, Haidara was charged with subversion and then served with an expulsion order which he ignored. The following day he sent a letter to his followers in Kambia exhorting them to revolt.

Troops were despatched to arrest Haidara on the grounds that he preached sedition and was fomenting peasant discontent. Haidara resisted arrest. He was killed although his men succeeded in killing the British commander, Captain H. J. Holmes.

*

Those Africans who had been elected or nominated into the Legislative Council spared no efforts in opposing unpopular government policies. During debates on the government budget, for instance, they vehemently attacked the Government's discriminatory attitude in raising salaries and allowances of only European officials. They also complained about the appointment of more Europeans than Africans to civil service posts, the slow promotion rate of, and poorer conditions of employment for, African civil servants, and related matters.

In due course, the Government made two important concessions. In November 1938 it established a Standing Finance Committee (which had more Africans than Europeans) to check on supplementary expenditure after the budget was passed. And in 1943 two Africans were appointed in the Executive Council – J. Fowell Boston and Paramount Chief Albert George Caulker.

These constitutional concessions were a prelude to the movement towards independence which actually started after the Second World War.

8.6 Wallace-Johnson and the Youth League

The NCBWA's pre-eminence in Sierra Leone politics was to be effectively challenged by a new force which was led by I. T. A. Wallace-Johnson. Wallace-Johnson was born at Wilberforce village on 6 February 1895, and after his early education, worked for various employers, including the Customs Department and the Freetown City Council. His attempts to organize strikes for better pay and working conditions were to lead to his dismissal from each of these places.

A great traveller, political agitator and journalist by profession, Wallace-Johnson had visited many countries in Africa and Europe where he edited several newspapers. He briefly attended Moscow University in the Soviet Union. He helped to organize trade unions in the Gold Coast and Nigeria. He and some trade unionists in the Gold Coast founded the West African Youth League in 1934 to champion the cause of workers and defend the constitutional rights of all people in the Gold Coast.

Wallace-Johnson returned to Sierra Leone in 1938 with a

lot of communist literature, some of which was destroyed by government officials. He immediately proceeded to form the Sierra Leone branch of the West African Youth League. The League's membership was open to all Sierra Leoneans. As a mass organization, it had members in most provincial towns. Less than a year after its formation, the League boasted a membership of at least 30 000.

Aims of the Youth League

The Youth League aimed to mobilize urban labour, ensure an equitable distribution of the country's wealth, unite the people of the Colony and the Protectorate and end colonial rule in Sierra Leone. It established a newspaper (the *African Standard*), organized mass meetings, founded trade unions and contested elections.

The labour situation in the country at the time of Wallace-Johnson's arrival was deplorable. Most Sierra Leonean workers were poorly paid and were subjected to long hours of work. Their salaries ranged from fourpence to twenty-five pence a day or ten shillings to £3 a month, and they worked between eight and 14 hours a day. Europeans fresh from school were paid an initial annual salary of £400 with many fringe benefits as against £264–372 paid to African chief clerks with thirty or more years of service. The living conditions at the mines were also terrible – congested, squalid, insanitary, with practically no medical facilities.

The Youth League criticized the Government and the foreign companies for the low wages and poor conditions for workers. It then began to organize trade unions. These included Public Works Workers Union, All Seamen's Union and Yengema Diamond Workers Union. Although the unions were not legalized by the Government, they started collective bargaining with employers.

The formation of trade unions was followed by a wave of labour unrest in the country. For instance, War Department employees staged two strikes in 1939 over wage reductions, dismissals, boots and uniforms. In the Marampa Mines at Lunsar, the workers downed their tools for higher pay and better conditions. As in previous labour unrest, the government came down heavily on the leading strikers.

In the realm of politics, the Youth League called for more

Mrs Constance Cummings-John, one of the Youth League candidates in the 1938 Freetown City Council elections; the first woman mayor in Freetown, 1965–66. She is in the centre of the photograph.

African representation in the Legislative and Executive Councils, universal adult suffrage and improved social and economic benefits for Sierra Leoneans. That the Youth League was able to articulate these socio-economic problems was one factor in its great appeal to the people. Wallace-Johnson was also an eloquent speaker and a capable mass organizer. He knew his audience and talked to them in the language they understood.

The Youth League fostered competitive party politics in Freetown. It effectively challenged the NCBWA and swept the polls in the November 1938 City Council elections.

These developments worried the colonial authorities and leading members of the NCBWA. They regarded Wallace-Johnson as 'a dangerous agitator and demagogue' who was 'inimical to good government.'

When the Second World War broke out in 1939, Wallace-

Johnson began to write articles that were critical of the British Government. It was feared that he would prejudice workers against government during the war. He was arrested for sedition and imprisoned together with other league officials. So the movement collapsed.

In 1942 the British Government sent a trade union officer, Edgar Parry, to Sierra Leone to help organize the labour movement. Parry formed the Sierra Leone Trade Union Congress and reduced the number of trade union movements in the country. He also created two bodies for collective bargaining at industry-wide level – Wages Boards and Joint Industrial Councils. They were heavily influenced by government agents.

Parry gave a lot of encouragement to moderate labour leaders. He secured scholarships for them to study overseas and ensured their appointment on important government bodies. Siaka Stevens, General Secretary of the Marampa Mines Workers Union, was sent to Britain to study industrial relations and trade unionism. J. Akinola-Wright of the reconstituted Railway Workers Union became a member of the Legislative Council, while Siaka Stevens became a member of the Protectorate Assembly. They were also elected President and General Secretary, respectively, of the Sierra Leone Trade Union Congress.

Wallace-Johnson's influence on the labour movement in Sierra Leone had by now declined considerably. He died in Ghana in 1965 in a road accident on his way to a conference. His burial in Freetown attracted a large crowd.

Assessment of the Youth League

It is not easy to assess the Youth League, for it meant many things to many people. Most Sierra Leonean nationalists and trade unionists, for instance, regard Wallace-Johnson as the father of trade unionism in West Africa, as a fearless militant journalist, and as one of the pioneering pan-Africanists.

There is general agreement that the fast rise of the Youth League and its success during the first seven months of its existence were partly due to Wallace-Johnson's ability and effectiveness in articulating public grievances, and partly due to the existence of a responsive society.

The Freetown City Council showed its high regard for

City Hall, Freetown

I.T.A. Wallace-Johnson (1895–1965) addressing a political meeting

Wallace-Johnson by naming an important street in central Freetown in his memory in the 1970s. His statue was erected on this street just outside the City Hall.

The Youth League, more than any earlier organization, played a very important role in reducing the social gap in the Colony and the Protectorate.

But some people have argued that the League failed to identify and establish priorities. Its leaders appeared to be in a hurry and attempted to do too much within too short a time. They were also over-ambitious. In addition, there was a wide gap between the leaders and their followers. They put forward certain demands which were not understood by the majority of their followers.

Furthermore, Wallace-Johnson lacked the organizational ability necessary for running a big movement. True, his dynamism and boldness gave the movement its initial strength, but he was tactless and lacked the ability to assess the strength of opponents and odds. This exposed the movement to destructive forces.

Youth League agitation, however, hastened the adoption of certain measures, such as slum clearance, legalization of trade unions and compensation of workers injured during service.

8.7 Decline of the Krio

The process of the decline of the Krio began in the 1880s when the governments of Western Europe, having completed the first stages of the partition of Africa, were now ready to effectively occupy the continent by replacing Africans with Europeans in their colonial establishments. The Krio were the worst-hit in West Africa.

Various factors accounted for the decline of the Krio. First, there was the rise of racism and the propagation of Social Darwinism in Europe, a philosophy that preached the superiority of the white races. Second, improvement in transportation systems and in science and medicine made it possible for greater numbers of Europeans to come out and stay much longer in West Africa and in greater comfort. Third, colonial economic policies tended to favour European and Asian businessmen at the expense of Krio traders. Fourth, the rise of a new Protectorate educated elite and the post-Second World War constitutional provisions which had the effect of transferring power to the Protectorate.

Governor Cardew did much to hamper Krio aspirations. He kept them out of the Protectorate and he and other governors elsewhere made it a rule that whenever a Krio civil servant died or retired, he would be replaced by a European. When, for example, Enoch Faulkner, the District Commissioner for Waterloo died in 1908, his district was amalgamated with an adjacent one under a European District Commissioner.

In 1892 there were about 40 senior government posts in the Colony and the Krio held 18, nearly half. By 1912 there were 92 senior posts, but the Krio held only 15 of them, and five were abolished during the next five years as their holders retired. Even the few posts held by the Krio carried no political authority. For instance, the Krio Assistant Colonial Secretary could not act in the absence of the British Colonial Secretary.

In 1910 the Colonial Office expressed the opinion that Africans should give way to Europeans in the colonial establishments. This gave official Colonial Office approval to a policy which was already being followed in West Africa. In that same year J. E. Dawson, Assistant Head of Customs in Sierra Leone, was replaced by a European.

Krio medical doctors were also discriminated against. They were considered inferior to white doctors and many European women did not like to be treated by Krio doctors. Thus, few Krio doctors were employed by the colonial government. Even the Christian churches attempted replacing black pastors with white ones.

The influx of foreign traders (Europeans and Syrians) into the interior following the course of the railway adversely affected Krio business interests. The foreign firms moved into retailing and with their capital resources drove the Krio out of a sector of the economy they had controlled for decades. These firms and the banks gave credit to Syrians to expand their business where they refused it to the Krio, who bitterly resented this discrimination against them.

The rise of a new class of Protectorate Africans from the 1920s also contributed to the decline of the Krio. They too had gone overseas for professional and higher training and on their return became actively involved in national politics. This

class included the Margai brothers – Milton and Albert,
James C. Massally, Arthur Massally, John Karefa-Smart,
Banja Tejan-Sie, I. B. Taylor-Kamara, S. T. Navo, Doyle L.
Sumner, W. H. Fitzjohn and Frank S. Anthony. In the
post-Second World War period, it was this Protectorate-
educated elite who challenged the Krio and successfully took
over the country's leadership from them.

Krio reactions   The Krio were very bitter about the changing
attitude of the British towards them. They embarked on a
number of measures to restore their lost glory, but achieved
very little. Krio appeals to British justice and their loyalty to
the British Crown were slighted.

Some of them attempted a cultural rebirth through the
formation, for example, of the Dress Reform Society in 1887.
Members of the society wore gowns instead of European
suits. They also rejected their European names and took
African names. Claude George called himself Esu Biyi; W. J.
Davies rechristened himself Orishatuka Faduma; Metzger
hyphenated his to Tuboku-Metzger. James Horton, while re-
taining his English names, adopted Africanus to make his
origins and identity very clear.

Others became super-sensitive in front of Europeans, and
they sometimes attempted to defend the indefensible. For
instance, a distinguished Krio head of department who had
embezzled £1 000 of government funds was acquitted twice by
a Krio jury, although his guilt was clearly evident.

The Krio also began to oppose any legislation that tended
to favour the people of the Protectorate. The 1924 and 1947
constitutions were vehemently opposed, especially the latter,
because it gave more seats to the people of the Protectorate
(see 10.2).

But Kriò opposition, no matter how sound, could not
change the attitude of the British towards them. And as the
twentieth century rolled on, the Krio continued to lose all the
privileges they had enjoyed in the nineteenth century.

The end-result was that the Krio remained politically mar-
ginalized. But all was not lost. Their culture continued its
socializing task, for it appealed to the upwardly mobile. The
Krio language has offered an easily accessible channel of
mediation. It is not only a medium of daily speech between
the Krio, but is a *lingua franca* for trade and communication

in Sierra Leone and beyond. It is the only language that is common or potentially common, to all Sierra Leoneans.

References

Collier, Gershon (1970), *Sierra Leone: Experiment in Democracy in an African Nation* (New York).

Crowder, Michael (1968), *West Africa Under Colonial Rule* (Hutchinson).

Fashole Luke, David (1985), 'The Development of Trade Unionism in Sierra Leone' (Part 1), *International Journal of African Historical Studies* (IJAHS), Vol. 18, no. 3.

Fyfe, Christopher (1979), *Sierra Leone Inheritance* (Oxford University Press).

Fyfe, Christopher (1987), '1787–1887–1987: Reflections on a Sierra Leone Bicentenary', *Africa*, Vol. 57, no. 4.

Kaniki, M. Y. H. (1977), 'The Idara Rebellion of 1931: A Re-appraisal', JHSSL, Vol. 1, no. 2.

Spitzer, Leo (1974), *The Creoles of Sierra Leone* (University of Wisconsin Press).

Spitzer, Leo & LaRay Denzer (1973), 'I. T. A. Wallace-Johnson and the West African Youth League', IJAHS, Vol. VI, nos 3 and 4.

Webster, J. B. et al. (1980), *The Revolutionary Years: West Africa Since 1800* (Longman).

Wyse, A. J. G. (1981), 'The 1926 Strike and Anglo-Krio Relations: An Interpretation', IJAHS, 14, 1.

Wyse, A. J. G. (1989), *The Krio of Sierra Leone* (London, Hurst for the International Institute).

Questions PART A

1 What were the main provisions of the 1863 Constitution?
2 What caused the anti-Syrian riots in 1919?
3 What major constitutional development took place in Sierra Leone during the administration of Governor Slater?
4 Why did the railway workers strike in 1926 and what was the outcome of the strike?
5 Who was Haidara Kontorfili? Why did he fall out with the colonial administration?
6 How did the West African Youth League contribute to the social and political development of Sierra Leone?
7 Why did the West African Youth League collapse?
8 Write on the career of I. T. A. Wallace-Johnson.
9 What factors were responsible for the decline of the Krio?

Questions PART B

1 How far is it true to say that the constitution of 1863 was a 'device for the more efficient government of an expanding Colony, rather than a concession to the principle of representation'?
2 'The anti-Syrian riots were a protest against British discriminatory practices.' Discuss.

3 Consider the view that Haidara's movement was a political rather than a religious movement.
4 Of what importance were the constitutional concessions of 1938 and 1943 to the people of Sierra Leone?
5 Assess the importance of Wallace-Johnson in the history of Sierra Leone.
6 Critically assess the factors that led to the decline of the Krio.

9 *Economic and social changes during the colonial era*

In discussing this topic two points must be borne in mind. Firstly, one needs to understand that the British colonialists (like their other European counterparts) were not interested in promoting internal economic development in their colonies. Their economic policy was guided by two main factors: the desire to encourage the production and export of raw materials for their home industries, and the need to create in the colonies an ever-expanding market for British manufactured goods. It was the attempt to meet these two demands – raw materials and markets – that largely dictated the nature and pace of Sierra Leone's economic development during the colonial period.

Secondly, the colonial era in Sierra Leone began at different times for the two parts of the dependency. In the Colony this period started in the 1790s with the advent of company administration, which gave way to British colonial rule in January 1808. Formal British rule in the hinterland commenced in 1896 when a British Protectorate was declared over that area.

Freetown's natural harbour facilitated trade between the Colony and Britain. The import-export trade flourished throughout the nineteenth century, thereby giving rise to a prosperous trading and professional bourgeoisie among the Krio population. The *nouveaux riches* built solid, well-furnished houses and gave their children quality education in the mission schools and in British universities.

Krio society thus became stratified. Below the bourgeoisie

The Queen Elizabeth II Quay

were the petty retailers, craftsmen and artisans and at the lowest rung were the manual workers, who were often despised by their more fortunate kinsmen.

The economic opportunities in the Colony, however, were insufficient to meet the demands of most Colony citizens, many of whom ventured into the hinterland in search of greater economic benefits. There subsequently developed greater trade relations between the Colony and the hinterland.

Despite the huge profits accrued from the trade, many hinterland people nevertheless stuck to subsistence agriculture, using the family structure as the unit of production.

The advent of colonialism in the hinterland radically altered the subsistence mode of production, as a greater premium was now put on the production of those crops that were in highest demand in Europe. To facilitate the transportation of these products to the Freetown harbour for eventual shipment to Europe, railway and rudimentary road network systems were developed.

9.1 Transportation

In 1872 a West Indian in the pay of the Freetown colonial establishment, Dr Edward Blyden, had mooted the idea of building a railway from Freetown to the north, where much produce was then obtained for the Freetown and overseas markets. But the idea did not gain much support. It was revived in the 1890s after Governor Cardew's tour of the hinterland. The Governor strongly believed that the construction of a railway across the export produce-bearing regions of the south and east would bring huge economic benefits to British industries.

The railway, after preliminary surveys had been completed in 1895, was started in January 1896. The main line of 227.5 miles (355 km) went across the country, from Freetown in the west to Pendembu in the east. It was completed in 1908. A branch-line, completed in 1916, started from Bauya, 64 miles (103 km) from Freetown, and terminated in Makeni. It covered a distance of 83 miles (133 km). Both had a narrow gauge of two feet six inches (76 cm). The early roads of the interior were designed to 'feed' the railway, hence they were called 'feeder roads'.

The railway served productive oil palm, cacao and coffee-producing areas. Another reason for building the railway was for the quick despatch of British troops into the interior.

The main line entered the palm belt in 1904 and had a clear impact on palm kernel exports. From the average of around 20 000 tons in 1896, exports reached 30 000 in 1906, rising to 43 000 in 1909. The Bauya-Makeni line too had some effect on exports, boosting them to 50 000 tons in 1912. Thereafter, the progress was very rapid; in 1936 the peak of 84 600 was reached, after which exports declined to an average of 50–60 000 tons in the 1950s, for two main reasons. Firstly, kernels were obtained through 'forest gathering' and no serious effort was made to cultivate oil palm trees until the 1940s. Secondly, a lot of farmers were attracted to more easily harvested cash crops and to illicit mining.

European firms and Lebanese traders were quick to seize the opportunity which the railway system provided. Prior to the construction of the railway, foreign traders bought their goods through African middlemen (mainly Krio) and sold their manufactured goods through the same media. Now they moved to control the source of supply of the produce and the means of distribution for their imported goods. This meant that the foreign traders, with access to greater capital resources, were soon to edge the Africans out of the produce and retail business. By the 1920s many large businesses were represented at Moyamba, Bo, Blama, Segbwema, Pendembu and Makeni. Between 1900 and 1918 exports rose from £362 471 to £1 516 871 in 1918. Over the same period, imports rose from £55 271 to £1 680 336.

Many people moved to the railway stations either to trade or to work in government departments or for traders. Consequently, population increased in these centres. The railway facilitated communication, which made administrative procedures more efficient. This was largely why all the provincial capitals – Makeni (Northern), Bo (Southern) and Kenema (Eastern) – and five district headquarters – Makeni, Magburaka, Moyamba, Bo and Kenema – were situated along the railway line. The railway, however, speeded up the decline of older ports like Sumbuya and Port Loko. They were only boosted by the building of the road network.

The railway fostered the education of the Protectorate's youth as it opened the doors of Colony schools to them. It has been suggested that the railway made it easier for a lot of criminals in the provinces to escape justice. The construction of more roads in the interior in the 1940s adversely affected the volume of traffic carried by rail as many people now preferred to use lorries, which were faster. Consequently, the number of passengers using the railway began to diminish. Mismanagement also led to a decline of profits, and government began to seriously consider phasing out the railway. This was finally effected in the early 1970s.

Aviation Air transport began in Sierra Leone in the 1940s. An airfield was constructed at Waterloo but was later abandoned because of its close proximity to high hills. Lungi, situated north of Freetown, was then chosen as the site for an international airport in 1947.

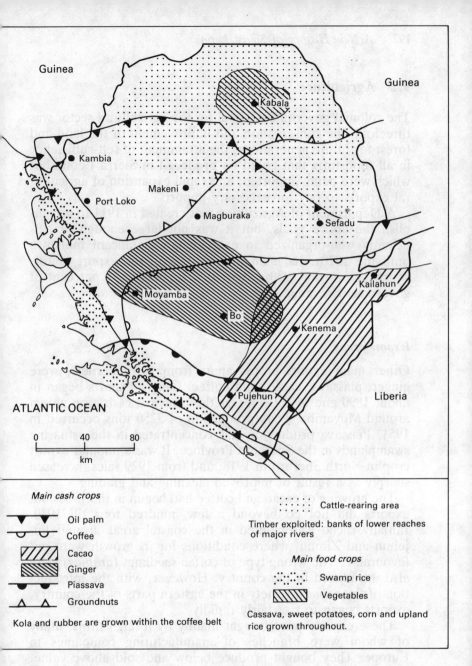

Guinea

Guinea

Kambia

Makeni

Port Loko

Magburaka

Sefadu

Kabala

Kailahun

Moyamba

Bo

Kenema

ATLANTIC OCEAN

0   40   80

km

Pujehun

Liberia

Main cash crops

▼ Oil palm

○ Coffee

///// Cacao

▨ Ginger

● Piassava

△ Groundnuts

Kola and rubber are grown within the coffee belt

::::: Cattle-rearing area

Timber exploited: banks of lower reaches of major rivers

Main food crops

::::: Swamp rice

▧ Vegetables

Cassava, sweet potatoes, corn and upland rice grown throughout.

12 *Agricultural production. Two further cash crops, tobacco and sugar cane, were cultivated after independence, mainly in the Northern Province.*

9.2 Agriculture

The colonial government's goal for the agricultural sector was threefold: the conservation and improvement of the land and forest for future generations; the attainment of self-sufficiency in all foodstuffs that could be produced in Sierra Leone but which were being imported; and rapid expansion of agricultural exports to pay for necessary imports.

A Department of Agriculture was created in 1911 to accomplish the above goals, but it was not large enough or sufficiently well-organized to exercise any significant influence until the 1920s. Its main interest was in the export sector, which before the 1930s, accounted for nearly 75 per cent of government revenue.

Export crops

Other main export crops, apart from palm kernels, were ginger, piassava, cacao, and coffee. Ginger exports began in about 1890 and by 1930 it was the principal cash crop grown around Moyamba. Peak production of 3250 tons occurred in 1951. Piassava production was concentrated in the estuarine swamplands in the Southern Province. It was a popular export crop in North Sherbro in 1918, and from 1929 sales increased sharply as a result of improved cleaning and grading.

The growing of cacao and coffee had begun in the 1900s but exports did not go beyond a few hundred tons till 1940. Initially cacao was planted in the coastal areas around Pujehun and Zimmi, where conditions for its growth were not favourable. The wrong type of coffee seedlings (*arabica*) were also introduced in the country. However, with the introduction of the *robusta* variety in the eastern parts of the country, exports began to rise fairly rapidly.

These exports were bought mainly by foreign firms, many of whom were branches of manufacturing companies in Europe. They bought produce below and sold above value. Profits realized from their operations in Sierra Leone went to their shareholders in Europe. No attempt was made to process these raw materials locally.

In 1949 the colonial government set up a trading enterprise, the Sierra Leone Produce Marketing Board (SLPMB), to take over the buying of produce from the foreign companies. The companies were to act as buying agents for the SLPMB. The Board aimed to give a guaranteed price to farmers whether world prices were high or low, which would act as an incentive to farmers to produce more crops. World prices for agricultural products, however, remained high and most of the surpluses accumulated by the SLPMB were not ploughed back to increase agricultural production. Instead they were invested in Britain.

The subsistence sector

In 1932 the Agriculture Department initiated a programme designed to arrest deforestation and at the same time increase rice production. Government's concern over self-sufficiency in rice production was borne out largely by political considerations. Shortage of rice had been a major factor in the 1919 anti-Syrian riots (8.2). After these riots the government realized that it was dangerous to be negligent in the matter of rice. So it became a top priority of colonial policy to ensure sufficient rice for Freetown and, later, the mining areas – Lunsar, Yengema, Bo and Kenema – where troubles were likely to erupt in the event of a fall in rice supply.

In an attempt to conserve the land and forests, swamp rice cultivation was to be sustituted for upland production, because the latter was destructive to the palm oil and kernel industry on which the government depended for revenue.

Swamp rice cultivation in Sierra Leone was begun in the late nineteenth century by Temne farmers in the Scarcies river basin. Some of these farmers were later deployed in other areas to help plant and establish nurseries. By 1928 swamp-rice cultivation was being taken up spontaneously on inland swamps. But most farmers still continued working on dry land. For although the swamps could give them more yield, this yield was limited to rice, whereas a variety of food crops such as yams, cassava, millet and vegetables could be grown together with rice on the upland farms. Moreover, land in wetland areas involved more labour-intensive devices and labour was scarce.

An agricultural school was established at Njala in 1919 to

assist with research. It trained agricultural instructors who went into the villages to teach farmers new farming techniques. In 1934 the Rokupr Rice Research Station was established for the explicit purpose of developing and testing improved varieties of swamp rice seeds. Then the Revolving Seed Schemes were initiated with a twofold objective: to distribute improved varieties of seeds and extend credit to farmers. The plan involved the grant of four bushels of rice to an individual farmer on condition that he return five after harvest. Between 1935 and 1946, 93 000 bushels of seed rice were distributed under this plan. A cooperative marketing society for swamp rice was also established.

In another drive to expand rice production, the Government embarked on swamp reclamation. By 1938 surveying and reclamation of new swamp-lands were being pursued vigorously. The Government then began to give loans to farmers for reclamation work. In the 1940s a large-scale project to drain 500 000 acres of flood plains along the Sewa and Wanje rivers was initiated. This ran into difficulties, however. Excavation equipment could not be secured because of wartime pressures, and skilled operators could not be trained on time. Problems of flooding arose in the small areas that had already been reclaimed.

In spite of these technical difficulties, the Government began to experiment with mechanical ploughing in 1949 in the hope that it would arrest the spread of weed-growth in previously-cleared land through deep ploughing, and expand rice cultivation into new areas. But the scheme failed because of the high cost of machinery, difficulty of moving it over the land, high incidence of wear and tear due to rough conditions and expensive repairs.

Not much effort was made though to promote the cultivation of other subsistence crops such as cassava, corn, millet, yams and beans. In the area of meat production, an experimental farm was constructed at Musaia, near Kabala, for the breeding of high-grade cattle for meat. But it was not successful, due largely to high maintenance costs. A pig farm and a poultry farm were also started at Newton.

Thus, its ambitious plans notwithstanding, the colonial government's role in developing subsistence agriculture was rather modest. Severe limitations of staff and lack of proper research and finance were mainly to account for this.

9.3   Mining

By the 1920s government began to realize the need to diversify the economy by encouraging mining activities in the country. This would help to increase the national revenue significantly. Consequently, experts were sent to Sierra Leone to search for minerals. From 1926 to 1927 the survey team discovered the existence of a number of minerals in commercial quantities. These included platinum, gold, chrome, iron ore and diamonds.

Platinum was the first mineral to be mined on a commercial basis. Platinum worth £252 was collected in the Freetown peninsula in 1929. Production continued up to the 1940s, when there was a break. It was restarted in 1957 but stopped completely at the end of the year when it was realized that the known deposits were nearing exhaustion. Gold-mining began in the Tonkolili District in the 1930s by small companies like the Pampana Mining Company and the Yemen Mining Company and by private individuals. Production ceased temporarily in the 1950s. The Sierra Leone Chrome Mines Company (which was a foreign enterprise) began mining chrome at Bambawo near Hangha in the Kenema District in the 1930s and continued until 1963.

Two foreign organizations – the Sierra Leone Development Company (DELCO) and the Sierra Leone Selection Trust (SLST) – became involved in large-scale mining ventures. DELCO and SLST secured mining monopolies for iron ore and diamonds, respectively, for 99 years. Each firm only had to give to the Sierra Leone Government five per cent of its net profits, if made.

Large deposits of iron ore were found at Marampa in the Port Loko District which DELCO sought to exploit. In order to aid its mining activities, DELCO undertook to build a 52-mile railway line from the mine at Marampa to the port of Pepel, where a jetty would be constructed for exporting the ore. DELCO was given a huge loan to construct the railway.

Iron ore exports began in 1933. By 1940 iron ore was not only an established foreign exchange earner: it had also outstripped gold as the second leading export sector. In the 1950s 40 per cent of Britain's iron came from the Marampa Mines and by 1960, DELCO was exporting annually 1.5 million tons

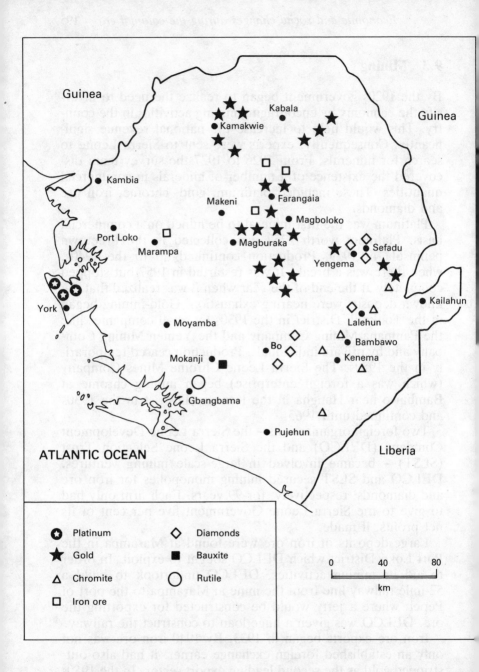

13 *Main minerals exploited in Sierra Leone during the colonial period. Bauxite and rutile were mined subsequently.*

[196]

of high-grade ore valued at £5 million. In the early years of its operation DELCO depended on migrant workers.

SLST was formed in 1934 to mine diamonds in Kono District and, later, in other areas in the country (except in DELCO-controlled areas). It was a subsidiary of Consolidated African Selection Trust (CAST) which had been engaged in mining activities in the Gold Coast.

Once production started, the rate of exploitation became quite intense. For example, total diamonds recovered by CAST in 1933 was 10 246 carats; by 1943 SLST had recovered 1 098 132 carats.

In 1955 an agreement was reached by which SLST restricted its operations to an area of about 500 square miles (1300 sq. km) in the Kono and Kenema districts. For this it was compensated with £1.5 million.

The following year the Alluvial Diamond Mining Scheme was introduced, which allowed capital other than SLST's to move into the industry. It was thought that this would combat smuggling and pilfering from SLST's lease. Licence-holders under this scheme sold their diamonds to a dealer who, in turn, sold to the Government Buying Office.

The impact of mining

Mining had a tremendous impact on the economy. In 1931 minerals accounted for less than five per cent of total domestic exports. By 1950 they rose to 43 per cent, in 1957 72 per cent, one-and-a-half times the value of agricultural exports. By the time of independence in 1961, minerals contributed 86.7 per cent of total exports. Diamonds alone contributed 60 per cent of total mineral exports and 43 per cent of all exports at this time.

Another major impact was on the agricultural economy. 1952 saw the great diamond rush. Many farmers abandoned their farms and rushed to the diamond-mining areas in search of quick wealth. Rice production in the villages consequently declined, while the demand for rice shot up. The simultaneous increase in demand for, and the decrease in supply of, rice caused an inflation which was politically unsuitable. Government was forced to import rice. The 1955–6 countrywide riots were partly attributable to the economic effects of the diamond rush (see 10.3).

Export industries in general suffered some reduction from losing labour to diamond-mining. DELCO was forced to raise wages and expedite mechanization. The chrome-mine at Bambawo faced high wages along with the decline in world market prices, and eventually halted production entirely. Various Government departments, especially public works, lost workers. In 1955 the Government was compelled to increase salaries and wages; this, in turn, brought pressure on the private sectors to do likewise.

Nevertheless, other sectors gained. As soon as the miners began to spend the money which they had earned in the rush, some sectors of the economy, like the importing firms, began to make huge profits. Luxury goods like cars, refrigerators and musical instruments were imported in large quantities for the newly rich. And many houses were improved with corrugated-iron roofing and cement-plastering, while new houses were built by successful diggers. Furniture production and other woodwork increased considerably.

Another favourable factor was the construction of roads and investment in motor transport. Many farmers and traders were thus able to transport their wares to the mining areas where they sold for higher profits. The Queen Elizabeth II Quay, completed in 1954, proved a valuable investment. Work on the ships, on the quay and in the importing firms provided considerable employment. A substantial portion of the imports was sent to the mining areas and this caused an important stream of traffic up-country.

The Government was also able to derive some revenue from mineral royalties and from import duties, even though there was a decline in agricultural exports. Consequently, some money became available for infrastructural development and other social services.

There was also a tremendous population increase in the mining towns – Lunsar (iron ore), Yengema, Koidu, Bo and Kenema (diamonds). Koidu, for example, had a population of about 100 in 1927; by the late 1950s its population was about 12 000.

9.4 Banking and manufacturing industry

Another economic revolution that took place in Sierra Leone during the colonial era was the introduction of a new mone-

Table 9.1 Quantity and value of minerals exported from Sierra Leone (other than illicit exports of diamonds), 1953-7

	Gold (oz)	Chromite (tons)	Iron Ore (tons)	Diamonds (carats)	Columbite (tons)	Platinum (oz)
1953 Q	3835	26096	1200240	416742	—	—
V (£)	37619	331737	4345429	1198133	—	—
1954 Q	2530	15120	877306	443598	4	—
V (£)	26573	165025	2543939	1389003	7874	—
1955 Q	241	17750	1331573	401423	3	—
V (£)	2542	192331	3709595	1400478	7558	—
1956 Q	452	18774	1328019	647799	—	—
V (£)	4741	194630	4003016	3467385	—	—
1957 Q	—	16378	1444542	863202	—	4.61
V (£)	—	170196	4330343	6425197	—	106

(Q = Quantity)
(V = Value)

Compiled from Colonial Reports: Sierra Leone, 1953-7, London, HMSO.

tary and taxation system. Metal coins and paper currencies replaced the system of barter and commodity currencies like country cloths and iron bars. The West African Currency Board was set up in 1913 to supply currency to British West Africa. Its currency of pounds, shillings and pence (£ s d) was closely tied to the British Sterling at certain rates of exchange. The Board had its office in London, but was represented locally by a Currency Officer and its local agents were the Bank of British West Africa which was established in Freetown in 1898. This bank together with Barclays Bank (established in Freetown in 1917) dominated the banking industry in Sierra Leone.

Not much effort was made to encourage local industries. In fact, colonial regulations speeded up their decline by restricting their production and waiving taxes on those foreign goods that were locally produced. Dr Abayomi Cole, a Sierra Leonean entrepreneur, was banned from producing tobacco, brandy, soap and sugar in the early twentieth century. Cadbury's of England flooded the Sierra Leone market with cheap chocolates in order to force D. B. Curry out of business. The Government gave a huge subsidy of £10000 to Freetown Cold Storage Company to aid its business, but denied such assistance to the locally-owned Freetown Mineral Waters Company. The latter was forced to close down. During the period of decolonization some steps were taken to promote the development of secondary industries. The Development of Industries Board was established in 1947 to finance local industries. In 1949, for example, it gave loans to fund the following projects:

Rice-milling and nut-cracking	£1 500
Cabinet-making	100
Pig-rearing	1 500
Timber-sawing	600
Soap-making	4 500

The SLPMB set up oil mills at some of its oil-palm plantations – for example, at Masanke. In 1954 the United Africa Company moved into cigarette-manufacturing through the Aureol Tobacco Company.

So at independence Sierra Leone was still a producer of primary products and receiver of European manufactured goods. Distribution of the manufactured goods and marketing of the produce of the Sierra Leonean farmers were almost exclusively controlled by large European companies and their agents. It is thus obvious that through this system Sierra Leoneans were effectively excluded from participating in big business in the country and, inevitably became victims of economic exploitation.

9.5   Social developments

Education

Western education in Sierra Leone, and indeed in British West Africa, was promoted largely by Christian missionaries. They built many schools in various parts of the country.

The Fourah Bay Institution officially became Fourah Bay College in 1848. Twenty-eight years later it was affiliated to Durham University in England. The missionary bodies, principally the CMS and WMS, continued to administer the college until the end of the Second World War, when it was handed over to the Government.

In 1906 the Government established a notable school in the Protectorate – the Bo School – for the sons and nominees of

Fourah Bay College in the nineteenth century

chiefs. It was to be the cornerstone of Western education in that region. The school was meant to produce progressive chiefs who would uphold the indirect rule system. These future leaders of the people were to be given a cultural education and training in the duties of citizenship, and a sense of their obligations to the community.

Another male government institution was opened in Freetown in 1925, the Prince of Wales (secondary) School. The school laid emphasis on science teaching. It was non-denominational and non-discriminatory, and so attracted many pupils.

After the Second World War the Government took positive steps to expand and improve on the quality of secondary and higher education. Colonial development grants were used to open and develop more institutions. The Magburaka Training College was restarted in 1948 at a cost of over £100 000. In that same year grants were provided for the re-establishment of Fourah Bay College on Mount Aureol. In 1959 the college became, by grant of a Royal Charter, the University College of Sierra Leone. Dr Davidson Nicol was then appointed the first Sierra Leonean Principal.

The strides made in education since the Second World War could be attested to by the following figures. In 1945 there

Bo School

Dr Davidson Nichol in 1971

were 23559 pupils in primary schools, 2064 in secondary schools, none in technical/vocational schools, 145 students in teacher-training institutions and 48 in other higher institutions.

By 1961, there were 86224 pupils in primary, 7512 in secondary, 1183 students in technical/vocational, 629 in teacher-training and 300 in higher educational institutions. Impressive as these figures may appear, they represented only a small fraction of students actually eligible for Western education in Sierra Leone.

Medical establishments

In 1896 when a Protectorate was declared over the hinterland, general hospitals and smaller, specialized facilities for smallpox and incurable diseases existed in Freetown and Bonthe. Dispensaries were also located in the Colony villages and the small coastal customs stations, and these barely met the minimal needs of the people. In the Protectorate, medical facilities were only provided by the UBC mission hospital at Rotifunk and by the medical officers stationed at the five district headquarters. The services of the latter were mainly

Connaught Hospital

intended for the white District Commissioners and their staffs. In the early twentieth century medical facilities were extended to Bo, Shenge, Taiama and Jaiama.

In 1904 Hill Station was built exclusively for Europeans, so that they could avoid the unhealthy climate of Freetown. A special railway line was constructed to take officials to and from work in Freetown. The Connaught Hospital was opened in Freetown in 1922 to replace the Colonial Hospital that was destroyed by fire two years earlier. And in 1924 work began on the European hospital. The American Wesleyan Mission opened a health centre at Kamabai and the Methodists did the same at Segbwema. These centres, as well as those of the UBC at Taiama and Jaiama, were upgraded to full hospitals in the 1930s.

At the end of the Second World War, plans were made under the revised Colonial Development and Welfare scheme to build four new hospitals and 50 health centres, but progress was impeded by lack of materials and of technical and supervisory staff. In fact three of the existing hospitals in the Protectorate closed intermittently because of staff shortage. By 1952, none of the planned hospitals and only six of the health centres had been opened. However, there was some expansion of the epidemic diseases control programme, and some Native Administrations and District Councils managed to build dispensaries in their respective areas.

By 1957, the shortages of the immediate postwar years had been overcome and four new hospitals were opened and health centres were provided in many large towns. The Christian missions also expanded their operations; they opened a few new hospitals and several dispensaries all over the country. Compared to the population of the country, however, the medical services provided during the colonial era were only token services.

Pipe-borne water and electricity

These amenities have never been enjoyed by the majority of the Sierra Leone population. Most people have had to rely on small streams or underground water for their water needs.

The first pipe-borne water supply was laid in Freetown in 1872, whilst the first in the Protectorate was constructed at Panguma between 1923 and 1925. As the Freetown population grew, the Kongo Dam in the Orugu valley was constructed in 1953.

The first electricity-generating plant was opened in Freetown in 1928. Public electricity reached the provinces with the opening of installations at Lungi Airport in 1947, in Bo (1949) and Kenema (1953). Electricity was later extended to Magburaka, Rokupr, Njala, Bonthe, Port Loko, Makeni, Moyamba and Kambia.

References

Buscher, Ludger (1984), *Integrated Rural Development: The Case of Southern Sierra Leone* (Hamburg).

Clarke, J. I. (1969), *Sierra Leone in Maps*, 2nd edn (London University Press).

Collier, Gershon (1970), *Sierra Leone: Experiment in Democracy in an African Nation* (New York).

Crowder, Michael (1968), *West Africa Under Colonial Rule* (Hutchinson).

Dorjahn, Vernon and Isaac Barry (eds, 1979), *Essays on the Economic Anthropology of Liberia and Sierra Leone* (Institute of Liberian Studies, USA).

Foray, C. P. (1978), *Outline History of Fourah Bay College 1827–1977* (FBC).

Fyfe, Christopher (1964), *Sierra Leone Inheritance* (Oxford University Press).

Fyfe, Christopher (1979), *A Short History of Sierra Leone* (Longman).

Hoogvelt, Ankie M. M. and Anthony M. Tinker (1978), 'The Rise of Colonial and Post-Colonial States in Imperialism – A Case Study of the Sierra Leone Development Company', *The Journal of Modern African Studies*, 16, 1.

ILO (1981), *Ensuring Equitable Growth: A Strategy for Increasing Employment, Equity and Basic Needs Satisfaction in Sierra Leone* (JASPA, Addis Ababa).

Kaniki, M. Y. H (1973), 'Economic Change in Sierra Leone During the 1930s', *Trans-African Journal of History*.

Levi, John et al. (1976), *African Agriculture – Economic Action and Reaction in Sierra Leone* (Commonwealth African Bureau).

Richards, Paul (1985), *Indigenous Agricultural Revolution – Coping with Hunger: Hazard and Experiment in an African Farming System* (London).

Riddell, J. Barry (1970), *The Spatial Dynamics of Modernization in Sierra Leone: Structure, Diffusion, and Response* (Evanston, Northwestern University Press).

Saylor, R. G. (1967), *The Economic System of Sierra Leone* (Duke University).

Spitzer, Leo (1968), 'The Mosquito and Segregation in Sierra Leone', *Canadian Journal of African Studies*, II, 1 (Spring).

Sumner, D. L. (1962) *Education in Sierra Leone* (Freetown).

Van der Laan, H. L. (1965), *The Sierra Leone Diamonds: An Economic Study Covering the Years 1952–1961* (Oxford University Press).

Questions PART A

1 Of what importance was the railway with its feeder-roads to the economic and social development of Sierra Leone before the 1950s?

2 What attempts were made during the colonial period in Sierra Leone to improve agriculture, and what were the results?

3 What effects did the diamond rush of the 1950s have on Sierra Leone?

4 Describe the major economic developments that took place in Sierra Leone during the colonial period.

5 Outline the developments that took place in educational and health services up to the time of independence (see Chapter 3).

Questions PART B

1 How far did colonial policy contribute towards increased agricultural production in Sierra Leone?

2 Discuss the impact of mining and cash-cropping on the Sierra Leone economy during the colonial period.

3 *Either*
   (a) 'The export sector of the Sierra Leone economy experienced growth without development during the colonial period.' Discuss.
   Or
   (b) To what extent was colonial economic policy in relation to Sierra Leone merely 'extractive'?

4 Discuss the view that the economic changes in Sierra Leone during the colonial era benefited Europeans more than they benefited Sierra Leoneans.

10 Transfer of power

Before the start of the Second World War Britain had no intention of devolving power on her colonies' nationals. She still felt that they were not yet ready for independence. Britain, however, embarked on the road to decolonization as soon as the war ended. Several factors accounted for this change in British colonial policy.

The war had greatly weakened Britain; she was therefore not strong enough to effectively resist nationalist pressures. America and the Soviet Union, both of which had emerged from the war as the new superpowers, were opposed to colonialism, though for very different reasons. The United Nations also condemned colonialism. Most dependent peoples were now more eager than ever before to regain their independence. The postwar governments in Britain were committed to a more rapid transition to self-government and accordingly took steps to achieve their goal.

In Sierra Leone a semi-legislative body, the Protectorate Assembly, and a new constitution were inaugurated as initial steps towards the movement for independence.

10.1 The Protectorate Assembly

This was established in 1946 mainly to provide the people of the Protectorate with a central representative body which could speak with authority on Protectorate matters. The Assembly comprised Official and Unofficial members. The former included directors of some government departments. The Unofficial members included two representatives from each district (who were mostly chiefs) indirectly elected by District Councils, and the Governor's nominees. In all, the Assembly had 42 members.

It held its first meeting in Bo on 23–26 July 1946, and thereafter Bo became its annual meeting-place. The Assembly discussed national issues, including constitutional matters, social questions, and so on. Assembly members advocated the provision of more welfare services for the Protectorate since the largest share of the country's revenue came from that region.

The Assembly brought the chiefs together to share experience and compare problems relating to their respective chiefdoms. It also functioned as an electoral college for the election of Protectorate representatives into the Legislative Council. Above all, the Assembly served as a political training institution for Protectorate people. Thus, nationalist leaders like Milton Margai, Albert Margai and Siaka Stevens were all products of the Protectorate Assembly.

It held its last meeting in 1955. By this date, more Protectorate people had been elected into the Legislative Council and it became no longer necessary to discuss national issues in the Protectorate Assembly before debating them in the Legislative Council. The Protectorate Assembly became redundant and was formally dissolved in 1957.

10.2 The Stevenson Constitution

Governor Hubert Stevenson drew up a new constitution in 1947 as another step towards the movement for independence. The constitution provided for an elected Unofficial majority in the Legislative Council. Ten of the Unofficial members were to be elected from the Protectorate (nine by the Protectorate Assembly and one nominated by the Governor from among the members of the Assembly) and four from the Colony. There was no literacy qualification for the Protectorate representatives. The Executive Council was to remain an Official body, with its two nominated members. The Governor was president of both Councils.

Many Protectorate people, especially chiefs, welcomed the constitutional provisions, for they saw in the proposals a whole range of new opportunities for the social and political advancement of the Protectorate.

But most Krio bitterly opposed the constitutional arrangements, because they had the effect of transferring power to the Protectorate. In their petition to King George VI in 1948, Krio politicians called for literacy qualifications for Legislative Council members. They further argued that Protectorate people had no right to sit in the Council, since they were foreigners.

Another group that supported the call for literacy qualifications was the Sierra Leone Organization Society (SOS), which had been formed in Moyamba in June 1946 as an educational and improvement association. The SOS was annoyed at the predominant role chiefs played in Protectorate affairs. It argued that if illiterates were elected into the Legislative Council, 'they would not profit by the deliberation nor benefit the country by their presence in Council, since they would not contribute to the discussion'. All their petitions, like those of the Colony politicians, were largely ignored by British officials.

As Krio opposition to the constitution intensified, SOS

Dr H.C. Bankole-Bright (1883–1958)

members dropped their earlier demands and closed ranks with the chiefs. When people from the Colony formed the National Council of Sierra Leone (NCSL) under the chairmanship of Dr H. C. Bankole-Bright to block the constitution, Protectorate people formed the Sierra Leone People's Party (SLPP) to press for its implementation. The SLPP was led by a retired medical officer, Dr Milton A. S. Margai.

After a long and inconclusive debate, the new Governor, Sir George Beresford-Stooke, implemented a revised form of the Stevenson Constitution in 1951. The new Legislative Council was to comprise the Governor, seven Official members, seven directly-elected members from the Colony, 14 indirectly elected from the Protectorate and two nominated members. The new constitution was immediately followed by general elections which saw the SLPP emerge as the majority party.

After the elections, SLPP leaders were chosen to sit in a newly-constituted Executive Council. In 1953 the following African members in the Executive Council were given responsibility for ministries:

Dr M. A. S. Margai	Health, Agriculture and Forests
Mr A. M. Margai	Local Government, Education and Welfare
Mr M. S. Mustapha	Works and Transport
Mr A. G. Randle	Trade and Commerce, Post and telegraphs
Mr S. P. Stevens	Land, Mines and Labour

Paramount Chief Bai Farima Tass II was appointed Minister Without Portfolio.

Dr Margai became Chief Minister the following year.

On 1 July 1954, the Governor appointed the Keith-Lucas Commission to consider and advise on electoral reform in Sierra Leone. The Commission later made the following recommendations: an expansion of the Protectorate franchise to include women who paid tax, were literate or owned property; the Colony franchise was to include men and women over 21 years, who had resided in the Colony for over six months, and who could meet some minimal financial requirements. The Legislative Council members were to determine the size and composition of the Council.

NCSL and SLPP leaders failed to agree on the size of the

Council. Each party was then asked to submit separate proposals. A non-party conference adopted the SLPP proposals which called for a single House of Representatives consisting of 57 members, including four Official and two nominated members. Twelve of the 51 members were to be Paramount Chiefs elected by District Councils, 14 ordinary members from the Colony, two ordinary members from each of the 12 provincial districts, and one representative from Bo town.

10.3   1955–6 countrywide riots

While the colonial authorities were busy effecting changes that would lead the country to political independence, certain developments took place, especially in the provinces, which reminded them that their over-reliance on chiefs for the success of their administration was becoming more and more counter-productive. British officials and some Sierra Leonean ministers appeared equally surprised when in February 1955 four days of serious rioting engulfed Freetown, and then nine months later thousands of people took to the streets against chiefs in many big towns in the provinces.

Freetown general strike

The Freetown riots were sparked off by economic factors. They developed out of strike-calls by Marcus Grant, leader of the Artisans and Allied Workers' Union, and H. N. Georgestone, leader of the Transport and General Workers' Union, over wage increases, following a dramatic rise in food costs resulting from the diamond rush. Grant and Georgestone had submitted an application for a general increase of one shilling and sixpence per day for their union members, but the employers were prepared to pay only fourpence. After a series of unsuccessful meetings between the employers and the workers, the latter went on strike on 9 February 1955.

There was large-scale rioting in Freetown when unemployed youths joined the strikers. The houses of three ministers – Siaka Stevens, Albert Margai and M. S. Mustapha – were stoned. It was felt that these ministers were not sympathetic to the workers' cause.

The strike was called off on 12 February and work resumed

two days later. The workers in the end received a pay increase of one shilling a day, effective 1 February.

A commission set up to look into the causes of the strike and accompanying riots acknowledged that economic hardships were mainly responsible for their outbreak.

The provincial disturbances

These were caused by economic and political factors. Local tax rose from 11 shillings and sixpence in 1950 to 25 shillings in 1955. The tax rules had also been amended to include many young men who had hitherto not been taxed. Many people were further angered by the abuse of power by Paramount Chiefs and other chiefdom personnel. These officials engaged themselves in malpractices such as forced labour and extortions.

The disturbances began in November 1955 in Maforki chiefdom, Port Loko District, when a large crowd protested at the District Commissioner's Office against chiefdom tax increases, abuses and extortions in tax assessment and other levies. The District Commissioner was unable to contain the situation and it exploded into violence.

Opposition elements in many other northern chiefdoms also mobilized many angry young men to rise against their chiefs. In the Bumpe and Ribbi chiefdoms of Moyamba District, ethnic antagonisms provided an important source of conflict underlying the acts of violence in these areas. In Bumpe, leaders of the Loko people, who had been bitterly aggrieved at not being allowed to nominate a candidate in the all-Sherbro paramount-chieftaincy election of 1954, joined forces with supporters of the defeated Sherbro candidates to attack the Sherbro ruling elite in the chiefdom. Temne and Loko people in Ribbi cooperated against the Sherbro who controlled the chieftaincy.

These disturbances resulted in considerable loss of life and property. Many people were killed when troops moved in to contain the rebels, sometimes with machine-gun fire.

The Herbert Cox Commission appointed to look into the disturbances found that they were mainly caused by the maladministration and dishonesty of local government bodies, and recommended, among other things, that chiefdom administrations should be thoroughly overhauled. Five chiefs were deposed, and five resigned their offices. Many rioters were given stiff jail sentences.

The 1958 Constitution

More constitutional changes took place in 1958. The Chief Minister became Prime Minister; the four Official members were removed from the House – its new composition now comprised the Speaker, 51 directly-elected members and two appointed members. The Executive Council consisted of the Governor as president, the Prime Minister, and the other ministers, who were appointed by the Governor on the recommendation of the Prime Minister from among the members of the House. The Governor still retained his reserve powers and was responsible for foreign affairs, defence, internal security and the public service. Apart from his reserve powers, he was required to consult the Executive Council and act on its advice in all matters. Thus by 1958 Sierra Leone had virtually attained self-determination in internal affairs. This was the last stage towards achieving independence.

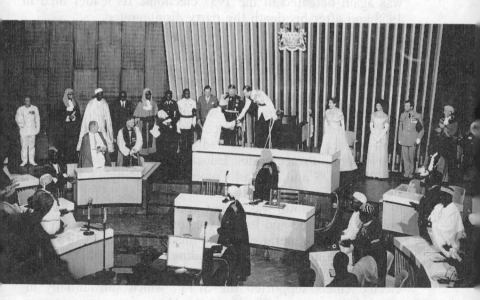

The Duke of Kent, representing Queen Elizabeth II, shakes hands with Sir Milton Margai after handing over the independence documents

10.4   Political parties

Many political parties sprang up in Sierra Leone immediately prior to independence. Politicians wanted their respective groups to enjoy the distinction of leading the country to independence.

The National Council of Sierra Leone (NCSL)

This was the oldest political party in Sierra Leone on the eve of independence. It was founded in August 1950 out of a fusion of various semi-political organizations in the Colony. Following its defeat in the 1951 elections, the party's leader, Dr Bankole-Bright, introduced a motion in the Legislative Council demanding independence for the Colony. The motion was rejected without debate. Thereafter, the party resorted to violent attacks on the SLPP and opposed several government measures.

The NCSL did not make much impact in Sierra Leone. It was again defeated in the 1957 elections. Its leader died in 1958 and after his death the party disintegrated.

The Sierra Leone People's Party (SLPP)

The SLPP was the largest party in the country. Its establishment came in direct response to the activities of the NCSL. As a counterforce, the SLPP was intended to be the party to represent, defend, and advance Protectorate interests. Three semi-political organizations had merged to form the SLPP. They were Protectorate Educational Progressive Union (PEPU), SOS and a small Colony-based People's Party, led by Lamina Sankoh (see 10.6).

The party's motto was 'One Country, One People' its symbol the palm tree and its party colours, bright green.

In the 1957 general elections the SLPP won 25 of the 39 popularly contested seats, including nine out of 12 in the Colony. Eight successful independent candidates and the elected chiefs supported the SLPP, which substantially increased the party's majority in the House.

The SLPP was essentially a patron party, composed of various groups loosely held together. It did not make any serious effort to mobilize the masses and the party's leadership was opposed to mob action. It was largely conservative in leadership and gradualist in its approach to national issues. It preferred peaceful compromise to open confrontation, bargaining to *diktat* (a dictated settlement).

The United Progressive Party (UPP)

The UPP was formed in 1955 and was led by a Krio lawyer, C. B. Rogers-Wright. It is believed that the UPP came into existence as an organization through which opposition against the central and local governments could be ventilated.

In the 1957 elections the party won five seats, thereby becoming the main opposition party in the House. In 1959, however, the potential of the UPP was seriously weakened by a split within the party. A minority then emerged as an independent political organization calling itself the Independent Progressive People's Party (IPP), and sat separately in the House under its new name.

The Kono Progressive Movement (KPM)

KPM was perhaps the most effective of the smaller parties. It was formed in the early 1950s and was led by a druggist, Tamba S. Briwa. It wanted to ensure that the Kono people derived maximum benefits from the diamond industry. The KPM, though a daring display of guts and high-powered organizational skill, completely dominated the politics of the Kono District during this period.

The KPM later merged with the Sierra Leone Independence Movement (SLIM), to form the Sierra Leone Progressive Independence Movement (SLPIM). This new group again merged with the People's National Party in 1959 and began to pose a serious threat to the SLPP.

The People's National Party (PNP)

The PNP came into existence in 1958 as a result of ideological differences and struggle for power within the SLPP leadership. Dr Margai and the rest of the SLPP old guard were happy to continue with their gradualist approach to national issues, and also wanted to maintain the party's alliance with the chiefs. These policies were rejected by the young and more dynamic members of the SLPP. They wanted quick action. This group was led by Dr Margai's younger brother, Albert. He successfully bid for the leadership of the party but severe pressure was put on him to step down for Dr Margai. Albert and some of his colleagues, including S. T. Navo, A. J. Massally, Maigore Kallon and Siaka Stevens, then quit the SLPP to found the PNP.

From its inception, the PNP tended to be more radical and critical of chiefs. It demanded faster progress towards independence. PNP leaders also promised vastly increased social facilities and better economic opportunities for Sierra Leoneans. In the matter of foreign affairs, the PNP called for non-alignment.

The vigour of the PNP did pay off. It attracted many young intellectuals and progressive elements over the whole country. Albert Margai appeared to have a kind of magnetic force which drew a lot of people to his movement.

The United National Front (UNF)

The UNF was the brainchild of Sir Milton Margai (knighted in 1959). The emergence of many political parties with varying ideologies and sometimes radical approaches to national issues had threatened to undermine his party's pre-eminence in Sierra Leone politics. So he became convinced that if he did not work out a compromise with these parties, he would lose the country's leadership. By 1960 Sir Milton had got the main political parties and other prominent politicians to agree to form a United National Front which would discuss the country's independence arrangements with the British Government. He became head of the Front.

In return for their cooperation, the leaders of the other parties were rewarded with ministerial posts in the government. Albert Margai, leader of the PNP, became Minister of Agriculture and later Minister of Finance; C. B. Rogers-Wright of the UPP became Minister of Housing and Country Planning, and later Minister of External Affairs. G. Dickson-Thomas and John Nelson-Williams, both of IPP, became Minister of Social Welfare and Minister of Information and Broadcasting, respectively.

Sierra Leone therefore sent a united delegation with a

single voice to London for the Independence Constitutional Talks, which were held from 20 April to 4 May 1960. Siaka Stevens, who was one of the PNP delegates, marred the talks by his refusal to sign the constitutional documents. His reason was that he disagreed with Sierra Leone's defence agreements with Britain.

Despite his opposition, the other participants duly signed the documents and it was agreed that Sierra Leone should become a politically independent state within the Commonwealth on 27 April 1961.

The All People's Congress (APC)

Siaka Stevens returned to Sierra Leone two weeks before the rest of the UNF delegation and proceeded to form a party. He launched the 'Elections Before Independence Movement' in July 1960, which transformed itself into the All People's Congress two months later. Stevens became the leader. The APC adopted as its symbol the red sun – its motto 'Now or Never' (now 'Live for Ever').

Like the defunct PNP, the APC was also a radical party. It professed a vague socialism, promising equal opportunities for all. The APC soon attracted a large following, particularly from the north. Some northerners were dissatisfied with what appeared to them to be 'Mende hegemony' in government.

Just before the formal declaration of independence the APC leadership was accused of attempts to wreck the celebrations by violence and sabotage. Some 43 of its leaders, including Stevens, were detained though they were released shortly afterwards.

10.5   The Independence Constitution

The Sierra Leone Independence Constitution contained many important provisions, some of which are discussed below.

Citizenship rights   were conferred on any indigenous person whose paternal grandfather was a Negro African. Basic rights were guaranteed by entrenched clauses which meant that they could not be altered by the normal process of legislation.

Parliament   was the supreme legislative body and comprised the Head of State, the Speaker and elected members. The Queen of England was made Head of State in Sierra Leone and she was represented by the Governor-General who was also Commander-in-Chief. The Speaker presided over Parliament. The elected members were voted for by single-member constituencies. And each provincial district sent an additional Paramount Chief member to Parliament.

The Governor-General appointed as *Prime Minister* the person who appeared to him likely to command the majority in Parliament. The Prime Minister advised the Governor-General on the appointment of ministers of government. The Governor-General, Prime Minister and the ministers formed the Executive.

The Judiciary   A hierarchy of courts was established with the Chief Justice as head. He was appointed by the Governor-General on the advice of the Prime Minister. Other judges were appointed by the Governor-General on the advice of the Judicial Service Commission. Judges held office *quamdiu se bene gesserit* (during good behaviour) though they retired at the age of 62 years.

A Public Service Commission and an *Electoral Commission* were established. Members of Parliament and parliamentary secretaries were barred from becoming members of the latter commission which was responsible for the conduct of general elections in the country. The Public Service Commission had power to appoint, promote, dismiss and exercise disciplinary control over any person holding an office in the public service.

10.6   An architect of Sierra Leone's independence

There were certain people to whom the phrase 'One Country, One People' was not just political talk. They were determined to put it into practice. We shall have a profile of one such person – the Reverend E. N. Jones.

E. N. Jones was born at Gloucester on 28 June 1894. He was educated at Fourah Bay College and at Wycliffe College, England. Jones had a taste of racial prejudice while at Wycliffe. The college bishop refused to ordain him because he was black. When he was eventually ordained a deacon in 1923, the bishop wore white gloves to protect himself against Jones's blackness. These sad experiences, coupled with Rev. Jones's expression of solidarity with the Protectorate people, made him drop his European name and take the new name of Lamina Sankoh.

Lamina Sankoh returned to Sierra Leone in 1924 and was ordained a priest. He taught for some time at Fourah Bay College before returning overseas for further studies.

On his second return in the early 1940s, Sankoh embarked on political and civic work of all kinds. He wanted to found a People's Church which would be Christian in outlook, but with its main accent on an African approach to God. He initiated a People's Forum in Freetown, which was a cultural organization intended to examine the views and values held by Sierra Leoneans.

Sankoh stood for the oneness of Sierra Leone. He appealed to both Colony and Protectorate leaders to bury their differences and work for the progress of the country. His People's Party was the only Colony organization that merged with two Protectorate organizations to form the first truly national party (the SLPP) in 1951. He became the party's second Vice-President.

However, Sankoh did not live to see the results of his untiring work. He died in 1954 and was given a decent and honourable burial.

10.7   The impact of colonialism

We would like to conclude this chapter with a brief look at the effects of colonialism in Sierra Leone. Although the colonial period lasted for less than 200 years, it nevertheless brought profound political, economic and social changes to the Sierra Leone society. Some of these changes were good while many were bad.

It is argued that colonialism succeeded in bringing together some 17 divergent communities to form a nation-state called Sierra Leone. Colonialism provided a stable government which ended the savage destruction of life through inter-communal rivalries, violence and slave raids. Colonial legal and moral codes proclaimed equality of all before the law.

But colonialism denied the Sierra Leonean the right to self-determination. It weakened the traditional institutions of chieftaincy and destroyed the indigenous systems of govern-

Houses of Parliament, Freetown

ment. For instance, colonialism introduced the system of ruling houses among the Mende. These people had laid emphasis on individual qualities and achievements rather than on birthright in the acquisition of political leadership. Colonialism further aimed to divide the people. And the colonial administration was so far removed from the majority of the people that many never identified themselves with such administration.

Some people have argued that the colonialists made an attempt to improve the communications network. Railways, motor roads, harbours and airports were constructed and telephone and telegraph lines were laid. These facilitated the movement of people, goods, exchange of ideas and information. Colonialism made it possible for greater exploitation of the country's resources and this helped to increase Sierra Leone's prosperity. The economy of Sierra Leone was integrated into that of the world in general.

Many people, however, believe that the improvements in communication systems were not primarily designed to benefit Sierra Leoneans and any benefits they might have derived from them were purely accidental.

Economic development was lopsided. Cash-crop production and mining were encouraged at the expense of industrialization or subsistence agriculture. The economy was export-orientated and therefore not very relevant to the nation's developmental needs. It was also largely in the hands of foreigners.

Socially, colonialism brought certain benefits. The new administrative, commercial and mining centres were provided with some amenities, such as hospitals, better housing and sanitary facilities. These led to an improvement in the quality of life of people living in these centres. Western education was made available to some people, which gave them an opportunity to improve their social status.

There were some harmful effects, though. Colonialism widened the gap between the urban centres and the rural areas, and between the rich and the poor. As more rural workers migrated to the urban centres in search of work, the villages became depopulated. Many rural workers, however, found urban life unbearable. They could not find jobs or decent accommodation and were forced to live in crowded homes with very poor sanitary facilities. In an attempt to earn a living against great odds many migrants indulged in all kinds of criminal activities.

The education and other services provided during the colonial era were grossly inadequate and were heavily concentrated in the capital, Freetown, and the provincial headquarter towns. Colonialism left behind a large illiteracy problem and an education system that was not suited to the needs of the people. For the education system was designed to teach the Sierra Leonean to be British instead of remaining Sierra Leonean.

Attitudinal change was perhaps one of the most lasting negative social effects of colonial rule in Sierra Leone. Many Sierra Leoneans imbibed Western values and developed insatiable tastes for European goods and services. They were made to believe that anything African was bad and inferior and anything European was good and superior. And sadly enough, this attitude has persisted to this day and some Sierra Leoneans continue to measure their own way of life by Western standards.

References

Alie, J. A. D. (1988), 'The (Sierra Leone) Protectorate Assembly, 1946–1957: An Experiment in Tutelary Democracy?' MA (USL).

Boahen, A. Adu (1985), 'Colonialism in Africa: Its Impact and Significance', in Boahen (ed.), *UNESCO General History*, Vol. VII.

Boahen, A. Adu (1986), 'The Colonial Powers and West Africa', *Topics in West African History*, new edition, (Longman).

Cartwright, John (1970), *Politics in Sierra Leone 1947–1967* (University of Toronto Press, Canada).

Cox, Herbert (1956), *Report of the Commission of Enquiry into Disturbances in the Provinces, November 1955-March 1956* (Freetown).

Darwin, John (1984), *Britain and Decolonization 1945–1965* (Macmillan, London).

Deveneaux, Gustav (1983), *Power Politics in Sierra Leone* (AUP, Nigeria).

Dumbuya, A. R. (1977), 'Emergence and Development of the PDG and SLPP: A Comparative Study of the Differential Development of Political Parties in Guinea and Sierra Leone', JHSSL, Vol. 1, no 1.

Encyclopaedia Africana, Vol. 2.

Fashole-Luke, David (1985), 'The Development of Trade Unionism in Sierra Leone' (Part 1), *The International Journal of African Historical Studies*, Vol. 18, no. 3.

Fyfe, Christopher (1964), *Sierra Leone Inheritance* (Oxford University Press).

Hargreaves, J. D. (1979), *The End of Colonial Rule In West Africa: Essays in Contemporary History* (Macmillan).

Kilson, Martin (1966), *Political Change in a West African State – A Study of the Modernization Process in Sierra Leone* (Harvard).

Pearce, J. D. (1982), *The Turning Point in Africa* (Frank Cass).

Sekgoma, Gilbert (1981), 'Decolonization in Sierra Leone 1938–1961', MA (Dalhousie).

Tangri, Roger (1976), 'Conflicts and Violence in Contemporary Sierra Leone Chiefdoms', JMAS, Vol. 14, no. 2.

Questions PART A

1 Why was the Protectorate Assembly founded in 1946 and what did it achieve?

2 What were the main provisions of the Stevenson Constitution?

3 Why did riots occur in Sierra Leone in 1955–6?

4 Write notes on *two* of the following:
   (a) National Council of Sierra Leone
   (b) United Progressive Party
   (c) Kono Progressive Union
   (d) People's National Party.

5 Why was the United National Front formed in 1960 and what were its achievements?

6 Trace the process by which Sierra Leone attained independence between 1945 and 1961.

7 What part did Lamina Sankoh play in the history of Sierra Leone?

8 How did colonial rule affect Sierra Leone?

Questions PART B

1 What part did the Protectorate Assembly play in the political history of Sierra Leone from 1946 to 1955?

2 How true is it to assert that the Protectorate Assembly was an experiment in tutelary democracy?
3 Discuss the importance of the 1947 Constitution (implemented in 1951) to the political development of Sierra Leone.
4 'The colonial government's proposals for constitutional reforms after the Second World War caused the formation of political parties in Sierra Leone.' Discuss.
5 How valid was the Krio claim that the Protectorate was a foreign country?
6 In what circumstances did Sir Milton emerge as Leader of Government Business, and how did these affect his subsequent career?
7 Critically examine the factors that gave rise to the APC.
8 Attempt a balance sheet of colonialism in Sierra Leone.

11 *Politics since independence*

Sierra Leone achieved independence on 27 April 1961. In the following years this achievement was affected by certain developments, namely, growing tension between the political parties and among the major ethnic groups, corruption and lavish display of wealth by the ruling elites, involvement of the military in politics and moves towards republicanism and one-partyism.

11.1 The Milton Margai era

Sierra Leone's first Prime Minister, Sir Milton Margai, was born at Gbangbatoke on 7 December 1895. He was educated at Fourah Bay College and at the Durham College of Medicine in England. He was the first Protectorate man to enter Fourah Bay College and the first British-trained medical doctor from the Protectorate.

Sir Milton returned to Sierra Leone in 1927. During his long medical career he worked in nearly all the provincial districts. He took a keen interest in the training of midwives through the Sande society. He was made a Member of the British Empire (MBE) in 1947 in recognition of his midwifery services.

Sir Milton retired from government service in 1950 and then became an active politician. He was for several years an unofficial adviser to many chiefs; he helped them to found their conference from which the District Councils and the Protectorate Assembly evolved. He served on the Protectorate Assembly for many years. He became leader and president of the SLPP in April 1951.

[224]

Sir Milton Margai

In the 1951 general elections the SLPP obtained a majority in the new Legislative Council and Sir Milton was appointed to an Official seat on the Executive Council. Soon he was Minister of Health, Agriculture and Forests, Leader of Government Business and Chief Minister. Under the increasing burden of responsibility, Sir Milton's policy remained constant in holding the interests of the country as a whole to be paramount. Recognition of his position in Sierra Leone public life was shown when he received the honour of knighthood in 1959.

When some radical members threatened to quit the SLPP because of his gradualist approach to national issues, Sir Milton's wise leadership prevented the party from collapsing. He achieved a United Front of all political parties in 1960 to work out the Independence Constitution with the British Government. Sir Milton became the country's first Prime Minister on 9 July 1960, and three days later Durham University awarded him an honorary degree of Doctor of Civil Law.

Sir Milton's astute leadership made it possible for Sierra Leone to achieve independence in a relatively peaceful atmosphere. The country could not have produced a better leader at independence. He became a founder member of the Organization of African Unity (OAU) in 1963.

Sir Milton was a conservative ruler who was opposed to change. He had great respect for traditional authority and attached much importance to age, maturity and experience. Thus, he refused to be pressurized into elevating young Sierra Leoneans to positions of supreme authority.

For the most part Sir Milton seemed to hold the view that he knew what was best for Sierra Leoneans. And although he listened to conflicting views, he most often stubbornly held on to his own, no matter how tenable. He once remarked that 'it would be awkward for a leader to say one thing at one time and then change later'.

But he was very cautious and hardly took hasty decisions. It was said that Sir Milton 'drove with the brakes ready'. He made no lavish display of wealth, although he did not ensure that his ministers emulated his fine example. He detested mass participation in politics, for he felt this would lead to dictatorship. This was why his party worked mainly through chiefs and other influential people.

Sir Milton was very tolerant with opposition members. In

1962, for example, Siaka Stevens was part of Sierra Leone's delegation to the United Nations General Assembly in New York, USA. Opposition leaders received personal loans from the government and were allowed to campaign freely in their constituencies.

He was sickly and as his illness became more severe, he lost interest in long meetings and arguments. Politics stagnated for the most part of his administration.

1962 elections   The first general election after independence was held in 1962. The SLPP won 28 seats out of 74 seats, the APC and allied parties 20, independents 14 and Paramount Chiefs 12. Most of the independents later declared for the SLPP, which substantially increased its majority. The Paramount Chiefs also supported the ·SLPP. But the APC emerged as the official opposition party in Parliament.

The election results clearly indicated that the SLPP was losing significant ground to the APC and that it was only a matter of time before the SLPP was voted out of power. What delayed this change was the personality and style of leadership of Sir Milton. He was highly respected even by the opposition; moreover, he tried hard to keep ethnic tensions down, for he formed a broad-based government.

Sir Milton died on 28 April 1964 without naming a successor. There were three possible contenders – his brother Albert, Dr John Karefa-Smart, the 'darling of the North' and M. S. Mustapha who on many occasions had acted as Prime Minister.

11.2   Sierra Leone under Sir Albert

The Governor-General appointed Albert Margai Prime Minister, but this appointment was bitterly opposed by leading SLPP and APC men. Most people had felt that a non-Mende would succeed Sir Milton. Sir Albert reacted by dismissing the four non-Mende ministers who had criticized the Governor-General's action. They were M. S. Mustapha, John Karefa-Smart, Y. D. Sesay and S. L. Matturi. This dismissal turned out to be a political blunder as it caused considerable dissatisfaction in the country, which did not turn out well for the new leader. The dismissed men were influen-

Sir Albert Margai

tial people in the SLPP who represented important areas in the country.

Albert was very different from his brother. He was a radical, an innovator, meticulous, articulate, acquisitive, robust and had an imposing personality.

He was also born in Gbangbatoke on 10 October 1910. He studied law in Britain (1944–8) and returned to Sierra Leone as the first Protectorate lawyer. He took a seat on the Protectorate Assembly and made a mark there as a critic of the government's policies. He held a number of cabinet posts – education, agriculture, and finance – between 1951 and 1964. During this period he carved for himself a high reputation for hard work and organizing ability and for getting things done efficiently and quickly. He represented Moyamba South Constituency in the central legislature from 1957 to 1967.

As Minister of Finance he established the 'leone' (Le) as

legal tender, and created the Bank of Sierra Leone as the country's central and national bank in 1963. (The leone was launched on 4 August 1964 when Sir Albert was now Prime Minister.)

Politics and diplomacy Sir Albert (knighted in 1965) made a number of attempts to broaden his base of strength. First he increased the size of the Freetown City Council and changed its tenure of office. His confidence that the SLPP could carry the election and take control of the Council was misplaced, for the APC won 11 seats on the enlarged Council as against the SLPP's seven.

Next he embarked on a strong effort to counter the APC. Provincial chiefs were advised to discourage the party from entrenching its position in the chiefdoms, and the Sierra Leone Broadcasting Service (SLBS) was directed not to publicize the APC. A rule-change was pushed through Parliament, depriving four APC members of their seats for absenteeism; these members were then in jail and could hardly help being absent. (The APC was to use the same legislation in 1977 against four SLPP members, one of them being Sir Albert's son, Charles.)

Sir Albert also determined to reorganize the SLPP. To this end he called for a national headquarters, a party press, a clear-cut policy on how candidates were to be appointed, and an organization of the party at the local level. This attempt at reorganization was vehemently opposed by many of the SLPP old guard who had never forgiven Sir Albert for his departure from the SLPP in 1958, which led to the near-collapse of the SLPP. They viewed the changes as an attempt by the Prime Minister to strengthen his position. Sir Albert then pushed most of this old guard aside and brought in more of his former PNP colleagues into the cabinet, some acting as advisers to the government.

Sir Albert regarded himself as the servant of the people. He set aside a day each week when ordinary people would come to him with their problems. He believed in mass rallies.

During Sir Albert's premiership women played a very important role in national politics. Certain respectable women were apointed Mammy Queens, and were given the responsibility of organizing their fellow women into small groups to give political support to the government.

One woman who became very prominent in national politics was ex-Paramount Chief of Kaiyamba Chiefdom, Madam Ella Koblo Gulama (daughter of Paramount Chief Julius Gulama). She had been actively involved in politics since the 1950s and was the first Sierra Leonean woman to be elected into the national legislature in 1957. She was re-elected Paramount Chief Member of Parliament for Moyamba District in 1962, and appointed Minister Without Portfolio (later Minister of State I) and a member of the Cabinet in 1964, the first Sierra Leonean woman to be so honoured. Madam Ella was a close ally of Sir Albert and enthusiastically supported Sir Albert's radical policies. In fact, she was one of Sir Albert's closest advisers.

In 1966 Sir Albert attempted to introduce a one-party system of government, but the judiciary, university community and the APC took a strongly negative stand. The general feeling was that a single party would lead to dictatorship. The issue was later dropped.

Sir Albert was also accused of tribalism because certain key positions in the government were held by Mende or by people who had a close affinity with the Mende: Peter Tucker, a Sherbro, was Secretary to the Prime Minister; John Kallon was Establishment Secretary; and S. B. Daramy was Financial Secretary. David Lansana was elevated to the post of Brigadier and Force Commander. In terms of seniority and levels of training these individuals merited their positions.

Sir Albert translated Sierra Leone's intended non-alignment into reality. He strengthened diplomatic relations with the Soviet Union. He participated personally and made significant contributions in Commonwealth Prime Ministers' Conferences, and in meetings of the OAU and of the UNO, earning the name 'Albert of Africa'. He thus earned for Sierra Leone, internationally, new prestige and effectiveness. The Prime Minister also sought closer ties with Guinea and better trade relations with other West African countries.

Sir Albert and the economy Sir Albert sent his Finance Minister abroad to negotiate aid and loan agreements with many Western countries. He also encouraged the SLPMB to embark on large-scale plantation projects which absorbed many unskilled workers. But the projects were unrealistically costed and some were badly located. The SLPMB was also

Oil refinery, Freetown

regularly plundered by politicians. Soon the Board faced serious financial problems and was unable to pay farmers for their produce. This led to massive smuggling of produce to neighbouring countries.

The Government further embarked on a policy of encouraging small-scale industries in which it had large part-holdings. A cement plant and an oil refinery were located in Freetown. But these projects, including the Cape Sierra Hotel, were undertaken with highly-inflated contractor-financed loans which adversely affected the economy. At the end of 1966 the government took a loan of 7.5 million US dollars to help put the country's finances in order. The opposition then began to accuse Sir Albert and his ministers of corruption and extravagance.

The 1967 elections

Sir Albert determined to make Sierra Leone a republic, with a President appointed by the cabinet. In order to amend the constitution two sessions of Parliament had to pass the amendment, with a general election having been held in between. In January 1967 Sir Albert got the necessary two-thirds vote in one session. He then proceeded to call general elections.

In the run-up to the 1967 elections, the Prime Minister pushed through Parliament a series of tough measures that would hamper opposition candidates. Paramount Chiefs were given control of public meetings in their chiefdoms, and a special court was proposed to try election petition cases. Candidates' election deposits were raised from Le200 to Le500 as a means of discouraging non-SLPP aspirants from contesting the elections. The Chief Electoral Commissioner, M. A. Khazali, who was a Northerner, was replaced by I. B. Sanusi, a Westerner who was an SLPP sympathizer. Finally, a strong ally of the Prime Minister, Gershon Collier, was appointed Acting Chief Justice.

On 8 February 1967 the government uncovered an alleged *coup* plot three weeks before the elections were due. Eight officers including Colonel John Bangura, the Deputy Force Commander (he was a Northerner), were arrested. Sir Albert quickly signed a defence pact with Guinea, and Guinean troops were despatched to the Sierra Leone/Guinea border to help preserve peace.

The officers arrested included three Southerners. But the arrest, particularly of the Krio and Northern officers, was seen as the last desperate attempt by Sir Albert to complete his mastery over the army in preparation for the elections. This gave the APC a propaganda tool to appeal for both Krio and Northern solidarity.

The SLPP contested the elections as a deeply-divided and weakened party and was no match for the highly-organized and formidable APC. The elections were scheduled for 17 March and 21 March, for ordinary and Paramount Chief members, respectively. Sir Albert had fallen out with a number of able young men in his own party, some of whom were either opposed to his policies or harboured political ambitions which threatened his leadership. These men were denied the SLPP symbol and so contested the election as independents. When they won, they refused to support Sir Albert, a decision which ruined his chances of regaining the premiership.

The elections exposed once again the dangerous ethnic tension in the country. The APC won all the seats in the North but one, all contested seats in the Western Area and some in Kono District, while the SLPP won almost all seats in the South and most seats in Kenema and Kailahun districts. The Governor-General was wrongly informed that at the close of the polls the state of the parties was SLPP 32, APC 32, independents two; when the true results were SLPP 28, APC 32 and independents six.

Tension began to mount in Freetown. Many of the newly-elected parliamentarians had travelled to Freetown with their supporters and there was much jubilation in the city. The academic staff of the university, students and many leading personalities made representations to the Governor-General to appoint a Prime Minister. The Governor-General, in an attempt to avoid a major crisis, appealed to SLPP and APC leaders to form a national government. But the APC leader, Siaka Stevens, objected on the grounds that the elections had been fought on two crucial issues – one-partyism and republicanism – which the electorate had rejected by voting the APC to power. Any association with the SLPP, he argued, would be a betrayal of trust. (It is, however, not true that the one-party idea was an issue in the 1967 elections.)

The Governor-General then wrote to Sir Albert, leader of the SLPP, informing him that he was going to appoint a Prime Minister, but that he had no intention of appointing *him*. Stevens was duly appointed and sworn in on 21 March, the day of the Paramount Chiefs' elections. Stevens was on the verge of appointing his ministers when the army commander, Brigadier Lansana, seized power and imposed martial law. The Governor-General and the new Prime Minister were detained. Lansana's reasons for staging the *coup* were contained in a broadcast on Wednesday, 22 March.

Lansana argued that the Governor-General had acted unconstitutionally because he had not waited for the advice of the elected chiefs before appointing a Prime Minister. Moreover, none of the parties had had an absolute majority (the House had 78 seats). He also felt that the elections had been fought on an ethnic basis. He had therefore taken over the government in order to avert a civil war.

Some people supported these arguments, but many others disagreed. They felt that it was the duty of the chiefs to support any government that was in power. They further argued that the SLPP did not have an absolute majority in the 1962 elections, yet Sir Milton was appointed Prime Minister. When he died in 1964 his brother Albert was appointed Prime Minister although no one counted how many persons in the House supported Sir Albert.

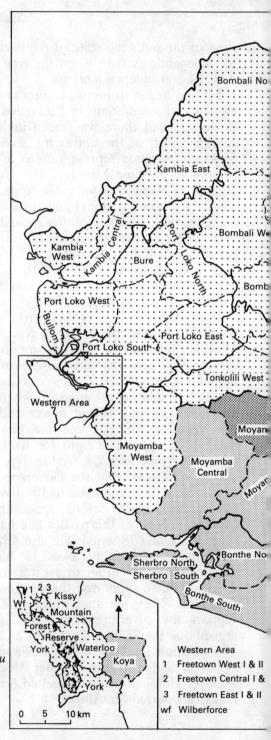

14 General election results, 1967, by constituency. The following four constituencies are not represented, being added just before the election: Kono Central (APC win), Kenema North-East (SLPP win), Koinadugu South-East (APC win) Port Loko South-West (APC win).

Bombali No

Kambia East

Bombali W

Kambia Central

Port Loko North

Kambia West

Bure

Bomb

Bullom

Port Loko West

Port Loko East

Port Loko South

Tonkolili West

Western Area

Moyar

Moyamba West

Moyamba Central

Moya

Bonthe No

Sherbro North
Sherbro South

Bonthe South

1 2 3
Wf — Kissy
N
Mountain
Forest
Reserve — Waterloo
York — Koya
York

0   5   10 km

Western Area
1 Freetown West I & II
2 Freetown Central I &
3 Freetown East I & II
wf Wilberforce

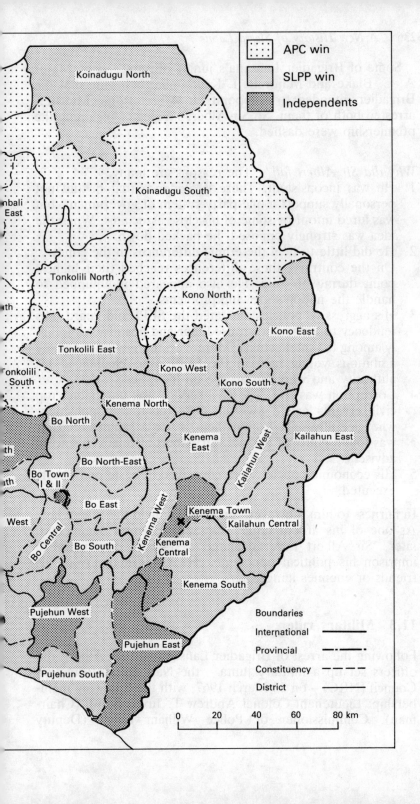

Some of Brigadier Lansana's junior officers, led by Major A. C. Blake and Major B. I. Kai-Samba, believing that the Brigadier intended to reappoint Sir Albert Prime Minister, arrested both of them. So Sir Albert's hopes of regaining the premiership were dashed.

Why did Sir Albert fall?　The reasons are many.

1　He was inconsistent. There is evidence that he did not personally support a one-party system of government, but was lured into it by some of his close associates. When the idea was strongly opposed, he backed down.
2　He did little to heal the ethnic differences in the country. On the contrary, these differences reached their highest point during his rule. He also appeared ill-equipped to handle the nation's growing problems.
3　His aggressive policies alienated the SLPP old guard. His tendency to autocracy aroused fear and hostility, especially among the intellectuals. Moreover, there were too many ambitious young men in the SLPP who challenged his authority and who had an eye on his office.
4　Corruption was rife. The civil service was unreliable; top civil servants leaked government secrets to the opposition, who gleefully seized upon them. Even a cabinet minister was found guilty of this act. Sir Albert also lacked sincere advisers.
5　His economic policies were conceived in haste and poorly executed.

In fairness to him, however, Sir Albert upheld the rule of law. As one of his ardent critics, Dr Sarif Easmon commented later, 'Sir Albert never declared a state of emergency to imprison his political opponents. He never had any of his friends or enemies hanged.'

11.3　Military rule

Following the arrest of Brigadier Lansana and Sir Albert, the officers set up a military junta – the National Reformation Council (NRC) – on 23 March 1967, with the following membership: Lieutenant-Colonel Andrew T. Juxon-Smith (Chairman), Commissioner of Police William Leigh (Deputy

Chairman), Majors A. C. Blake, S. B. Jumu, K. I. Kai-Samba, Abdul R. Turay and Assistant Commissioner of Police Alpha Kamara.

Juxon-Smith's first major move was to streamline the government ministries. He reduced the 14 ministries of the previous regime to nine departments. He took over the finance department while his deputy took charge of foreign affairs. Blake was in charge of trade, industry and agriculture; Kai-Samba works, transport and communications; S. B. Jumu health and Abdul R. Turay education; Alpha Kamara was responsible for social services.

The NRC proclaimed as its goals the ending of ethnic antagonisms, nepotism, corruption and the imposition of an austerity national budget. All political activity was made illegal and critical newspapers were silenced.

A National Advisory Council was set up and commissions were instituted to probe into certain issues. The Forster Commission enquired into the assets of ex-ministers and senior

Lieutenant-Colonel Juxon-Smith

civil servants. It met from May 1967 to February 1968. Its findings indicated that Sir Albert and his men had illegally used several thousand leones of state funds. They were ordered to pay it back.

The Dove-Edwin Commission, appointed to investigate corrupt electoral practices, submitted its report in September 1967. The findings emphasized that the SLPP had employed irregular means to win the elections, that the APC victory had been legitimate, and that Stevens's appointment as Prime Minister was valid. The commission also clarified the relationship between Paramount Chiefs and the central government. It stated that Paramount Chiefs were above party politics and that it was their bounden duty to support the government of the day.

The NRC leader ignored those sections of the report that were unfavourable to him, for example, the speedy return to civilian rule. He even accused the Commission chairman of partisanship when it became known that the latter had been one of those prominent people at State House who had pressurized the Governor-General to appoint Stevens as Prime Minister.

The delay in handing over power to civilians led to the formation of certain underground movements in and out of the country which aimed to overthrow the NRC. There were also open attacks on the regime by intellectuals and professional bodies like the Bar Association.

The NRC adopted some radical economic policies. These included the closing down of many uneconomic projects undertaken by the previous regime, the retrenchment of workers, levying more taxes on personal income and on diamond dealers and an austerity budget. These policies, although necessary, imposed heavy burdens on the populace, and resentment became widespread. A West German loan of Le 400 000 was secured for the Tonkolili-Kono Road project.

Meanwhile, those APC leaders and supporters who had gone to Guinea were busy training guerrillas to invade Sierra Leone. They were later joined by Siaka Stevens and Colonel John Bangura. These developments greatly worried the NRC leader and attempts to dissuade President Sekou Touré to expel the dissident group proved fruitless. In the circumstances, some NRC leaders decided to make arrangements for the return of civilian rule, if only to save their necks.

The rank and file of the army were also annoyed with the NRC leadership. They alleged that while their bosses lived in luxury and comfort, nothing was done to improve their own conditions. In the face of these difficulties, the privates, apparently under the influence of Colonel Bangura and other dissidents, decided to take matters in their own hands. So on the night of 17 April 1968 a 'Sergeants' Revolt', led by Private Morlai Kamara and Warrant Officer Patrick Conteh, overthrew the NRC. They formed the Anti-Corruption Revolutionary Movement (ACRM) and announced an immediate return to civilian rule.

A National Interim Council was created to oversee this process. Colonel Bangura was recalled to head the junta. The council also recalled the former Governor-General, Sir Henry Lightfoot-Boston, from leave. He did not come; instead Justice Banja Tejan-Sie was sworn in on 23 April as Acting Governor-General (his position was later confirmed).

The Acting Governor-General then invited all successful candidates in the 1967 general elections for consultations at State House on 26 April. Siaka Stevens was again appointed Prime Minister with Salia Jusu-Sheriff (the new SLPP leader) as his deputy. A national government was proposed with a cabinet of 15 made up as follows: APC six ministers, SLPP four, independents two and Paramount Chiefs three. But Siaka Stevens did not adhere to this arrangement. Thus, the national government was shortlived.

11.4 The Siaka Stevens regime

Siaka Stevens was a Limba and a trade unionist. He was born in Moyamba on 24 August 1905. After his secondary education he worked in the police force and later at the Marampa Mines, where he began his trade-union activities. He co-founded the United Mine Workers Union and for 15 years was secretary of the union.

He took a seat on the Protectorate Assembly and on the Freetown City Council as the Governor's nominee. His first really strategic appointment came with the Legislative Council in 1951 and he was subsequently made Minister of Lands, Mines and Labour.

When the PNP was formed in 1958, Stevens became its

Dr Siaka Stevens

Vice-President. He formed the APC party in 1960 after his refusal to sign the Independence documents in Britain. His party swept the polls in the 1967 elections, thereby becoming the first opposition party in post-colonial Africa to oust a ruling party through the ballot-box.

Stevens strengthens his position

A number of SLPP parliamentarians were unseated for alleged electoral malpractices, so it became necessary to hold by-elections. The APC, perhaps because it was now visibly in power, won a lot of seats in these elections, thereby increasing substantially its representation in Parliament. The elections were characterized by violence and intimidation.

Stevens also replaced some Mende military officers with Northerners. Colonel John Bangura was promoted Brigadier and Force Commander in May 1969. Stevens then promised to better the lot of the army.

. The economic situation offered little to celebrate. Stevens inherited a government that was heavily burdened with public debt. Personal property belonging to former Prime Minister, Sir Albert, and his colleagues in Sierra Leone was impounded in partial repayment of the fortunes they had amassed illegally. Arrangements were made with the IMF for standby loans and technical assistance in refinancing Sierra Leone's debts. Sierra Leone took 51 per cent ownership in the mining companies and negotiations were begun with SLST which resulted in the transfer in 1971 of its diamond-mining operations to the newly-formed National Diamond Mining Company (NDMC).

In spite of the severe economic problems facing the country, Stevens still thought it fit to order a fleet of armoured cars for the use of the army. He also created a second battalion in Teko near Makeni and a paramilitary force called the Internal Security Unit (ISU; later State Security Division, SSD).

Establishment of the republic

Many people had thought that the republican issue would die with the 1967 general elections. But they were mistaken, for barely a year after coming to power Siaka Stevens reopened discussions on the matter. The SLPP, now in opposition, argued that it was morally wrong for the APC to revive the issue. The opposition had its say while the APC had its way.

While the debate over the republican issue was going on, the leadership of the APC was temporarily torn apart in September 1970 when some of the party's top men such as Ibrahim Taqi (former Minister of Information), Mohamed S. Forna (Minister of Finance) and Mohamed O. Bash-Taqi (Minister of Development) quit the party. They accused Stevens of corruption and dictatorship. Stevens was then attending a Non-Aligned summit in Lusaka, Zambia. These men then joined the newly-formed National Democratic Party (NDP). NDP leaders aligned themselves with Dr John Karefa-Smart, an important political figure who had occupied a UN post in Geneva for several years, to found the United Democratic Party (UDP).

The bulk of this new group's support came from Freetown and the Northern Province, particularly from the Temne (most UDP leaders were Temne). This was a major threat to Stevens, for his major appeal throughout his political career had been to the Freetown community and the Temne. As soon as he returned from Zambia, Stevens declared a state of emergency. The UDP was accused of being financed by foreign interests to destabilize the country. The UDP's followers reacted with violence, staging attacks on APC offices and other government targets in the Northern Province and in Freetown.

The violence was suppressed, the UDP and its newspaper banned, and its leaders jailed. Some fled the country. On 13 October the government arrested 12 army men on the grounds of plotting a *coup*. The arrested officers were dismissed from the army. Parliament gave the Prime Minister emergency powers, including sweeping censorship and detention powers.

On 23 March 1971 an attempt was made on Stevens's life by a group of soldiers, including Brigadier John Bangura. Army personnel loyal to the government suppressed the revolt. Because the government had lost confidence in many of the military officers, Guinean troops were invited to Sierra Leone to help preserve peace. The rebellious Brigadier Bangura and others involved in the *coup* were hanged, in spite of Bangura's impassioned speech in which he recalled his long association with Stevens and the role he had played to ensure that Stevens became Prime Minister.

Shortly after the failed *coup* certain changes were made in the law which were followed by rapid moves to republican status on 19 April 1971.

The Governor-General had been forced to resign and so the Chief Justice, C. O. E. Cole, was immediately sworn in as the ceremonial president in accordance with the constitution. On 21 April, Stevens secured a simple majority in Parliament to change the ceremonial presidency to an executive office. He then became the first Executive President of Sierra Leone. Justice Cole reverted to his position as Chief Justice. S. I. Koroma, who was a founding member of the APC, became Prime Minister and Vice-President. The Constitution conferred enormous powers on the President. With the declaration of a republic and Siaka Stevens's ascendancy to the executive presidency, many of those intellectuals who had given their unqualified support to the APC began to lose confidence in Siaka Stevens and his party. Some became bitter critics of the APC government, but Stevens lost no time in silencing them.

General elections were scheduled for May 1973, under a state of emergency. At the close of nominations 46 APC candidates were returned unopposed, giving that party a majority in the House before elections ever took place. The SLPP then withdrew its candidates, professing fear of violence. The election campaign continued, but on polling day, the APC had all its candidates virtually returned unopposed.

Between 1973 and 1977 the APC was the only political party in Parliament. During this period two serious attempts were made to rock the APC foundation. In July 1974 some soldiers and civilians attempted to assassinate the new Prime Minister, C. A. Kamara-Taylor, by bombing his house. Twenty-two people were sentenced to death for the bombing, and the eight finally executed included ex-Brigadier David Lansana and two founding members of the banned UDP, Mohamed S. Forna and Ibrahim Taqi.

Then in February 1977 university and other students effectively challenged the APC hegemony in nationwide demonstrations that forced the government to call a general election. The SLPP contested the 1977 elections with a great determination, though under very unfavourable conditions. In the end the party won 15 out of 29 contested seats (APC candidates had again been returned unopposed in the other constituencies). Thus, the SLPP again became the official opposition in Parliament.

One-Partyism Several calls were again made (this time by APC stalwarts) to change the constitution and introduce a one-party state, as the only practicable way of eliminating the political violence which some people believed was inherent in the multi-party system. A further argument was that in a

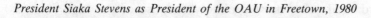

President Siaka Stevens as President of the OAU in Freetown, 1980

one-party state all hands would work together for the economic, political and social advancement of the nation. These were the same arguments put forward by the SLPP leadership in 1966.

These calls received a new impetus after the 1977 elections, with the coming back to Parliament of the SLPP. In June 1978, after a referendum, Sierra Leone became a one-party state. Under the new constitution Dr Siaka Stevens (he had been given honorary degrees by the universities of Sierra Leone and Lincoln in the USA) was given a seven-year term of office.

Stevens as a trade unionist had on occasions led strikes against the British colonial administration. In 1981 he was on the receiving end. His headache began in July when the Sierra Leone Labour Congress sent an eight-point memorandum to the Government calling for economic reforms. Congress officials, apparently under pressure from their union members, called for a nationwide peaceful strike on 1 September when it was realized that the Government was dragging its feet on the memorandum. By 3 September the strike had become so successful that on the following day President Stevens announced that 'any worker who does not report for duty tomorrow....will lose his or her job and steps are in hand to fill the vacancies thereby created'. The threat got the desired effect. Workers began drifting back to work to safeguard their jobs, most probably because of the high rate of unemployment, but no doubt with the hope that they would fight another day. Most Congress officials, including the Secretary-General, James Kabia, were rounded up and taken to Pademba Road Prisons. The *Tablet* newspaper, which for some years had embarrassed the Stevens regime with its incisive comments and exposés, was forced to go underground. Its editor, Pios Foray, then fled the country.

On 12 January 1984, Fourah Bay College students staged a demonstration which coincided with the official opening of the Eighth APC National Delegates' Conference held at the City Hall in Freetown. The students too were calling for major economic reforms. Unemployed youths took advantage of the situation to embark on wide-scale looting and destruction of property. The university was closed for eight weeks following the disturbances.

11.5 The New Order

Since the 1970s President Stevens had been talking about his retirement from public life. Delegations from the provinces and the Western Area would then 'plead with the Pa' to stay on. So when in late 1984 there were rumours that Stevens was going to retire and would be succeeded by an army officer, Major-General J. S. Momoh, few people believed it. Then Momoh began to accompany the President on his provincial tours in the President's attempt to show Momoh to the chiefs as his possible successor.

In July 1985 Parliament amended sections of the Constitution which effectively cleared the way for Momoh to contest the presidential election. And at a National Delegates' Conference at the Bintumani Hotel in early August, Stevens, who was 80, gave final notice that he would not stand for re-election when his extended term of office expired in December. Momoh was then elected Leader and Secretary-General of the APC. In the presidential election of 1 October in which he was the sole candidate, he had a landslide victory.

Why Momoh?

Alan Rake, a political correspondent for the *New African*, believes Stevens wanted Momoh to succeed him for three main reasons. Firstly, Stevens had lost confidence in his First Vice-President, S. I. Koroma, and therefore feared that if Koroma succeeded him, he (Stevens) could be put before a commission of enquiry to account for everything that had gone wrong during his 17-year rule.

Secondly, the President did not believe that any of the other APC old guard would make a good leader. If he left the party in the hands of a weak and incompetent leader, there would be much in-fighting and he would be blamed for this.

Thirdly, Stevens was concerned for his own and for national security. 'I don't want to be disgracefully carried out of power', he had told journalists a few days before the National Delegates' Conference. Stevens wanted a peaceful and stable transition of power in order to prevent a repetition of the Guinea *coup* after the death of Sekou Touré in 1984.

Perhaps a fourth reason was that Stevens convinced himself

President Momoh at the State Opening of Parliament, 1986

that in the existing circumstances, Major-General Momoh, with his strong military discipline, would be the most suitable person to put things back on their right course.

On 19 November the University of Sierra Leone awarded the Degree of Doctor of Civil Law (*honoris causa*) to President-Elect Momoh. Nine days later Major-General Dr Joseph Saidu Momoh was installed President of Sierra Leone at a colourful ceremony held in the chambers of Parliament. After reciting the oath of office in the presence of Chief Justice S. M. F. Kutubu, President Momoh was handed the gold and green staff representing the power and authority of the presidency by retiring President Stevens. Stevens thus again made history, as the first African leader to hand over a civilian-constituted government to an army head. This ushered in the 'New Order' as the new leader chose to call his regime.

Born on 26 January 1937 at Binkolo in the Bombali District to Limba parents, President Momoh attended the West African Methodist Collegiate School in Freetown before joining the West African Frontier Force as a private in 1958. He later took courses at the Nigerian Military Academy, Kaduna, where he won the baton of honour as the best cadet in 1962, and at the Mons Officer Cadet School in Aldershot, Britain, where the won the sword of honour for being the best overseas cadet in 1963. He was commissioned as a second lieutenant in the Sierra Leone Military Force later that year. He was appointed Commanding Officer of the First Battalion in 1971 and Force Commander 1972. Since then he had been awarded the Order of the Rokel and the Order of the British Empire. In 1974 he was appointed into Parliament and into the cabinet. He became the first Major-General in Sierra Leone's military history in 1983.

The new leader has inherited a number of difficult problems, some of which require urgent attention and draconian measures to solve. In his maiden speech, President Momoh expressed determination to work hard for a brighter tomorrow, not only in building on the foundations that have been laid but also breaking new ground. He promised to instill discipline into all aspects of Sierra Leonean life, cut out corruption, bribery, mismanagement, smuggling, hoarding of vital commodities, and tax evasion, and to resurrect the economy (including agriculture which has been totally neglected), and make all public corporations profitable.

In a very stern voice he emphasized the need for accountability and issued a warning to

those people who made it a habit to ignore stipulated rules and regulations by virtue of their standing or connection in society... as from this moment, their days have come to an end. Henceforth the question will not be 'who you are' but 'what you can do' In other words, as from today your recognition in society will be determined by the contribution you make to its welfare rather than by your assumed airs of arrogance.

Chronic problems such as shortage of rice, frequent power-cuts and inadequate transportation will receive immediate attention in the new order, he went on. He also disclosed that plans were underway to reorganize the civil service to make it more effective, review salary structures with an aim to increase them and ensure the prompt payment of salaries and wages.

He concluded by saying that Sierra Leone can no longer continue to accept a situation in which its resources are exploited only to benefit foreign countries. He called on foreign companies to identify themselves with the aims and aspirations of the new order and to respect and observe its rules and regulations. He reaffirmed his active participation in all organizations of which Sierra Leone was a member and promised to stand by oppressed peoples the world over.

If the President is able to achieve his objectives, he will have done a great service to his country.

An assessment of the Siaka Stevens regime

Siaka Stevens ruled Sierra Leone for 17 years and throughout this period he was firmly in control, despite a few setbacks. One of his greatest achievements was that he was largely able to unite the country. He was himself the symbol of this unity, for he never closely associated himself with any single group. He claimed to belong to varous ethnic groups by birth, marriage or otherwise.

He was an extremely lucky man who knew when to take crucial decisions. He survived an assassination attempt in 1971 and another attempt to overthrow his regime in 1974. Stevens used such incidents to tighten his grip on the country. A republican constitution was rushed through Parliament soon after the assassination attempt and Stevens assumed the executive presidency. The failed *coup* provided the driving force for the adoption of a one-party state in 1978.

In a further attempt to consolidate his rule, Stevens established clientist relations with potentially powerful opposition groups such as the labour unions and the academic staff of the University, although he had less success with the students. He got the University dons to confer on him the degree of Doctor of Civil Law and in January 1973 he was installed Chancellor of the University of Sierra Leone.

Compared to many African leaders, Stevens was not a very violent man. State-organized violence was slight during his era and occurred mostly at election periods. But he did not hesitate to imprison opponents, striking at labour leaders and students, investigative journalists and other critics, if only for short periods of time.

Stevens was a skilful manipulator who exploited the weaknesses and divisions among his supporters and opposition elements to political advantage. For example, he took advantage of the squabbles in the SLPP hierarchy to wreck that party. He brought one of the SLPP leaders, Francis Minah, together with his followers, into the APC. Minah was given the lucrative post of Trade and Industry Minister. He later became Second Vice-President in Stevens's government.

Stevens used state resources lavishly to maintain himself in power. Special privileges were extended to the armed forces to keep them quiet. For example, they were usually the first to be paid at the end of the month and were assured of regular rice supply at heavily subsidized rates. He also appointed the heads of the army and the police into Parliament and into the cabinet. He regularly dished out large sums of money to his supporters.

Stevens tolerated a high degree of corruption. He himself amassed a lot of wealth and was always desirous to have more. The economy suffered heavily during his era. However, some attempt was made to improve the infrastructure, and some roads and bridges were constructed.

Stevens always ensured that his policies brought material gains. They were also geared towards his political survival. For example, the APC had proclaimed itself as a socialist party, thereby creating the impression that it cared for the ordinary man. But it hardly cared. When Communist China promised to offer more aid than the Taiwanese, he threw the latter out. Stevens allowed Sierra Leone to join the Islamic Council not necessarily because the majority of Sierra Leoneans were Muslim, but because there were greater opportunities to be exploited.

His regime made nonsense of the electoral system, for elections were always rigged in favour of his party. Stevens did not also show a high regard for the constitution which he always manipulated to suit his own ends.

Stevens was a conservative leader who had little admiration for radical and military regimes, especially those led by young soldiers like Flight-Lieutenant Jerry Rawlings of Ghana. He preferred to work with older conservative rulers like Sir Dauda Jawara of the Gambia or Felix Houphouët-Boigny of the Ivory Coast.

That Stevens could cling to power for so long and then set up his political disengagement without violence as happens in most Third World countries clearly demonstrated that he was adept in political manoeuvring.

Siaka Stevens died on 29 May 1988 and was given a state funeral.

Foreign policy

Sierra Leone's foreign policy since independence has been based on the principle of non-alignment. She is a member of UNO and of the Commonwealth and was a signatory to the Charter of the OAU. She is also a member of the UN Economic Comission for Africa, and of the African, Caribbean and Pacific (ACP) states. For the most part, she maintains a principle of non-interference in the internal affairs of other countries and respects each state's sovereignty and territorial integrity. In spite of her small size and limited resources, Sierra Leone wields tremendous influence both in UNO and in the OAU. She has served on the Economic and Social Council, the Security Council and on several committees including the Committee on Peace-keeping Operations. She lends her full weight to the liberation movements in southern Africa and was one of the observer countries appointed by the Commonwealth Secretariat to ensure free and fair elections in Zimbabwe in 1980.

At the request of the OAU, Sierra Leone was host to an Ad Hoc Mediation Commission in Freetown in December 1977, to look into the dispute between Sudan and Ethiopia. A follow-up meeting was held in Freetown in February 1979. These meetings went a long way towards lessening the tension between the two states. Between July 1980 and June 1981 Sierra Leone's President Stevens was Chairman of the OAU.

To give meaning to her policy of neutrality and non-alignment, Sierra Leone's representation abroad is diversified.

Missions have been established in several countries including the People's Republic of China, the Soviet Union, the USA, Saudi Arabia and Egypt. At the regional level Sierra Leone has cooperated with her neighbours and other countries in the sub-region. Sierra Leone is a member of the Economic Community of West African States (ECOWAS), Mano River Union (MRU) and several other sub-regional organizations such as the Federation of West African Chambers of Commerce and the West African Conference of Surgeons. In addition, she holds several bilateral agreements with states in the sub-region.

The Mano River Union

Sierra Leone and Liberia have a combined population of less than six million. Their economic output is also relatively weak. As a result, the governments of the two countries had long felt the need to forge some kind of cooperation to facilitate the economic development of their respective countries. Initial attempts at economic cooperation in the mid 1960s were frustrated by the unfavourable political climate in Sierra Leone. However, the issue of bilateral cooperation between Sierra Leone and Liberia was revived in 1971. A

The Mano River Union Bridge

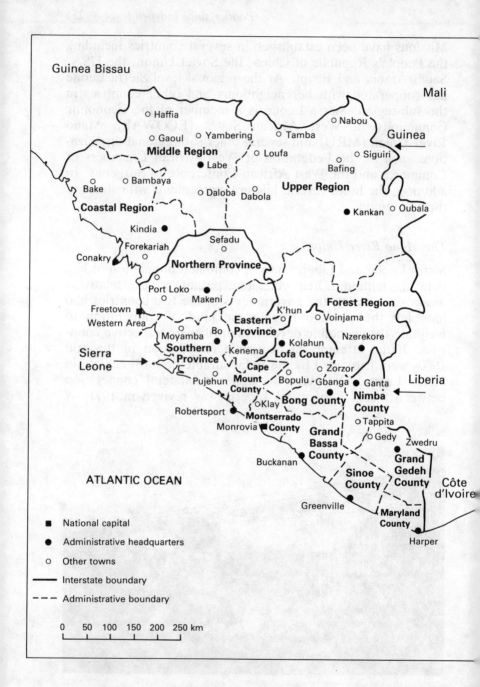

Guinea Bissau

Mali

Guinea

○ Haffia

○ Nabou

○ Gaoul   ○ Yambering   ○ Tamba

Middle Region   ○ Loufa   ○ Siguiri

● Labe   Bafing

○ Bambaya   **Upper Region**

Bake   ○ Daloba Dabola

Coastal Region   ● Kankan   ○ Oubala

○ Kindia   ○ Sefadu

○ Forekariah

Conakry ■   **Northern Province**

○ Port Loko   ● Makeni

Freetown ■   **Forest Region**

Western Area   ○ K'hun   ○ Voinjama

Eastern

○ Moyamba   ● Bo **Province**   ● Nzerekore

Sierra   ● Kenema ● Kolahun

Southern   **Lofa County**

Leone →   **Province**

○ Pujehun **Cape**   ○ Zorzor   **Liberia**

Mount ○ Bopulu · Gbanga ● Ganta ←

○ Klay **County**   **Nimba**

Robertsport ●   **Bong County**   **County**

Monrovia ■ **Montserrado**   ○ Tappita

County **Grand**

Bassa   ○ Gedy   Zwedru

Buckanan ● **County**   **Grand**

Gedeh

Sinoe **County**

County   **Côte**

ATLANTIC OCEAN   **d'Ivoire**

Greenville ●

Maryland

County

Harper

■ National capital

● Administrative headquarters

○ Other towns

─── Interstate boundary

- - - Administrative boundary

0   50 100 150 200 250 km

15   Mano River Union States: Sierra Leone, Liberia and Guinea

[252]

series of joint ministerial council meetings in Monrovia and Freetown led to the formation of a customs union in 1973. The declaration establishing the Union was signed by President William Tolbert of Liberia and President Siaka Stevens of Sierra Leone at Malema, a small town on the Mano River in Sierra Leone, on 3 October 1973. The Union was named after the Mano River, which forms the border between Sierra Leone and Liberia. The Mano River Union declaration emphasized the importance of extending economic cooperation within Africa. A Union Secretariat was established in Freetown and certain organs were also created to implement the Union's programmes. These were:

(a)   The Union Ministerial Council, comprising ministers of both states responsible for planning, finance, education, trade, industry, agriculture, transport, communications, power and works.

(b)   The Union Standing Committee, comprising key officials of the two governments.

(c)   Five Union Sub-committees responsible for
  (i) trade and industry;
  (ii) agriculture, forestry and fisheries;
  (iii) transport, communications and power;
  (iv) finance and administration;
  (v) education, training and research.
The Sub-committees consisted of senior professional officials of both governments.

(d)   Working groups as are found necessary to give expert detailed information and formulate recommendations.

(e)   Liaison officers appointed for specific projects.

As part of its programme for the development of infrastructure, the MRU built a bridge over the Mano River in 1976, which linked the two countries and reduced the journey from Freetown to Monrovia by 300 miles (481 km). In that same year it was agreed that locally-manufactured products from either member state would qualify for freedom of movement in the other, free of customs duties or quota restrictions. A harmonized protective policy to help local producers against outside imports was put into force in 1978.

The MRU declaration had made provision for other countries in the West African sub-region to join the MRU if they so desired. Thus, Guinea became a member on 25 October

1980. Shortly after, the Union felt the need to streamline its organs into three divisions in addition to the Office of the Secretary-General, so that the Union's programmes could be more effectively carried out. The new divisions were Development Planning, Project Implementation and Management and Administration, and Finance. The Secretariat was also reorganized. The original declaration had provided for the appointment of a Secretary-General by Liberia and a Deputy Secretary-General by Sierra Leone. With Guinea's accession, some amendments were made. The Secretary-Generalship would now rotate between Liberia and Guinea and there would be two Deputy Secretaries-General, one responsible for technical services and the other for administration and finance.

Achievements of the MRU   There has been some development in intra-union trade. Some 25 Liberian enterprises and 49 products have so far participated in the trade; in Sierra Leone 30 enterprises and 62 products, and in Guinea 11 enterprises and 26 products. In 1983 alone the value of trade by Sierra Leone to Liberia was estimated at 722 519 US dollars, while that of Liberia to Sierra Leone was estimated at 54 328 US dollars and the trade from Liberia to Guinea was estimated at 75 000 US dollars. A Customs Training School has been established in Monrovia.

A number of industries have been identified for implementation at Union levels. These include a cassava processing plant, a salt-refinery project, a pharmaceuticals-projects industry, and integrated fruit juices and jam industry and a glass-containers factory, using local materials. In agriculture there has been close cooperation between the produce marketing boards of the member countries. They regularly exchange information on sale prices, operational costs, export orders, and so on. A land resources survey of the Mano River Basin is in progress. It is hoped that such a survey would help in the integrated development of the basin by member states. Agreement has also been reached on the location of the forest-training, silvicultural research, wood-utilization research and forest-workers' training programmes.

The Mano River Bridge and six miles of approach on each side of the bridge have been constructed and a MRU postal union has been established. Training of middle-level man-power in the fields of communication and ports, forestry, marine and customs, excise and trade statistics has begun.

Financial and technical assistance for most of the projects has come from UN agencies such as UNDP, UNCTAD, UNIDO, FAO, and from ITU, the EEC, West Germany, the United Kingdom and the USA.

Problems The successes outlined above notwithstanding, the MRU is faced with numerous problems which have made it very difficult for the union to realize most of its objectives. Traders plying the Freetown–Monrovia and Freetown–Conakry highways are subjected to harassment at the numer-ous checkpoints along the routes, the freight charges are high and certain sections of the highways are impassable during the rainy season. There is massive smuggling of goods from non-member countries, that are similar to and compete with pro-ducts of local origin in the Union markets. The production capacities of the member states are also very low. Further-more, there is absence of an effective project implemen-tation capacity within the Union Secretariat, to translate feasibility studies into viable projects. And there is no region-al industrial development bank or fund to facilitate the mobilization of financial resources within the member states.

The Union is also faced with serious financial problems. Contributions of member states to the Union's budget are irregularly paid and some members still have arrears which are quite outstanding. Then there are the political problems. The Liberian *coup* of April 1980, in which one of the founding fathers of the MRU was killed, adversely affected the smooth running of the Union. For a long time President Stevens was unprepared to recognize Samuel Doe as President of Liberia. As a result it became extremely difficult for the Union's leaders to meet. Liberia also harboured ill-feelings against the Sierra Leone Government when it was learnt that Sierra Leo-neans participated in a *coup* to topple the government of President Doe in November 1985. The Liberia–Sierra Leone border has been closed many times because of these unfortun-ate developments. All these have slowed down the early im-petus towards economic union. It is hoped, however, that this impetus will be restored.

References

Africa Now, October 1981.

Cartwright, John (1978), *Political Leadership in Sierra Leone* (Toronto, Canada).

Clifford, Mary L. (1974), *The Land and People of Sierra Leone* (New York).

Collier, Gershon (1970), *Sierra Leone: Experiment in Democracy in an African Nation* (New York).

Cox, Thomas S. (1976), *Civil–Military Relations in Sierra Leone* (Harvard, USA).

Deveneaux, Gustav (1983), *Power Politics in Sierra Leone* (AUP, Nigeria).

Fashole-Luke, David (1988), 'Continuity in Sierra Leone: from Stevens to Momoh', *Third World Quarterly*, Vol. 10, no. 1 Jan. 1988 (London).

Fisher, H. J. (1969), 'Elections and Coups in Sierra Leone', JMAS, VII.

Foray, C. P. (1977), *Historical Dictionary of Sierra Leone* (Metuchen, New Jersey).

GIS (1961), *Sierra Leone: An Illustrated Souvenir of the Birth of a New Nation* (Freetown).

Lavalie, A. M. (1983), 'The SLPP – A Study of the Political History of the Sierra Leone People's Party with Particular Reference to the Period 1968–1978', MA (USL).

Mansaray, F. B. L. (1977), 'The Growth of the Mano River Union', The African Association for Public Administration and Management.

New African, October 1985 (IC Publications, London).

Report of the Dove-Edwin Commission of Inquiry into the Conduct of the 1967 General Elections (Freetown, 1967).

Report of the Forster Commission of Inquiry on the Assets of Ex-Ministers and Ex-Deputy Ministers (Freetown, 1968).

Stevens, Siaka (1984), *What Life Has Taught Me* (Kensal Press, England).

Taylor, Richard (1973), 'Sierra Leone, What Next?' *Africa*, 20 April.

Turay E. D. A. and Arthur Abraham (1987), *The Sierra Leone Army: A Century of History* (Macmillan).

Webster J. B. et al. (1980), *The Revolutionary Years: West Africa Since 1800* (Longman).

West Africa, 2 and 9 December 1985.

Questions PART A

1 'His place in history has been assured.' Do you think Sir Milton Margai deserves this praise?

2 Why did the APC win the 1967 general elections?

3 Why did Sir Albert fall from power in 1967?

4 What led to the formation of the NRC in 1967 and how did its rule come to an end?

5 What major political problems did Sierra Leone face between 1961 and 1971?

6 What problems did the APC government face from 1968 to 1971 and how were these problems overcome?

7 How and why did Sierra Leone become a republic in 1971?

8   Outline the reasons for the decline of the SLPP between 1964 and 1978.
9   Why did Sierra Leone become a one-party state in 1978?
10 What did Dr Siaka Stevens achieve for Sierra Leone?
11 Why was the Mano River Union formed in 1973 and what has it achieved since its formation?
12 Describe some of the problems facing the Mano River Union.

Questions PART B

1   'Sir Milton was a conservative ruler whose term of office brought few political innovations.' How far do you agree with this statement?
2   'Sir Albert was an enlightened leader whose policies were, however, misinterpreted by certain wicked people in order to discredit him.' Do you agree?
3   'Sir Albert's downfall came largely from within his own party.' Elaborate on this statement.
4   To what extent was Sir Albert responsible for his downfall?
5   Was the NRC a legal government?
6   'Certain flaws in the 1961 Independence Constitution paved the way for the ascendancy of the military to power in 1967.' Discuss.
7   To what extent has ethnicity affected Sierra Leone politics since independence?
8   'Man is a brute and it is only brute force that he understands.' To what extent did Siaka Stevens use brute force during his tenure of office as Prime Minister and later as President of Sierra Leone?
9   'President Stevens exploited the weaknesses and divisions among his supporters and opposition elements to political advantage.' Elaborate on this statement.
10 Discuss the view that President Stevens was not influenced by any remote intellectualism in his approach to politics.
11 Make an assessment of the Siaka Stevens regime.

12 Social, cultural and economic developments since independence

12.1 Social developments

Education

Educational facilities expanded greatly after independence. Primary and secondary education became more readily available to all sections of the country. The primary school curriculum was reformed to make it more relevant to the needs of society. Technical assistance for the programme was secured from the United Nations Development Programme (UNDP) and UNESCO. The International Development Association (IDA) also provided funds and technical assistance to rehabilitate some secondary schools and revise syllabuses in science, mathematics, English and social science.

Two technical institutes (one in Freetown and another in Kenema) and three craft centres – Kissy and Magburaka Trade Centres and Opportunities Industrialization Centre (OIC) in Bo – were also built. They train skilled craftsmen and artisans. The Roman Catholic mission recently established a male vocational centre in Lunsar.

Two private institutions – the Young Women's Christian Association (YWCA) Vocational Institute in Freetown and St Mary's Vocational Institute in Bo – train women and girls in home science, catering, commercial subjects, and so on. There are also specialized in-service or pre-service training arrangements in some government ministries and large companies such as NDMC.

The nine teachers' colleges were consolidated into six colleges in the late 1960s for reasons of economy and more effective use of their training staff. Five of these colleges prepare teachers for primary schools. They include Freetown, Port Loko, Makeni, Bo and Bunumbu teachers' colleges. The sixth institution is Milton Margai Teachers' College which prepares teachers for the lower forms of secondary schools. The training of teachers for the upper secondary forms and most teachers of technical subjects in secondary schools is carried out at Fourah Bay College and Njala University College.

The Institute of Education was set up in 1968. It coordinates the activities of the teacher training colleges and organizes in-service courses for teachers.

Njala Training College was upgraded to university status in 1964. Njala and Fourah Bay became constituent colleges of the University of Sierra Leone in 1972. A University Secretariat was then created and headed by a full-time Vice-Chancellor. A College of Medicine was established in April

Fourah Bay College

1988; it then became the third constituent college of the University of Sierra Leone.

Four schools for the physically handicapped, all primary schools, have been established. These include two Cheshire homes and schools for the deaf and for the blind. Children completing the course of instruction in any of these schools go on to regular secondary schools. SOS children's villages have also been built in Freetown and Bo.

Adult education has been promoted largely by non-governmental organizations (NGOs) such as the German Adult Education Association (DVV), People's Educational Association (PEA), Canadian Universities Service Overseas (CUSO), Christian Extension Services (CES), Sierra Leone Adult Education Association (SLADEA), and the Provincial Literature Bureau and Bunumbu Press in Bo.

Health and social facilities

A National Health Plan came into force in the early 1960s. The plan called for, among other things, a rapid expansion of medical services and the training of ancillary staff. The main hospitals in Freetown and Bo were to be improved to serve as the foundation of a system of rural hospitals in each of the district headquarters. Each chiefdom was to be provided with a health centre. Further, the Endemic Diseases Control Unit was to intensify its work in the treatment of sleeping-sickness, yaws and leprosy.

This plan was revised in 1975. Provision was again made for the improvement of the quantity and quality of health services in the country.

The government hoped to recruit more doctors and train more nurses at the National School of Nursing. This school, set up in Freetown, began preparing male and female nurses for certificates of State Registered Nurse and of State Enrolled Nurse in December 1969. The school's curriculum was to include courses in maternal and child health. More sanitary inspectors, laboratory technicians, and endemic diseases control assistants were to be trained. The health infrastructure was to be expanded by putting up and equipping more hospitals, dispensaries and health centres, and by the provision of more vehicles and medicines. Greater efforts were to be made to control communicable diseases and malaria and to intensify the immunization of pregnant mothers, infants and young children. Rural water supply and sanitation schemes were to be embarked upon to control the high rate of water-borne diseases such as dysentery and cholera. A Paramedical School was opened in Bo in 1982 and a Department of Community Health set up at Fourah Bay College in 1984 to train community health officers and community health nurses.

The role of NGOs

Although health services are primarily a function of government, considerable health work is carried out by NGOs, such as the Peace Corps, Catholic Relief Services (CRS), Cooperative for American Relief Everywhere (CARE), and church missions and organizations. They work closely with the newly created Ministry of Rural Development, Social Services and Youth in implementing community development projects.

Projects undertaken include construction of access roads and bridges, schools, social centres, pit latrines and digging of wells. Family nutrition programmes are planned for the welfare of children, pregnant and nursing mothers. Mobile under-five clinics are run in conjunction with the Ministry of Health and CRS, and demonstrations of general hygiene and sanitation are carried out in homes and villages.

The Rural Development Ministry also runs approved schools and remand homes in addition to the King George VI Memorial Home for Paupers, and the Farmcraft Training Centre for the Blind at Kenema. It has a National Training Centre in Bo for the training of rural and social workers.

Pipe-borne water facilities have been extended to some major towns. In Freetown the Guma Valley Dam was completed in the mid-1960s with a reservoir covering 250 acres and yielding 19.25 million gallons (87 395 000 litres) daily. An agreement was reached with the French Government which made it possible for the Degremont Water Company to construct pipe-borne water systems in many provincial towns. However, many of these have long since ceased to function.

In spite of the efforts made by the government and NGOs to improve health facilities in the country, the situation is still far from satisfactory. Drugs have become so prohibitively expensive that the majority of the people can no longer afford them. More infants are dying at present than was the case during the first few years of independence largely because the government has not paid greater attention to primary health care.

Electricity supply has been extended to all the provincial district headquarter towns. The Kingtom Power Station, which supplies the bulk of the Western Area's electricity, was completed in 1965. The nation's power will receive a major boost when the hydroelectric station being constructed at Bumbuna, on the fringes of the eastern highlands, comes into operation. A mini-station at Dodo, near Panguma, was completed in 1985. It supplies electricity to Kenema and Bo town.

Recreational facilities are provided largely under the auspices of the Education and Cultural Affairs Ministry. In the late 1970s the Chinese built a modern stadium at Brookfields to facilitate sporting activities particularly among the Freetown population.

A major feature of the Government's policy of self-reliance was the institution of self-help schemes all over the country. These community projects provided additional infrastructural amenities. The Maforki Scheme, which was inspired and sponsored by Vice-President S. I. Koroma, resulted in a 74-bed extension to the Port Loko Hospital and the erection of a large community centre. The 700-foot (214 m) former railway bridge at Daru was converted for motor-traffic through self-help.

12.2 Cultural developments

During the colonial era certain white missionaries and colonial officials had made efforts to discourage Sierra Leoneans from practising their culture. The former had wrongly believed that African culture generally was inferior to Western culture and was also anti-Christian. But they never really succeeded in wiping out African culture, for culture is an integral part of man's existence. There are no peoples without culture and as long as people exist they will also always practise their culture.

With the dawn of political independence in 1961, the indigenous Sierra Leone Government began to promote the country's cultural heritage. To this end a National Dance

The Siaka Stevens Stadium, Freetown

In traditional costume, a dancer celebrates Moslem New Year in Port Loko

Troupe was established which, within a relatively short time, became the pride of many. The troupe, under the dynamic leadership of John Akar, who was also Director of the Sierra Leone Broadcasting Service, won several laurels at international fairs. It has continued to thrill many visitors to Sierra Leone.

Music

Sierra Leone has a very rich and varied music, and prominent traditional musicians can still be found all over the country. These include Mende artists like Salia Koroma (who is the most famous Sierra Leone accordionist in living memory), Boi Nancy Koroma and Isatta Nyambae, the Temne *kondi* player Bassie, the Koranko *siraman* player Manti Nyankume Kabba and the Krio comedian Chris During. Ebenezer Calender, who died in 1985, was well-known for his *maringa* and later *milo* music, and so was Ali Ganda (he died in 1964) who was crowned 'West Africa's Calypso King' in the late 1950s. Ali Ganda's Independence calypso, 'Freedom, Sierra Leone' reflected the joy and happiness about the new freedom achieved by Sierra Leoneans.

The blossoming of Sierra Leone music in the period after independence was significantly aided by the existence of a number of recording studios in Freetown. Among them were Daramola with its MOOLA label, Penaphone, Attalah, Rogiephone and Zachariah (this one was based in Bo). But Jonathan Adenuga's Nugatone and the Bahsoon's Bassophone were the most successful ones.

The wave of Afro-American soul music which swept across many countries in the 1960s may have influenced the formation of popular soul dance bands in Sierra Leone, the first major one being Geraldo Pino and the Heartbeats. Others included the crowd-pullers Super Combo Kings, Afro National, Sabanoh 75 and Ochestre Muyei. The Military Dance Band, which for a number of years was headed by 'Big Fayia', was especially popular in the provinces for its native songs. S. E. Rogers's was a 'one-man band'.

Literature and drama

The non-existence of publishing houses in Sierra Leone has to a very large extent affected the growth of its written literature. Nevertheless, some effort has been made by interested individuals and organizations to produce materials for the general public. In 1971 the broadcaster, actor and journalist Ulisa Pat Maddy came out with *Obasai and other Plays*. In the area of oral literature the PEA has done tremendous work in collecting stories and songs, riddles and proverbs. Their most ambitious project, *Fishing in Rivers of Sierra Leone*, which contained some 125 entries from 13 ethnic groups in the country, was published in 1987.

A number of theatre groups have also been formed. Many of their plays are acted in Krio so that they can attract a very large audience. These plays are generally comedies, though a few venture to attack some of the ills in society. Dele Charley's *Tabule Tiata* represented Sierra Leone at the Second World Black and African Festival of Arts and Culture (FESTAC) in Lagos, Nigeria in 1977 with *The Blood of a Stranger*, and in 1983 presented Ray de Souza George's *Borbor Lef* at the London International Festival of Theatre 'LIFT 83'.

In the mid-1970s the Ministry of Education introduced an annual cultural gala in the schools and colleges which aimed at interesting the youth in their country's culture. This gala became known as the Schools and Colleges Arts Festival (SCAFA). The festival became very popular, especially dur-

Craft centre, Freetown

ing the first few years of its foundation. In 1986 the Institute of African Studies, Fourah Bay College, began a diploma course in cultural studies.

Art and craft

Small-scale art and craft centres have developed especially in the urban areas, and these cater mostly for foreign visitors. Sierra Leoneans like Miranda Burney Nicol, who paints as Olayinka, Phoebe Ageh Jones, John Vandi, Hassan Bangura, Idriss Koroma and Marco Conteh have had their works widely distributed abroad. A traditional craft that has also been given fresh vitality is the gara-dyeing of cloths.

12.3   Economic developments

Minerals

Bauxite and rutile have been added to the list of exploitable minerals. The Sierra Leone Ore and Metal Company (SIEROMCO) started bauxite mining operations in 1963 on the Mokanji Hills in Moyamba District. By 1969 this company was exporting 435 000 tons of ore valued at Le380 160. The Sherbro Minerals Limited (later Sierra Rutile Mining Company) began rutile production in May 1967 around Gbang-bama in the Moyamba and Bonthe districts. In that same year 19 000 tons were exported. This figure began to rise steadily when it was established that Sierra Leone had the largest known reserves of rutile in the world. Gold mining has been re-started in many places in the Northern Province.

Industry and commerce

The Government initiated certain measures in an attempt to encourage the rapid development of manufacturing industries. These measures were as follows:

  (i) issuance of a non-nationalization policy statement;
 (ii) enactment of the Development Act of 1960;
(iii) establishment of an industrial estate;
 (iv) increased governmental participation in industrial undertakings; and
  (v) creation of Sierra Leone Investments Limited.

The Government made it clear that it had no intention of nationalizing any form of commercial mining or industrial undertaking, but that in the event of such occurrence a fair compensation would be paid.

A Development Act also stipulated that companies wishing to invest in Sierra Leone would be allowed to import or buy in Sierra Leone duty-free all the equipment they might need for the mine or factory, or pay reduced customs duties on raw or semi-processed materials required by the mine or factory. A lot of investors seized the opportunity to open small industries, especially in Freetown.

A further inducement to investors was the creation of an industrial estate at Wellington in the Greater Freetown area. It was equipped with water, electricity, transportation services, banking facilities and so forth. The plots were rented from the Government for a nominal fee. Factories located at Wellington produced a whole range of consumer goods including cigarettes, confectionery, rum, wine, beer and soap.

Two separate loan schemes were also established by the Government in an effort to attract investors. The first was the Development of Industries Board (created in 1947 but given more weight after independence) to serve the credit needs of wholly-African enterprises. The Government and the Commonwealth Development Corporation (CDC) established Sierra Leone Investments Limited (SIL) in 1961. It lent money to companies only. SIL funds were used to build a flour mill, a tyre-retreading factory, a plastics firm and a palm-kernel processing mill in Freetown. A furniture factory was established at Kenema.

In 1983 a new Development of Industries Act replaced the 1960 Act. The main features of this new Act included greater participation of the Trade and Industry Ministry in the identification and formulation of industrial projects.

The Government established some economic projects. A National Trading Company was set up in Freetown in 1971. It imported essential consumer commodities for local distribution at reasonable prices. It had branches in the provincial headquarter towns.

The former Railway Workshops at Cliné Town were converted into a viable National Workshop for the production of tools. It offered mechanical engineering services to local government institutions, local industries and ships.

The Sierra Leone National Shipping Company was formed in 1972 for clearing and forwarding of cargo. It bought two vessels a few years later.

A Sierra Bricks Factory was located at Kissy in 1976 for the manufacture of bricks for domestic building purposes. The Bennimix factory in Bo produced infant food from locally-grown benniseed. In 1979 the Mabole Fruit Company was opened near Makeni for the production of fruit juice, jam and marmalade.

With the help of the United States Peace Corps Volunteers, the government established the Tikonko Agricultural Extension Centre at Bo in the 1970s for the manufacture of a range of locally designed farm implements and equipment.

Air transport   Massive improvements were made at Lungi Airport and in 1969 it reached international Class A standard. The nation's airline – Sierra Leone Airways – operated a domestic network from Hastings to Bo, Kenema, Yengema, Kabala, Gbangbatoke and Bonthe, in addition to its international flights.

Agriculture

The agricultural economy has continued to absorb some three-quarters of the adult population and to provide about 20 per cent of the country's exports. The main exports are still cacao, coffee, palm kernels, ginger and piassava. Rice, cassava, millet, maize and tobacco are grown, but mainly for home consumption. To boost agricultural production, the IDA and other international agencies have been giving several million US dollarsworth of credit to help finance integrated agricultural development projects in several areas of the country. Mechanical farming has been introduced in some areas.

Under a technical cooperation agreement with the Republic of China (Taiwan) a Chinese technical mission successfully demonstrated a multiple cropping system for rice production, whereby it is now possible to grow two or even three crops of rice a year with yields averaging 1.5 to 2.5 tons per acre.

The role of the SLPMB   After independence the SLPMB continued to be the main exporter of agricultural produce. This was done through a network of buying agents, transport, storage and packing facilities.

The SLPMB floated two companies in the late 1970s – the National Agricultural Produce Company (NAPCO) and the Sierra Leone Agricultural Production Company (SLAPCO). NAPCO trades in export crops and domestic staples and operates through a network of buying centres. It also serves as liaison between the SLPMB and other agro-based institutions. SLAPCO aimed at developing some five units of 3 000 acres of tree crops, mainly coffee and cacao estates. To date, it has developed a plantation of nearly 2 000 acres of coffee and cacao in Gaura Chiefdom, Kenema District.

The Government established two large oil-palm plantations and mills at Gambia (Mattru Jong) in 1968 and at Daru (Kailahun District) two years later. Two privately-owned plantations and mills were located in Port Loko and Mobai (Kailahun District) in the 1970s. They were owned by former Vice-President S. I. Koroma and Dr M. B. Kobba (a medical practitioner who is keenly interested in rural development), respectively. The government plantations and mills were privatized in the mid-1980s.

Government also established a sugar-cane plantation at Magbass in the Tonoklili District in the 1980s mainly with funds from the Chinese (Communist) government.

A mechanized fishing industry – Fish Products Limited – was started in Freetown in 1963. Presently, the industry, under the name of Sierra Fisheries Limited, is jointly being run by the Sierra Leone Government and the Government of the Soviet Union. It exports fish and shrimps to many Western countries. A number of private companies are also engaged in the fish trade.

Financial institutions

The Bank of Sierra Leone was created in 1963 to perform the following functions:

  (i) to issue legal currency in Sierra Leone and maintain external reserves in order to safeguard the international value of the leone;

 (ii) to act as banker and financial adviser to the government; and

(iii) to promote monetary stability and a sound financial structure.

16 *Integrated Agricultural Development Project Areas (IAPP) aimed at maximising agricultural production and improving the living standards of people in the provincial areas. Farmers were to be given credit to buy seeds, fertilisers and farming equipment. They were also to be advised on improved farming methods. The projects also involved the construction of access roads, markets, wells and storage facilities for the farming communities.*

   The Eastern IADP included large oil palm, cacao and coffee plantations. It assisted farmers to plant some 12000 acres of swamp rice.

[270]

The Bank issued its own notes and coins for the first time on 4 August 1964.

A National Development Bank (NDB) was set up in 1968 to extend financial and technical assistance to private enterprises which were economically viable and likely to make significant contributions to economic development. Other financial institutions created since independence include the government-owned Sierra Leone Commercial Bank and many insurance companies such as the National Insurance Company (NIC) and Transworld Insurance Company. The NIC was the first indigenous insurance company; it aimed at mobilizing funds for development purposes.

Some encouragement has been given to the tourist industry. A Hotel and Tourist Board was set up to cater for tourist attractions, from the ancient relics in the national museum to the scenic beauties of the many beaches near Freetown. New, imposing hotels such as the Cape Sierra Hotel, Hotel Bintumani, and Hotel Mammy Yoko have also been built along the beaches to attract tourists and other foreign visitors.

12.4 Some factors affecting rapid economic development

1 Sierra Leone has depended too much on mineral wealth, and the minerals are nearing exhaustion. The mining companies pay small royalties to the Government. This, cou-

---

The Northern IADP concentrated on rice and cattle. Provision was also made for the construction of 300 miles (480 km) of access roads, 200 wells and five market centres.

The Koinadugu IADP was directed mainly towards the cultivation of cassava, rice, vegetables and fruits, the integration of animal and poultry husbandry with crop production on small farms and forest conservation and afforestation.

The Moyamba IADP aimed to developed inland valley swamps as well as constructing access roads and other infrastructure and upgrading health facilities and water supplies in the region.

The Magbosi IADP focused on the reclamatin of swamp land and on road and irrigation improvements in the area.

The Bo/Pujehun Rural Development Project concentrated on providing primary health-care facilities, building of classroom blocks, community halls and access roads. It also offered various forms of technical and financial assistance to farmers in the Bo and Pujehun districts.

pled with illicit mining and smuggling, have deprived the Government of substantial revenue.

2 Agricultural development has not been given the serious attention it deserves. Mechanized farming is done on a small scale. The integrated agricultural development projects introduced since 1972 have been so badly managed that most of them have been closed down. The financial institutions are unwilling to give credit to farmers. Food production is very low and government has regularly had to import rice, using its scarce foreign exchange.

3 The land tenure system in the provinces is another inhibiting factor to rapid economic development. In the provinces ownership of land is vested in the local authorities, and land is not readily available for sale. This system deprives capital, expertise and enterprise, which other Sierra Leoneans may possess, from finding their way in the provinces, where there is enough land and labour. It is estimated that under 10 per cent of the country's agricultural land area is being utilized.

4 Government has been heavily dependent on export and import dues for its revenue. The economy has therefore been heavily dependent on world price-fluctuations. This has made it extremely difficult for government to meet its internal expenditure. The country's import bills have been soaring annually since independence. Imports range from consumer goods like milk and butter, to manufactured goods like motor cars and machinery. Energy is almost entirely dependent on oil, which again leaves the country at the mercy of external sources. And since 1973 the price of oil has been increasing dramatically, which has hit Sierra Leone particularly hard.

5 The commercial sector is largely in the hands of foreigners which deprives indigenous Sierra Leoneans and government from making substantial profits.

6 The Government has not been very careful in its financial management. A common problem is that unplanned expenditure always runs much higher than expected. For instance, Sierra Leone spent some Le200 million to host the 1980 OAU summit, although Le100 million had been earmarked for the conference.

7 Massive corruption and embezzlement of state funds have also adversely affected the economy. Funds allocated for

general development have invariably found their way into the pockets of private individuals. Since 1981 certain government ministers and officials have been implicated in huge financial malpractices variously dubbed 'vouchergate', 'squandergate' and 'milliongate'.

8   The country has a poor road and communications network. The Siaka Stevens regime actually made some attempt to construct first-class roads and useful bridges. These included the Taiama–Bo road, the Bo–Kenema road, the Freetown–Waterloo road, the Lunsar–Makeni road, the Makeni–Matotoka road and the Makeni–Kabala road. A four-lane Congo Cross Bridge replaced the narrow single-lane bridge which had been both unsafe and inconvenient. Two new bridges over the Scarcies rivers, at Mange and Kambia, link Sierra Leone with Guinea. Some access roads were also built, but the road network in general needs a big boost. Many agricultural centres along the former railway routes and in remote parts of the country have declined because these centres have not been connected to the main road-systems.

9   Foreign exchange problems have resulted in the economy being practically stagnant, with industries operating at less than full capacity, since they lack foreign exchange to import essential items. Irregular supply of electricity has also adversely affected the productive capacity of the industries.

The future

Sierra Leone's economic situation is deplorable. Unemployment is high, and opportunities for school-leavers and university graduates are few; foreign exchange is in short supply, and inflation is running at over 600 per cent. IMF measures to salvage the economy, which involved, for example, delinking the leone from British sterling and attaching it to IMF Special Drawing Rights in 1978, devaluation and floating of the leone, and government removal of subsidies on basic commodities, have only aggravated the situation. Until serious efforts are made to radically restructure the economy and control mismanagement, smuggling and corruption, the living standards of the people will continue to deteriorate.

References

Bangura, J. S., Bob Conteh and E. Balansingham (1985), 'The Role of Central Banks in Export Production in Developing Countries – A Case Study of Sierra Leone', *Economic Review*, Vol. 19, nos 3 and 4, July–December (Bank of Sierra Leone).

Bangura, Sam L. (1978), 'We Must Concentrate on Agricultural Development', *New African Development* (IC Publications, London), April.

Bender, Wolfang (1978), *Sierra Leone Music* (Berlin).

Deveneaux, Gustav (1983), *Power Politcs in Sierra Leone* (AUP, Nigeria).

Foray, C. P. (1978), *Outline History of Fourah Bay College 1827–1977* (FBC)

Gutkind, P. C. W. and I. Wallerstein (1976), *The Political Economy of Contemporary Africa* (Beverly Hills, California).

Harrel-Bond, Barbara (1984), 'Sierra Leone: When Life-lines are Cut', *West Africa*, 28 May.

Hoogvelt, Ankie (1987), 'IMF Crime in Conditionality: An Open Letter to the Managing Director of the IMF', *Monthly Review: An Independent Socialist Magazine*, Vol. 39, 1, May.

Hopkins, A. G. (1973), *Economic History of West Africa* (Longman).

Johnson, Omotunde E. G. (1972), 'Comments on Certain Aspects of the Government Economic Policy Since Independence', *Aureol Review*, Vol. 1, no. 7, May (Fourah Bay College).

Momoh, Eddie (1984), 'Sierra Leone: Will the Railway Return?', *West Africa*, 7 May 1984.

Parfitt, Trevor (1985), 'The Politics of Aid to Sierra Leone: A Case Study of the Makeni-Kabala Road Project and Koinadugu IADP', in Jones, Adam and Peter M. Mitchell (eds), *Proceedings of the Fourth Conference, Sierra Leone Studies Symposium 13–15 July*, Fircoft College, Birmingham, United Kingdom.

Riddell, J. Barry *The Spatial Dynamics of Modernization in Sierra Leone: Structure, Diffusion and Response* (Evanston, Northwestern University Press).

Saylor, R. G. (1967), *The Economic System of Sierra Leone* (Duke University).

Sierra Leone Government (1975), *National Development Plan 1974/75–1978/79* (Freetown).

USL (1976), *Sierra Leone Education Review: All Our Future*.

West Africa, 23 June 1980; 12 May 1986.

Questions PART A

1 Trace the major developments in education since independence.
2 What economic and social progress has Sierra Leone made since independence?
3 Outline the economic developments that took place during the Siaka Stevens era.
4 Why did the Sierra Leone Government initiate the 'open-door' policy and what was its importance to the economy of the country?
5 Describe the main factors that have affected Sierra Leone's rapid economic development since independence.

Questions PART B

1 Make a case for the democratization of education in Sierra Leone.
2 'Health for all by the year 2000.' Will Sierra Leone attain this goal?
3 'Mining represents a wasting asset in Sierra Leone.' Discuss.
4 Critically examine the effects of the government's 'open-door' policy on the Sierra Leone economy.
5 'Poor extension facilities, low level of schooling of the farming population and the uncertainties created by the land tenure system,' are the major factors in the low output in agriculture in Sierra Leone. Comment.
6 The main reason for the failure of agricultural projects in Sierra Leone 'has been the lack of sufficient government input to match words with practical assistance to farmers'. Elaborate on this statement.
7 Estimate the degree of corruption among government ministers, officials and parastatal organizations in Sierra Leone since independence (see Chapter 11).

Appendix 1
Governors of Sierra Leone

Province of Freedom

May 1787	Richard Weaver
September 1787	James Reid
June 1788	John Lucas
1789	Abraham Ashmore

Company Administration

1792	Lieutenant John Clarkson
1792–3	Lieutenant William Dawes
1794–5	Zachary Macaulay
1795–6	Lieutenant William Dawes
1796–9	Zachary Macaulay
1799	John Gray
1799–1800	Thomas Ludlam
1800	John Gray
1801–3	Captain William Day
1803–5	Thomas Ludlam
1805	Captain William Day
1806–8	Thomas Ludlam

Crown Colony

1808–10	Lieutenant T. P. Thompson
1810–11	Captain E. H. Columbine
1811–14	Lieut. Colonel C. W. Maxwell
1814–24 (a)	Colonel Sir Charles MacCarthy
1825–6 (a)	Major-General Charles Turner
1826–7	Sir Neil Campbell
1828	Lieut. Colonel Dixon Denam
1828–34	Colonel A. Findlay
1833–4	Major O. Temple
1835–7	Major H. D. Campbell
1837–40	Lieut. Colonel R. Doherty
1840–41	Sir John Jeremie
1842–4 (b)	Colonel G. Macdonald
1844–5	Staff Surgeon W. Fergusson
1846–52 (c)	N. W. Macdonald

1852–4	Captain A. E. Kennedy
1854–62	Colonel J. S. Hill
1862–8 (d)	Major S.W. Blackall
1868–72	Sir A. F. Kennedy
1872–3	J. P. Hennessy
1873	R. W. Keate
1873–4 (e)	G. Berkeley
1875–7	C. H. Kortright
1877–81	Sir Samuel Rowe
1881–4	Captain A. E. Havelock
1885–8	Sir Samuel Rowe
1888–91 (f)	Captain Sir James Hay
1892–4	Sir Francis Flemming
1894–1900	Colonel Sir Frederic Cardew
1900–04	Sir C. A. King-Harman
1904–11	Sir Leslie Probyn
1911–16	Sir Edward Mereweather
1916–22	R. J. Wilkinson
1922–7	Sir Ransford Slater
1927–31	Brigadier-General J. A. Byrne
1931–4	Sir Arnold Hodson
1934–7	Sir Henry Moore
1937–41	Sir Douglas Jardine
1941–8	Sir Hubert Stevenson
1948–53	Sir George Beresford-Stooke
1953–6	Sir Robert de Zouche Hall
1956–61	Sir Maurice Dorman

Independent Sierra Leone (Governors-General)

1961–2	Sir Maurice Dorman
1962–7	Sir H. J. Lightfoot-Boston*
1968–71	Sir Banja Tejan-Sie

Notes
(a) From 1821 to 1827 the Governor of Sierra Leone was Governor-in-Chief of the British West African settlements, including the Gold Coast and Gambia. The Gold Coast was separated in 1827 but the Gambia remained under the Governor of Sierra Leone.
(b) In 1843 the Gold Coast was again placed under the Governor of Sierra Leone and the Gambia was separated.
(c) In 1850 the Gold Coast was again separated.
(d) In 1866 the Gambia, Gold Coast and Lagos were placed under the Governor of Sierra Leone.
(e) In 1874 Lagos and the Gold Coast became separate governments.
(f) In 1888 the Gambia became a separate government.

* Sir H.J. Lightfoot-Boston was the first Sierra Leonean Governor-General.

Appendix 2
Governor Clarkson's Prayer for Sierra Leone

O Lord, I beseech Thee favourably to hear the prayer of him who wishes to be Thy servant, and pardon him from presuming to address Thee from this sacred place. O God, I know my own infirmity and unworthiness, and I know Thine abundant mercies to those who wish to be guided by Thy will. Support me, O Lord, with Thy heavenly grace, and so enable me to conduct myself through this earthly life, that my actions may be consistent with the words I have uttered this day. Thou knowest that I am now about to depart from this place, and to leave the people whom it has pleased Thee to entrust to my care. Guide them, O merciful God in the paths of truth and let not a few wicked men among us draw down the vengeance upon this Colony.

Ingraft into their hearts a proper sense of duty, and enable them through Thy grace to conduct themselves as Christians, that they may not come to Thy House without that pleasing emotion which every grateful man must feel when paying adoration to the Author of life. But I have great reason to fear, O Lord, that many who frequent Thy church do not approach Thy presence as becomes them, and that they may partly be compared to the Scribes, Pharisees and hypocrites.

Pardon, O God, their infirmities; and as Thou knowest their weakness from the manner in which they have formerly been treated, and the little opportunity they have had of knowing Thy will and getting acquainted with the merits of Thy Son, our Saviour Jesus Christ, look down upon them with an eye of mercy and suffer them not to incur Thy displeasure, after they have had an opportunity of being instructed in the ways of Thy Commandments.

Bless, O Lord, the inhabitants of this vast Continent, and incline their hearts towards us, that they may more readily listen to our advice and doctrines, and that we may conduct ourselves towards them so as to convince them of the happiness we enjoy under Thy Almighty protection.

Banish from this Colony, O Lord, all heathenish superstition, and let the inhabitants know that Thou art the only true God in Whom we live and move and have our being. If these people who profess Thy religion will not be assured of Thy superior power, convince them O God, of Thine anger for their profession without their practice; for Thou knowest I brought them here in hopes of making them and their families happy, both in this world and to all eternity.

But I fear they may not be governed by my advice, and that they may ruin themselves and their children forever by their perverse and ignorant behaviour. I entreat Thee not to let their evil example affect the great cause in which we have embarked, but I would rather see this place in ashes and every wicked person destroyed, than that the millions we have now the opportunity of bringing to the light and knowledge of Thy holy religion should, from the wickedness of a few individuals, still continue in their accustomed darkness and barbarism.

Thou knowest that I have universally talked of their apparent virtue and goodness, and have praised Thy name for having permitted me to be the servant employed in so great and glorious a cause. If I have been deceived, I am sorry for it, and may Thy will be done; but I implore Thee to accept the sincerity of my intentions and my best endeavours to improve the talent committed to my care. Only pardon the infirmity of my nature, and I will trust to Thy mercy.

Should any person have a wicked thought in his heart, or do anything knowingly to disturb the peace and comfort of our Colony, let him be rooted out, O God, from off the face of the earth, but have mercy upon him hereafter.

Were I to utter all that my heart now indicates, no time would be sufficient for my praise and thanksgiving for all the mercies Thou has vouchsafed to show me, but as Thou art acquainted with every secret of my heart, accept my thoughts for thanks. I have no words left to express my gratitude and resignation to Thy will. I entreat Thee, O God, if nothing I can say will convince these people of Thy power and goodness, make use of me, in any way Thou pleasest, to make an atonement for their guilt. This is an awful and I fear too presumptuous a request yet if it should be Thy will that I should lay down my life for the cause I have embarked in, assist me, O Lord, with Thy support that I may resign it in such a manner as to convince these unbelieving people that Thou art God indeed.

May the heart of this Colony, O Lord, imbibe the spirit of meekness, gentleness and truth; and may they henceforth live in unity and godly love, following as far as the weakness of their mortal natures will admit, that most excellent and faultless pattern which Thou hast given us in Thy Son our Saviour, Jesus Christ, to Whom with Thee and the Holy Spirit be all honour and glory, now and forever. Amen.

Appendix 3
Sir Milton's Independence Message

Men, women and children of Sierra Leone, I greet you all on this historic day, and I rejoice with you.

Sierra Leone today becomes a unified and independent nation to take her place as an equal partner in the Commonwealth of nations and as an entity in the world at large. For this we rejoice, and may your own rejoicing wherever you are be really full of happiness.

We must also face up squarely to the problems which will confront us, and I want you all to understand clearly that the Sierra Leone Government in future will depend very greatly upon the active support and assistance of each one of you. The aim will certainly be to make our country a land worth living in, a land worth serving; but this can only be done by wholehearted service and hard work now. I have told you this before, and I call upon you to give the Government your active help and support.

I ask you to deal fairly and honestly with your fellow men, to discourage lawlessness, and to strive actively for peace, friendship and unity in our country.

We have much to do to bring improvements to all parts of our country. I am fully aware of this and I assure you all that my Government is determined that general progress shall be made as fast as possible.

But there is also much that can be done by yourselves to meet your own needs, and I shall continue to support and encourage voluntary local effort, whether it is directed to the building of a road, a bridge, a school, or a community centre, a sports field, a water supply, or any other communal requirement.

I would like to make it clear that Independence will not result in any sudden changes in our day-to-day life. Whether you are a farmer, a clerk, a trader, an artisan, a daily-wage worker, a fisherman, a lawyer or a judge, life will go on just the same, with the same rights and privileges safeguarded, the same type of laws, the same justice in our courts, the same taxes and other responsibilities, the same articles for sale in the stores. Mining companies, missions, trade unions, hospitals, schools, and government departments will go on as before.

The significant change is that we are now in complete control of our destiny and for the formulation of our external as well as our internal policies.

I wish you all to be assured that we in Sierra Leone will stand for the freedom and prosperity of men everywhere.

Sierra Leone is proud to be a member of the Commonwealth because this great family of nations has exactly the same aims. We believe in the dignity of man and the sovereignty of states, and we will oppose to the limit of our power any movement of aggression which may conflict with these ideals.

This is the time when all you men and women should strive to know what is being done, what your responsibilities are and what the responsibilities of your country are. The Government Information Service is working hard to help you to do so, and I and my Ministers will continue to come round and talk with you, but you must want to know, and you must bring others with you to listen to the authoritative words of the Government, and you must pass the true word to those who cannot attend.

As I have said before, Paramount Chiefs, Section Chiefs, Tribal Headmen, and Tribal Authority Members all have a great responsibility to do this, and I expect them all to do what is required of them.

Exactly the same applies to Town Councillors and more particularly to District Councillors. It is not enough to attend your Council meetings, and then go home to sit in your hammocks. Many of our people are thirsting for knowledge of what your Council and the Government are doing.

All your elected people must tell your constituents the true word and bring their questions and desires back to your Councils so that they may be answered.

I look forward to a long period of mutual cooperation and understanding between the Sierra Leone Government and the Sierra Leone Council of Labour.

Over the past years we have supported and encouraged the growth of trade unions in our country because these are accepted as the best means of ensuring good relations between the employers and employees, and of securing the rights and deserts of trade union members. Much of what I have said before in this message applies with great force to trade unions.

The Sierra Leone Government in the years to come will depend upon your cooperation and active assistance. You have an especial responsibility to maintain the high standards you have set in past years, to stand by the rules of procedure in the case of disputes, and to avoid conflicts which may be detrimental to the good of your country.

And to those of you who are studying at school or college I say: You are seeing history made this day. Work hard, for you are the future leaders of your country. We will lay traditions of which you will be proud. It will be for you to uphold them and to build upon them in the future.

I pray for God's help and guidance on this historic day and in the years to come, and for His blessing on you all.

Thursday
27 April 1961

Appendix 4
The National Anthem

1 High we exalt thee realm of the free
   Great is the love we have for thee
   Firmly united, ever we stand
   Singing thy praise, Oh native land.
   We raise up our hearts and voices on high
   The hills and the valleys re-echo our cry
   Blessing and peace be ever thine own
   Land that we love, our Sierra Leone.

2 One with a faith that wisdom inspires
   One with a zeal that never tires
   Ever we seek to honour thy name
   Ours is the labour, thine the fame
   We pray that no harm on thy children may fall
   That blessing and peace may descend on us all;
   So may we serve thee ever alone
   Land that we love, our Sierra Leone.

3 Knowledge and Truth our forefathers spread
   Mighty the nations whom they led
   Mighty they made thee, so too may we
   Show forth the good that is ever in thee.
   We pledge our devotion, our strength and our might
   Thy cause to defend and to stand for thy right
   All that we have be ever thine own
   Land that we love, our Sierra Leone.

(Words by C N Fyle)

Appendix 5
The National Flag

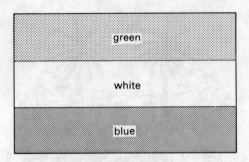

Sierra Leone's national flag consists of three horizontal stripes of green, white and blue of equal width, which have the following significance: leaf-green – for Sierra Leone's agriculture, natural resources and mountains: white – for unity and justice; and cobalt blue – for the hope that Sierra Leone's unique natural harbour may make its contribution to peace throughout the world in the years that lie ahead.

Appendix 6
Coat of Arms

The Arms A lion in gold (an allusion to the name of Sierra Leone which originates from the Portuguese words Serra Lyoa, meaning Lion Range) on a green background, a colour representing the country's agriculture and natural resources. The serrated top to the background is the heraldic representation of the mountains. The two blue wavy lines represent the ocean, coastline and unique natural harbour. Three flaming torches symbolize Sierra Leone's contribution to educational development in West Africa.
The Supporters On either side of the Arms is a lion in gold each supporting a palm tree, another symbol of the country's agricultural wealth. Below, on a white scroll, is the national motto: *Unity, Freedom, Justice.*

Appendix 7
National Honours and Awards

The National Honours and Awards Act of 1972 made provision for the granting of titles of honour, decorations and other eminent public awards, while the National Honours and Awards (Amendment) Act 1973 provided the necessary authority for their establishment, setting out the relevant procedures, conditions, etc.

There are two Orders of Dignity: **the Order of the Republic**, which is the premier order, and the **Order of the Rokel** (Civil and Military divisions). Each order is in four ranks, the highest being Grand Commander, the second, Commander, the third, Officer, and the fourth, Member. There are also various awards for gallantry; the Presidential Award Medal, which is awarded on the prerogative of the President; and the Certificate of Honour.

The insignia are as follows:

Grand Commander of the Order of the Republic (GCRSL). The rank of Grand Commander of the Order of the Republic is (except in the case of the President) an Honorary award only. It is conferred on the President of the Republic, and is otherwise reserved exclusively for foreign Monarchs, Heads of State or Government. This Order, which the President wears with the Presidential Baton, is part of his ceremonial uniform. It is the Premier Order.

Commander of the Order of the Republic (CRSL). One of the highest awards of dignity.

Officer of the Order of the Republic (ORSL). Order of dignity for distinguished and meritorious service.

Member of the Order of the Republic (MRSL). The fourth rank in this Order of dignity.

Grand Commander of the Order of the Rokel (GCOR). One of highest Orders of dignity.

Commander of the Order of the Rokel (COR). A high Order of dignity.

Officer of the Order of the Rokel (OOR). An order of dignity.

Member of the Order of the Rokel (MOR). The fourth rank in the Order of the Rokel.

Awards for Gallantry for both Civil and Military divisions are as follows:

The Bai Bureh Star (Military division) (BBS). For gallantry of the highest degree. Bai Bureh was the famous Temne warrior from Kasseh who figured prominently in the hut tax war in the north.

The Nyagua Medal (Military division) (NM). For gallantry of a very high degree. Nyagua was a warrior chief from Panguma who overran many other towns and fought against the British most gallantly to prevent British administration of the south-east. Like Bai Bureh, he also played a prominent part in the rising of 1898, known as the hut tax war.

The Matturi Medal (Military division) (MM). For gallantry of a high degree. Matturi was a chief of Jaiama in Kono District, acclaimed as a wise and capable ruler, who transformed his area of conquest into a model chiefdom.

The Siaka Stevens Cross (Civil and Military divisions)   (SSC). For gallantry of the highest degree. President Siaka Stevens started life as a policeman, and became the first African Leader of Opposition to defeat successfully by constitutional means, a government which had been in office for 15 years. He led Sierra Leone from a monarchical system of government to a republic and became the first Executive President.

The Milton Margai Medal (Civil and Military divisions)   (MMM). For gallantry of a very high degree. Milton Margai became the first Prime Minister of Sierra Leone after achieving independence for the nation on 27 April 1961.

The Wallace-Johnson Medal   (Civil and Military divisions) (WJM). For gallantry of a high degree. I. T. A. Wallace-Johnson was one of the earliest pioneers of pan-Africanism in Sierra Leone, and other parts of West Africa. Associated with the greatest and undaunted champions of pan-Africanism, he was detained in prison during the Second World War for his stand against colonialism.

The Medal of the Mosquito (Civil and Military divisions) (MM). Another award for gallantry. Sierra Leone became known as 'The Whiteman's Grave' in its early history largely through the mosquito which spreads malaria. It is believed that this insect through this dreadful disease prevented the whiteman from making a permanent settlement in Sierra Leone which may have otherwise been another Rhodesia.

The Republic Day Medal (Civil and Military divisions) (RDM). For award to all those in the armed forces and public service and others who rendered service in connection with the foundation of the Republic.

The Presidential Award Medal (Civil and Military divisions) (PAM) To be awarded as the sole prerogative of the President for the personal services of a lesser nature than would normally qualify for the Order of the Republic.

The Certificate of Honour (both large and small) (CH). For persons who do not qualify for award of the two Orders of dignity but who have nevertheless distinguished themselves in any walk of life.

Only citizens of Sierra Leone are eligible for appointment to any rank of the Orders. Non-citizens of Sierra Leone are eligible for appointment as honorary holders of any rank of the Orders.

Appendix 8
President Momoh's Inaugural Speech

MY LORD CHIEF JUSTICE
MR SPEAKER
HONOURABLE MEMBERS OF PARLIAMENT
MEMBERS OF THE DIPLOMATIC CORPS
PARAMOUNT CHIEFS
DISTINGUISHED GUESTS
FELLOW COUNTRYMEN

1 Let me start by offering my profound thanks and deep gratitude to you, my fellow Sierra Leoneans, for the tremendous confidence you so graciously reposed in me by overwhelmingly electing me to the Presidency of our nation. I pray that the Almighty may grant me enough strength to be able to measure up to your expectations.

2 I have had the good fortune of serving the just retired President, Dr Siaka Stevens, for seventeen years, the last eleven as a Member of his Cabinet. I have no doubt in my mind that this period of apprenticeship will stand me in good stead in the accomplishment of the enormous task that I have now inherited. I ought, therefore, at this stage, to express my appreciation and thanks to Dr Siaka Stevens for the unique opportunity he gave me to serve this nation both as Force Commander of the Republic of Sierra Leone Military Forces and as Cabinet Minister.

3 I would also like to offer my grateful thanks to His Lordship the Chief Justice for administering the prescribed oath to me and for the very cordial sentiments he so generously expressed about me in his congratulatory remarks.

4 Lastly, my thanks also go to many of you inside and outside these Chambers who stood by me from the very early days on to this moment that I now address you as President. Your contribution towards the fulfilment of this day will always be remembered.

5 Distinguished Guests, Fellow Sierra Leoneans, today, 28 November 1985, marks yet another significant milestone in the annals of this country's history; for, as we enter the dawn of a new era, we cannot help but thank the Almighty and praise ourselves for a peaceful transitional process, the uniqueness of which is that I, a Member of the Armed Forces, have been constitutionally elected to the leadership of a civilian administration. This is a clear manifestation of the high level of political maturity in this country. Therefore, it is my fervent hope that the remarkable events that have unfolded here since 4 August will

serve as a strong incentive to potential financiers and entrepreneurs to invest in Sierra Leone. They are assured of favourable business climate in this country.

6   It is on this note of hope and openness that I assume the mantle of leadership of our dear country. I can feel the weight of the aspirations of the vast majority of you on my shoulders. Let me, however, caution that while I am determined to work without respite for a brighter tomorrow, we must not lose sight of the fact that the tasks ahead are indeed formidable. I know that the global economic problems which confront all developing countries are not easy to contend with. It is against this background that the measure of achievement of my predecessor must be seen to be highly commendable. For my part, I am determined not only to build on the foundations that have been laid but also to break new grounds. On the other hand, I am aware that despite our past achievements, there are urgent problems facing us and that the solution to these problems must be found quickly. This is where the need arises for cooperation by all citizens and it must be accompanied by the will and determination to succeed, so that the proverbial light at the end of the tunnel will not take long in appearing.

7   Fellow Countrymen, Distinguished Guests, for close to four months, from the day I was elected Secretary-General and Leader of the All-People's Congress Party, to my election to the Office of President, culminating in my historic assumption of the Presidency of the Republic of Sierra Leone today, there has been a whole lot of jubilation. This jubilation is, no doubt, based on great expectations. A greater sense of patriotism has arisen along this new political development, clearly indicating that more and more of you, my Countrymen, also view this period as the most difficult period in our country's political history. It is a period in which the national economy is suffering severe setbacks, adversely affecting the standards of living of every citizen.

8   Even from a cursory look at the economic problems confronting the nation today, it is clear that the challenges ahead of my administration are tremendous; scarcity of fuel, limited availability of drugs in the hospitals, shortage of rice, our staple food, frequent power-cuts and inadequacy of public transportation – these are all grave problems which must be addressed with clear thinking, determination and speed.

9   It is obvious that the problems of this magnitude can only be solved if we Sierra Leoneans and others who have adopted this country as their home can make a new nation-building pledge aimed at the revitalization of the whole economy and, in the process, ensure that a new society evolves in which every man, woman and child can be sure of a decent standard of living.

10   My administration will have as its main priority, policies geared towards the downward trend of our economy and instituting measures effectively aimed at improving the quality of life of our people.

11   From an initial assessment of the situation, there appears to be much room for improvement in the existing machinery for harnessing our foreign exchange earning potential, as well as in the existing income-generating system to meet the needs of Government and the country as a whole.

12   It is from this stance that my administration, in an effort to improve the economic and financial status of the country will, as a first step, undertake a very critical examination of the operations of all the major and potential revenue-earning institutions of the country. Full details of these measures will be announced shortly. In the meantime, I can inform you all that the examinations of the institutions concerned will be carried out by a special committee set up by me. The committee will be given the full mandate to determine whether the operations of these institutions are in the best interest of the country, with particular reference to their capacity to generate revenue and manage their resources.

13   While the proposed committee will be performing its functions, my administration will put in place other measures to help ease the problems encountered by the citizens of this country, especially those relating to food, fuel, public transportation and medical care.

14   I have pointed out on more than one occasion, that some of the problems confronting the ordinary Sierra Leonean today are primarily related to the irregular business practices of a few individuals who, for self-interest, have always by-passed the laid-down laws and regulations of our land. The malpractices of smuggling, tax-evasion, profiteering, hoarding of vital commodities and black-marketing activities will be challenged with the greatest speed and most effective methods. I sincerely hope that, in this process, the use of harsh methods to achieve our desired end will not be necessary as a result of the cooperation of all concerned in the demonstration of their sense of responsibility in our attempt at building a better Sierra Leone.

15   Furthermore, my administration will insist on the maintenance of a high level of discipline in all sectors of our society and I would like to assure you that the enforcement of such discipline will be in the interest of the nation as a whole.

16   Fellow Countrymen, Distinguished Guests, there is very little point in talking about new programmes and the evolution of a better Sierra Leone if the nation in its majority is beleaguered by indisciplined citizens whose activities inevitably render impossible the implementation of the most beautiful of programmes. Let me, therefore, categorically state that, from me, your President and from my Ministers soon to be appointed; from Permanent Secretaries and other top-level Civil Servants, from students, teachers, labourers, taxi and *poda poda* drivers and, even from the ordinary man in the village a high degree of discipline is required at our various levels if we must tow this country out of the troubled social and economic waters on which it has been drifting.

17   To those people who made it a habit to ignore stipulated rules and regulations by virtue of their standing or connection in society, I say, that as from this moment, their days have come to an end. Henceforth, the question will not be 'who you are' but 'what you can do'. In other words, as from today, your recognition in society will be determined by the contribution you make to its welfare rather than by your assumed airs of arrogance.

18   Fellow Countrymen, another burning issue which demands immediate

attention is that of accountability. For too long, a well-placed and privileged group of public officials has considered itself above the law and therefore not answerable to the citizens they are supposed to serve. My administration will emphasize accountability not only in the area of actual performance, but also in the handling of public funds and property and, in doing so, just punishment will be meted out to offenders.

19   I have no doubt that for the implementation of the measures required for the smooth running of my Government, it will rely on the cooperation of the law-enforcement agencies. I am clear in my mind that the Judiciary will be allowed to function as a respectful institution with no outside interference. We therefore have every right to expect the Judiciary and the Police to stand up to the challenges of the moment. I sincerely believe that cooperation between my administration and the law-enforcement will yield the desired results in line with the expectations of every Sierra Leonean.

20   Follow Countrymen, Distinguished Guests, a Government can formulate policies, issue regulations and directives, but to realize their objectives, it is necessary to rely on an effective administrative machinery. As we are all aware, the Public Service is the organ that translates Government's programmes into concrete action. It is therefore evident that a weak Public Service can hardly stand up to the ordeals of running the affairs of a state in an economic emergency. Dependence on such a Service, I need not say, can only lead to failure and a serious compromise of Government's good intentions.

21   In this respect, my Government will take a serious look at the administrative machinery and the existing rules and regulations which are a vital instrument of Government especially as they are now required to respond to new tasks and provide innovative approaches to meet the aspirations of Government and the nation. I therefore intend to promote the revitalization of the Service so as to facilitate the installation of high standards and noble ideals in a new environment where appointments, promotions and other forms of rewards would be based on merit, ability and suitability in accordance with laid-down principles on these matters. In particular, undue interference with appointments and promotions within the Service will not be tolerated or encouraged. It is worthy of note that already, attempts have been made to review some of the regulations which are regarded as obsolete. The review is intended to suit the present circumstances and I intend to give the Report which is presently before Cabinet my most immediate attention.

22   I must admit, however, that with the present spiralling cost of living, the existing salary and wage scales in the Public Service are inadequate; I would like to assure all concerned that as soon as there is improvement in our economic and financial fortunes, this state of affairs will be reviewed, hopefully guided by the findings of the Commision on the Review of Salary Structures which has been appointed. I strongly believe that if we pay our officers well and provide them with the necessary tools and facilities, we will most likely get the good results expected of them. My administration will make serious efforts in that direction.

23 I have dealt at length on some of the problems facing our community, but since my main focus will be on the general improvement in the standard of living of our people, I must state here that the embarrassing development which has allowed irregular payment of salaries and wages to workers, mainly Civil Servants, teachers and Chiefdom workers, in many parts of the country, would be looked into immediately with a view to regularizing the situation.

24 Fellow Countrymen, I am of the opinion that this beautiful country of ours of just about four million people (I hope that the Chairman of the National Population Census is not pre-empted by my figures), is actually capable of graduating from the present hard times to a level of development that will be the envy of other countries. I have no doubt that this is an attainable goal if only we succeed in managing our resources properly. In this connection, I would appeal to the members of our business community, both Sierra Leonean and foreign, to cooperate with my administration in its endeavour to build a better society.

25 To foreigners who are engaged in business in this country, I appeal for identification with the aims and aspirations of the country which, to most of them, is second home. It is only but fair to state here that the country can no longer continue to accept a situation in which its resources are exploited only to benefit other foreign countries at a time when we ourselves are in dire need of economic salvation. It is a fact that foreign businessmen have for far too long enjoyed our hospitality and protection. It is now their turn, for once, to respect and observe our laws and regulations and to refrain from biting the fingers that feed them. Mutual respect and confidence, in the long run, can only come about when the rules of the game are observed and respected by our two sides. All sincere and law-abiding businessmen, be they foreigners, have absolutely nothing to fear.

26 To those friendly countries which have over the years identified themselves with the aspirations of Sierra Leone, I say a big thank you. I promise that we will continue to maintain the cordial relationship that happily binds our Governments and peoples. It is my hope, in particular, that the developed and industrial nations wll appreciate the present economic plight of poor nations like ours and demonstrate a sense of understanding and solidarity, remembering that each one is his brother's keeper.

27 To our next-door neighbours, I extend a warm hand of friendship and reaffirm our belief in and total commitment to the shared principles of good neighbourliness and non-interference in the national affairs of others. The peaceful nature of Sierra Leoneans is legendary. As a country we have never and will never engage in activities that are likely to bring discord and grief to other countries.

28 Under my administration, Sierra Leone will continue to play an active role in the United Nations Organization, the Non-Aligned Movement and the Organization of African Unity, among others. At the Sub-Regional level, membership in ECOWAS and the Mano River Union will continue to have a special place of importance. On the international scene, Sierra Leone will continue to firmly stand by all oppressed

peoples, particularly those in South Africa, Namibia and Palestine.

29 To all international organizations, I wish to say that the efforts they have made towards this country's development remain highly appreciated. I pledge to do all within my power to achieve a stronger and more fruitful relationship.

30 Fellow Countrymen, to realize the high standards we have set ourselves, it is no longer enough for the citizens of this country to sit aside as spectators while their Government makes all the mistakes. It is the binding duty of each one of us to participate in the noble task of nation-building. After all, when, in future, the success-story of Sierra Leone is written, the contribution of all Sierra Leoneans who, at a point in time, threw their weight behind their national administration in its programmes of reconstruction, will receive a place of honour.

31 That is why my dear Countrymen, I invite you to contribute in your various ways and capabilities, to the building of our Party, the State and the State machinery. Let us, under the banner of the All-People's Congress Party (APC), in unity, live in peace, dignity and harmony; let us learn to forbear one another and cultivate a sense of appreciation of our own values. Let us, together, design a strategy of self-reliance so that, at the end of the day, we can depend on our ability to manage our resources well for the benefit of all our people.

32 Finally, let us work towards the progress of our young nation and strive to preserve our national sovereignty that our forefathers fought so hard and fearlessly to attain.

> Long live the dignity of man!
> Long live the APC!
> Long live Sierra Leone!
> Thank you all and may God bless us all.

Index

APC (All People's Congress) 217,
   227, 239
   and elections 232, 235, 238
   against Albert Margai 229
   against Siaka Stevens 242–3
Abolition Act 65–6
abolitionists 54–5, 91–2
African Association 119
African Institution 66
African Standard 178
agriculture 26
   for export 192–3
   after independence 268–70
   and Kai Londo 148–9
   subsistence 193–4
   tropical 53–4
   see also food crops
All People's Congress, 217, 227,
   239
Almamy, Suluku 148–9
American War of Independence
   48–9
Amistad Committee 106
annexations, under Governor Hill
   114–15
apprenticeships abolished 67
Arabic script 44, 117
archaeological research 4, 6
art 266

BMS (Baptist Missionary Society)
   102–3
BRAC (British Royal African
   Company) 34–5, 36
Bai Bureh Star 285
Bank of Sierra Leone 271
Baptist Missionary Society 102–3
Barclays Bank 199
Barreira, Father Balthasar 101–2
barrenness 25
barter 26, 85, 199

basaraka 19
bauxite 266
beeswax 33
bembe 21–2
Bo 162
Bo School 200–201
Bonthe 162
Booth, Rev. James 109
British District Commissioner 134
British Government
   grants 63
   1865 Resolutions 117
British Royal African Company,
   34–5, 36
Bullom 11, 12
Bunce Island 35–6
Bureh, Bai 140, 141, 145–6

CEA (Committee of Educated
   Aborigines) 173
CMS (Church Missionary Society)
   69, 71
   and education 76–7, 103–4
   and Fourah Bay College 200
   and Recaptives 104
   and Short Course Men 105
cacao 192, 269
cannibalism 37, 38
Capuchins, as missionaries 102
caravel 32
Cardew, Colonel Sir Frederic
   133–5
   and Bai Bureh 145–6
   and house tax 139–40
   and Krio 183
Caulker wars 96–7
Certificate of Honour 286
Chalmers, Sir David 142
Chalmers Commission 142–3
chiefs 150, 152, 153
Christian Institution 76

[293]

Christianity 36
  difficulties with 110
  among Krio 79
  amongst Nova Scotians 64
  see also missionary societies
chrome 195, 198
chromite 199
Church Missionary Society 69, 71
Cintra, Pedro da 4, 33
circumcision 24
citizenship rights 217
clans, patrilineal 9–10
Clarkson, John, Governor 55–6,
  57–9, *quoted* 278–9
Clarkson, Thomas 49
cloth manufacture 28
coffee 192, 269
Colonial Office 135, 143
colonialism
  and agriculture 192
  and attitudes 221
  and British 187
  in Colony of Sierra Leone 187–
  8
  economic development under
  220
  education during 221
  and hinterland 188–9
  trade 220–21
  urban/rural dichotomy 221
Colony
  and colonial period 187–8
  founding 51, 53–5
  and local government 157
  organisation 53
  problems 59–60
columbite 199
Committee of Educated
  Aborigines 173
Commonwealth 250
communications network 220, 273
  see also roads
compass 32
Congress politics 169, 172–5
Constitutions
  (1863) 165–8
  (1924) 174–5
  (1958) 213
  Independence 217–18
corruption 236, 249, 272–3

cotton weaving 42
country cloths 28–9, 85
coups 232, 235
courts, under Protectorate 134
crafts 266
Creole 78
Crown Colony 62–3
  and education 69, 71
  under T. P. Thompson 67–8
Crowther, Samuel Adjai 80, 82
culture, after independence 262–6
currencies 60, 85, 198–9, 228–9
curriculum, for primary schools
  258

DELCO (Sierra Leone
  Development Co.) 195, 197,
  198
deforestation 89, 192, 193
Development of Industries Act
  (1983) 267
Development of Industries Board
  200
diamonds 197–8, 199
direct election 157
District Councils 156–7
drainage 194
Drake, Sir Francis 34
drama 264, 265
Dress Reform Society 184

ECOWAS (Economic Community
  of West African States) 251,
  292
economy
  under colonialism 220
  and Five Year Plan 160–61
  after independence 266
  under Sir Albert Margai 230–31
education 24, 153, 200
  under CMS 76–7, 103–4
  under colonialism 221
  in Crown Colony 69, 71
  after independence 258–60
  industrial 77
  attained by Krio 80
elections
  (1962) 227
  (1967) 231–2, 235–6, 238
  (1977) 243–4

under Stevens 249–50
electoral reform 210
electricity 204–5, 262, 273
ethnic groups 6, 9, 74
ethnic violence 212–13, 236
Executive Council 165–6
exports
    crops 89, 192
    of minerals *199* (fig.)
    timber 88

Falconbridge, Alexander 55
family, as working unit 21–2
famine 168
finance, post-independence 271
First World War 168
fishing 269, 271
Five-Year Plan for Economic
    Development 160–61
food crops 90, 148
foreign exchange 273
formation-fighting 40
Fourah Bay College 200, 201, 244
Fourah Bay Institution 77
Fox, Charles 65
Free Town 57, 59, 60
Freetown
    as army headquarters 72
    as cultural centre 82–3
    and French priests 77
    and general strike 211–12
    as natural harbour 187–8
    representation in 158
    and strategic importance 121–2
    and traders 87
    and tribal headmen 161–2
Freetown City Council 158–9
Freetown newspapers 82–3
French
    expansion by 121
    in Freetown 77
    and Samori 121, 122
friendship treaties 113, 114, 148
Frontier Police 124–5, 139
Fula 11, 13, 44
Futa Jallon 9, 43–4

Gallinas country 90–94
Georgestone, N. H. 211–12
ginger, as export 192

Gola 11, 13
gold
    as currency 85
    exported 199
    panning 28
    mining 195, 266
governors of Sierra Leone 276–7
Grant, Marcus, and strikes 211–12
Granville, Lord 65
Granville Town 53, 54
guerrilla warfare, against Mane 38
Gullah 36
Guma Valley Dam 261

Haidara rebellion 176
Harmattan wind 1, 4
Hawkins, John 33, 35
Hill, Governor S. J. 114–15
hinterland, and colonialism 188–9
hospitals 203–4, 260–62
    see also missionary societies
house tax 118, 135, 160
    and Bai Bureh 146
    and Colonel Cardew 139–40
    and Sir David Chalmers 142
    under Native Administrations
        153
    reintroduced 143
    and Madam Yoko 145
    see also hut tax war
Humonya, Madam 150
hundreds 53, 58, 64
hut tax war 140–42
    and Almamy Suluku 149
    and Bai Bureh 146
    and Nyagua 147

IMF (International Monetary
    Fund) 273
IPP (Independent Progressive
    People's Party) 215
imports 36, 198
incest 20, 25
independence 224
    and agriculture 268–70
    and culture 262–6
    and economy 266
    and education 258–60
    and finance 271
    and health facilities 260–62

Independence Constitution 217–
    18
Independent Progressive People's
    Party 215
indirect rule 133–4, 150
industrial school 105
industries 37, 254, 267
infant mortality 261–2
influenza epidemic 168
intermarriage 33, 35, 36
International Monetary Fund 273
invasions 31
iron 28, 42, 195, 199
Islam 31, 43–6, 102, 110
Islamic Council 249

Jesuits, as missionaries 101
Jones, Rev. E. N. (*later* Lamina
    Sankoh) 218–19
junta, military 236–7

KPM (Kono Progressive
    Movement) 215
kantha ceremonies 14
King Tom 51, 62
kinship system 20
Kissi 11, 13
Kono 11
Kono District 6
Kono Progressive Movement 215
Koranko 11, 12, 46
Koya Temne, against Sierra Leone
    Co. 62
Koya Temne Kings, title of 40
Kpaa Mende 9, 144
Kpo-veh wars 147
Krim 11, 13
Krio 11, 13
    and African names 184
    and Christianity 79
    cultural rebirth 186
    decline of 182–5
    discriminated against 143, 183
    educational attainments 80
    and First World War 168
    intellectuals 167
    opposed to constitution 209
    and political aspirations 165–8,
        173–4
    Recaptive influence 78

society 78–83, 187–9
    traders 82
    women, status 80
Krio language 184–5
Kru 11, 13
kugbe 21–2
kulahu, in Limba 19

land regulations, under
    Protectorate 138–40
land tenure system 272
languages
    Krio 78–9, 184–5
    Mande group 11
    Mel group 11
    Sherbro 41
Lansana, Brigadier 235–6
Lawson, Thomas George 116, 127
Legislative Council 165–6
leone, as currency 228–9
Lewis, Sir Samuel 128–9
Liberia 251–2, 255
Limba 6, 10, 18–20
literature 262, 264, 265
loan schemes 267
Loko 11, 12
Londo, Kai 147–8

MRU (Mane River Union) 251–5,
    292
Macaulay, Zachary 59–60
MacCarthy, Charles, 68–73
Mana, Prince 91–2
Mande language group 11
Mandingo 11, 12, 13
Mane invasions 37–8, 39–42
Mane sub-kingdoms 39–40
Mane warriors 12, 38
Mano River Union 251–5, 292
Margai, Sir Albert 215–16, 227–
    32
    economy under 230–31
    opposed 227–9
    removed 236
    and republic 231–2
Margai, Sir Milton 210, 216, 224,
    226–7, *quoted* 280–81
Maroons 61
martial law 235
Masimera–Loko wars 94–6

matrilineal descent 20
Matturi Medal 286
Mel language group 11
Mende 6, 9, 11, 16–17
Mendi Mission 105–7
Mercantile Association 165, 166
military rule 236–9
militia 60, 67
Milton Margai Medal 286
mining 195, 197–8, (fig.) 199
missionaries 46
  attacked 141
  Capuchin 102
  and education 200
  European 101
  and hospitals 203–4
  and hut (house) tax 139
  Jesuit 101
  Krio 82
  mortality 71, 73
  and slave trade 103–4
missionary societies 101–3
  see also specific society name
Momoh, Major-General J. S. 245,
  246, 248, *quoted* 287–92
Mosquito, Medal of the 286
music, after independence 264
Muslims, *see* Islam

NCBWA (National Congress of
  British West Africa) 172–3
NCSL (National Council of Sierra
  Leone) 210–11, 214
NDMC (National Diamond
  Mining Company) 241
NGO (non-governmental
  organizations) 261–2
NRC (National Reformation
  Council) 236–7, 238
naming
  among Krio 80, 184
  sequence for children 21
  of slave children 71
Napoleonic wars 59
National Advisory Council 237–8
National Congress of British West
  Africa 172–3
National Council of Sierra Leone
  210–11, 214
National Development Bank 271

National Diamond Mining
  Company 241
National Health Plan 260–62
National Reformation Council
  236–7, 238
Native Administration System
  152–4
Native Affairs Department 116–17
Ndawaa 147–8
New Order 247–8
newspapers 72, 82–3, 167, 178
non-annexation policy 112–15, 117
non-governmental organizations
  261–2
Nova Scotians 55–6
  and Christianity 64
  institutions 63–5
  and quit-rents 60
  rebelling 61–2
  reinstated 72
  and trade 64
Nyagua 146–7
Nyagua Medal 285–6

OAU (Organization of African
  Unity) 226, 230, 250–51
oil, as energy source 272
oil extraction 26–7
old people, status 23
one-partyism 230, 243–4
open towns 16
Organization of African Unity, *see*
  OAU

PNP (People's National Party)
  215–16, 239
palm products, as exports 189
Paramount Chiefs 134, 152
Parish Plan, and Recaptives 69
Parkes, James C. E. 129–30, 135
Parliament, under Independence
  Constitution 218
patrilineal descent 20
People's National Party 215–16,
  239
peoples, of Sierra Leone (fig.) *11*
Peters, Thomas 55, 57
piassava, as export 192
Pieh, Sengbe 106
plantations 36

platinum 195, 199
Pok, the 25
political parties 214–17
polygamy 20–21
population, increasing through
    mining 198
Poro 17, 18, 24–5, 42, 141
Port Loko 33, 44, 190
Port Loko mission 104
Portuguese 31–3, 37
postal union, under MRU 254–5
Prayer for Sierra Leone 58
Presidential Award Medal 286
pressure groups 167–8
Protectorate
    administration 134–5
    consolidated 149–50
    Courts under 134
    divided 155
    and education 200–201
    grievances against 135, 138–40
    and indirect rule 133–4
    proclaimed 126–7
    under Sir Samuel Rowe 119
    and socio-economic change 152
Protectorate Africans 183–4
Protectorate Assembly 207–8
Province of Freedom 51
provincial administration, changes
    154–5

Quakers Mission 77
quit-rents 59, 60

racism 182
railway 89, 189, 190
railway workers 168–9, 175
rainfall distribution 4
rates 160
Recaptives 66–7, 68
    and CMS 104
    evolving new culture 78
    organization 73–5
    religions of 74
    and rural villages 67
    status 75
    training 68, 69
religious beliefs, traditional 22–3,
    56
republic, established 241–2

Republic Day Medal 286
resettlement centres 67
Revolving Seed Schemes 194
rice 193, 194
riots 168–9, 211–13
ritual murder 133
roads 153, 189, 198
Rokupr Rice Research Station 194
Rotifunk, attacked 98–9
Rowe, Sir Samuel 118–19
Rural Area Councils 160–61
de Ruyter stone 25
rutile 266

SLPMB (Sierra Leone Produce
    Marketing Board)
    buying imports 193
    and oil mills 200
    role of 268–9
SLPP (Sierra Leone People's
    Party) 210–11
    1962 elections 227
    1967 elections 232
    1977 elections 243
    accused of election irregularities
        238
    under Sir Albert Margai 229
    under Sir Milton Margai 226
    policies 214–15
    under Sankoh 219
SMA (Society of Missions in
    Africa) 77
SLST (Sierra Leone Selection
    Trust)
    and diamonds 197
    and mining 195
    negotiating with Stevens 241
SOS (Sierra Leone Organization
    Society) 209
St George's Bay Company 54–5
salt, as currency 85
salt manufacture 26, 41–2
Samori Toure 121, 122–4
sanitation 152, 261–2
Sankoh, Lamina (*formerly* Rev.
    E. N. Jones) 218–19
Sapes 6, 38, 39
    and creativity 42
    as slaves 41
school populations 201, 203

sculpture 28
Second World War 207
secret societies 14, 15, 24–5, 74
self-help schemes 262
settlements, European 36
Seventeen Nations 74–5
Sharp, Granville 48, 49–51, 53–5
Sherbro 11, 12
    crops produced 90
    language 41
    matrilineal descent 20
    political organization 17–18
    trading 89–90
Sherbro Urban District Council
    162
Short Course Men 105
Siaka, King 91
Siaka Stevens Cross 286
Sierra Leone Branch, of Congress
    173–4
Sierra Leone Company 56, 57, 59,
    60, 62
Sierra Leone Development
    Company 195, 197, 198
Sierra Leone Gazette 72
Sierra Leone Labour Congress 244
Sierra Leone Organization Society
    209
Sierra Leone People's Party *see*
    SLPP
Sierra Leone Produce Marketing
    Board *see* SLPMB
Sierra Leone Selection Trust *see*
    SLST
Sierra Leone Trade Union
    Congress 180
Slater, Sir Ransford 173–5
slave trade 36
    and Abolition Act 65–6
    abolition of 48–51, 91–2, 139,
        151
    disallowed 54–5
    and Europeans 35
    and missionaries 103–4
slave-raiding 151
slaves 33
    children, named 71
    in economic system 151
    as labour force 23–4
    for plantations 36

redemption of 151
    as wealth 91–2
Smart family 94–6
Smeathman, Dr Henry 50, 51
smuggling 272, 255
soap-making 27
Social Darwinism 182
Society of Missions in Africa
    (SMA) 77
Sofa warriors 120–21
Solima state destroyed 120
Sommerset case 48
Soso 11, 12, 38
South Carolina, and slaves 36
sovereignty, lost 138
standard treaties 122
Stevens, Siaka 217
    and APC 235, 242–3
    and assassination attempt 242
    assessed 248–50
    appointed Governor-General
        235
    in Guinea 238–9
    and one-party state 244
    and regime 239–44
    retiring 245
Stevenson, Governor Hubert 208
Stevenson Constitution 208–11
strikes 168–9, 175
subsistence farming 193–4
    see also agriculture; food crops
succession disputes 92–4
suffrage, universal adult 179
Sumba 38
Syrians, riots against 168–9

Tablet 244
tariffs 118
Temne 6, 9–10, 11, 14–16
Temne–Loko conflict 95–6
territorial states 16–17
Thompson, Thomas Perronet
    67–8
Thornton, Henry 49, 54
timber 88, 96–7
tithings 53, 58, 64
totem 10
trade
    under colonialism 220–21
    conducting 35–6

expanding 118
indigenous 85–8, 91
long-distance 87
overseas 88–9
amongst Recaptives 75
regional 85, 87
in slaves 88
trade unions, and Youth League
     178
trade wars 94–9
traders
     British 33–5
     Colony 87
     Danish 36
     European 31, 190
     French 89
     Islamic 45–6
     Krio 82
     Lebanese 190
transport, improved 188–9
     see also communications
          network, roads
Travelling Commissioners 122, 124
treaties
     friendship 113, 114, 148
     standard 122
Tribal Authority 152
Tribal Headmen 161–2
tribalism 230
tribute collection 17
trypanosomiasis 89
Turner, Charles, and
     expansionism 113–14
twins 23

UBC (United Brethren in Christ)
     107–8, 203–4
UDP (United Democratic Party)
     241, 242, 243

UNF (United National Front)
     216–17
UNO (United Nations
     Organization) 250, 291
UPP (United Progressive Party)
     215
urban/rural dichotomy, under
     colonialism 221

Vai 10, 11
village improvement taxes 160

WMS (Wesleyan Methodist
     Society) 77, 98, 99, 108–9,
     200
Waima incident 125–6
Wallace-Johnson, T. A. 177–8,
     179–80
Wallace-Johnson Medal 286
war-medicines 42
war-towns 16, 17, 143
water supplies 204–5, 261
weaving 42
Wesleyan Methodist Society
     (WMS) 77, 98, 99, 108–9, 200
West African Currency Board 199
West African Youth League 177–
     8
Wilberforce, William 49, 65
witchcraft 25
women, status 21, 80
World War I 168
World War II 207

Yalunka 11, 12
Yoko, Madam 144, 145
Yoni 9, 99
Youth League 177, 178–80, 182

Zawo slave revolt 91